REV. VALERIE LOVE

Confessions of a Christian Witch

*How an Ex-Jehovah's Witness Lives Magickal & How
You Can Too!*

Third edition

ISBN: 9781659776850

This book was professionally typeset on Reedsy.
Find out more at reedsy.com

This work is lovingly dedicated to all the witches and magickal beings who've been told that you can't be magickal and love Christ at the same time.
It's time to dispel the myth that has been perpetuated on the mass consciousness of humanity and has lived on almost unquestioned.
Today this myth dies.

"You don't find Truth,
but Truth finds you. "

LUIS MARQUES
ASETIAN BIBLE

Contents

II   Magickal Resources

III Prayers for the Christian Witch

IV Soul-stirring Letters & Comments

Preface

I was terrified to write this book.

That's why it took all of 5 years plus to deliver to you the creation you now hold in your hands.

Terrified.

Of what?

My own inner demons, outpictured as everyone and everything.

I was, quite literally, afraid of my own shadow.

The shadow is a tricky devil, because it lives behind us. We can't see it. We can only see its nasty and frustratingly undesirable results. Since we see the effect really well, but can rarely see the cause, if at all, the perfect breeding ground forms to pin the whole thing on someone else. The person standing closest to us will do… lover, mama, daddy, anyone.

Since we can't always clearly see our own causation in the unwanted circumstances and experiences of life, we sincerely say to ourselves and the people around us, 'it's not me, so it has to be you!'

And we really believe it. Until we don't.

I swam in those waters for years, terrified to come out as a Witch because I was afraid of my shadow self… in one aspect afraid of my own power because of the immense energy locked up in the unacknowledged, unaddressed, unexamined shadow, and in another aspect afraid of the inner demons of unworthiness, not good enough and abandonment that had been relentlessly hawking me since childhood.

My choice was clear: take on my shadow, and with it immense power reclaiming, or blame it all on the first unsuspecting victim I could find.

For years I unconsciously chose the latter.

To be clear, here's a glimpse inside my inner terrors:

'Mom is a Jehovah's Witness, I can't come out the broom closet, it would catastrophic. Her and her Witness friends would be mortified.'

'Daddy is an elder in the Jehovah's Witness organization, I don't want to bring reproach on Jehovah's name and shame our family.'

Then later it was:

'My husband is a Baptist, it wouldn't be right to flaunt my Tarot deck in his face, seeing as how he hates it.'

On and on I went, denying myself and blaming it on other people.

All a mirror reflection of my own fear demons...

I was terrified of being marginalized as a Witch and not being taken seriously, of being a pariah, a laughingstock, a fool, and a public fool at that.

I was terrified of hurting people I love who are still in the Jehovah's Witness cult, especially friends and family members I cherish.

I was terrified of being ostracized, yet again, by any group I had grown close to (that old abandonment issue popping up again).

I was terrified of revealing so much of me in what energetically felt like a public self-stripping, a self imposed nakedness.

I was terrified of the answer to the dreaded question *what will people think of me?* The almost insatiable need for acceptance, love and validation from the outside was eating me alive on the inside. Therefore I spent more than enough time and energy languishing in the imagined deleterious effects of me expressing my truth would have on my mother, who transitioned out of this life in January of 2013, (and is now my biggest cheerleader in heaven). Even with the love and backing I felt on a soul level from mom, her mother and her mother before her from the other side of the veil, a long line of powerful Witches, my mind still plagued me with darts: was I doing the right thing to tell this much? To put this much out there? To bare my soul? To reveal the family 'business'?

The terror took the form of one helluva case of procrastination. I especially procrastinated on writing at every turn, even as the primal urge in me could NOT keep silent. The writer in me knows the power of the pen, and that it would out me for sure.

After sidelining my terrors long enough to write this book, my out-the-closet manifesto of sorts, the first edition was published in 2014.

Even after publication of the first edition of this work, I was so terrified about spilling the proverbial beans that I took the book out of publication on the grounds that I had to 'edit' more.

Pile on several more years of this terror procrastination and the muse would have no more. Though she had never ceased nipping at me, prodding me, inspiring me, urging me, this time, she put her foot down.

She had had ENOUGH of my hi-jinks: tussling with the manuscript, adjusting words, paragraphs and sentences here and there, promising myself to pull the trigger and publish soon, while attempting to assure myself that this every-so-often churning of the words and manipulating the manuscript was actually getting me somewhere, when indeed it was not.

The game's over.

It's time.

I always know when I've run out of excuses with the Uni-Verse. It's gentle yet insistent, powerful yet loving, and simply moves FORWARD NOW, like a giant wheel (not unlike the imagery on the Wheel of Fortune Tarot card).

I experienced the muse as Ambrosia, who never left my side, for as long as this work was still in my womb, like the best kind of midwife, that you can just FEEL is there to catch that baby and do whatever it takes for mama and offspring to be just fine; the kind of midwife who knows what position to put mama in during the long labor, and what essential oil to use next, and what herb to press in. Yes.

That's Ambrosia.

Thank you.

I'm happy to announce: the baby has arrived! And she's a fat one too! Healthy, fierce, bold, raw, boldly authentic and never apologetic.

This is my story...

KAISI

(Aka Rev. Valerie Love)

P.S. - This is the 3rd iteration of this book. The first edition was printed in

2016. The 2nd edition was released on 11/11/2018. This edition differs from the first 2 editions, and I thought it might be helpful to share with you exactly how this edition differs from the edition just prior to it.

This version has been edited again (a huge book like this one requires lots of edits and re-edits… thank you for understanding) to bring the work into a higher standard of excellence. My desire is to provide the best, highest quality work I can divinely provide.

In addition, this edition has been typeset and put into a handy 6 x 9 paperback format (if you're reading the paperback version of this work, and not the eBook version). The earlier editions of this work were 8 1/2 inches by 11 inches; a size that's not uniform for the publishing industry, and thus narrowing the distribution possibilities.

Also different in this edition is that the quotes formerly at the end of each chapter have been removed. Although I love quotes, and I did my best to include the authors of the quotes in the bibliography of the other editions, I did not procure permission for each quote from each author. Though I was okay with using quotes previously, I am no longer of that same mind. Hence, this is the quote-less version. For me, the quotes were a sort of decoration that I pray enriched the text in the previous editions. The major focus of this work is the message itself, not the quotes. I hope you'll understand. (The list of books that I previously sourced quotes from is in the back of this edition in the chapter titled *Recommended Reading*.)

The paperback edition of this work is also on fewer pages, since the font is smaller than the previous 2 editions. Making this book a bit more manageable in size may come in handy for our readers.

Lastly, if you have one of the previous editions of this work, either the original printing in 2016 (there are only 11 copies in print that I know of) or the 2018 edition (of which there are many more copies in print), know that you have a collector's item on your hands (while I cannot make any promises, one day it may be worth more on eBay than you paid for it… I'm being funny here).

Either way, whatever edition of this book you may own, I pray it serves you well. Please know that by divine providence, the edition that's perfect for you has found its way to you.

One more thing, would you kindly leave a review on Amazon and/or elsewhere online where this book is sold and/or discussed? Reviews help potential readers, and reviews support the author as well. I intend and desire to create many more works that reach and benefit many more readers. If you can find a brief window of time and energy to let others know how this book moved you, insights you gained, or any other helpful information, it would be greatly appreciated!

Acknowledgement

To Varonika, you're a jewel, a companion, a guide, a wonder and a blessing. I so appreciate you and the inspiration you prove to be for me every day. Plus you're smart as hell with guts to go with it. This will serve you well.

To Gaia, I love you and am SO proud of you. To Eazy Mack, thank you for being you, and for being the all-in dad to 3 phenomenal beings. We're looking to you to tear up the stages of the world! To Ether, you're a shining light. We don't know who you are, yet we are certain you will show us. To Enzo, supreme love for you as you walk the path that is uniquely yours! Keep being and doing you boo. To Empri, KEEP BEING A DIVA NO MATTER WHAT.

To Cory, who's literally reshaping the world with the creations of the cosmos, art rules!

My heart wells up with gratitude for my Inner Visions line sisters, I love you!

I humbly offer my gratitude to and for all the magickal authors and teachers I've read over the decades. Your words inspire me to be more of myself, and summon the courage in me to write what is true.

I am deeply grateful to Ambrosia, a spirit being who watched over and guided me in this work, even when I was near exhaustion and wondering if this creation would ever see the light of day. Thank you Ambrosia, my muse, for magick and mystery.

I'm grateful for the writer in me. She's persistent, insistent, if not always consistent. She's a gift and when I allow her to speak, miracles abound. Keep pouring it out Inner Writer, and I'll keep capturing it on paper.

With deepest love I thank you all,

KAISI (aka Rev. Valerie Love)

I

On Magick & How It All Unfolded...

*This is the genesis and unfoldment of the journey, up until now,
from Fundamentalist Christianity to coming home to the truth
of my soul as a practicing Christian Witch.
This is how I exited the cult of Jehovah's Witnesses and how that
outrageous act of courage continues to feed my soul to this day.
Enjoy.*

The Intention

The intention here is to inspire you to *be and express* your Authentic Self, and only this, and to present only this to Self and the world, and to inspire, support and teach others, through your bearing and being, to the same. Do you have the courage to be the *real you*? *Authenticity.*

In essence, it's to be free... free of what people think of you, free of your terrors, free of the judgments secretly born within that are reflected to us as the judgments of society, free of anything that encumbers you. Free to be you, like you've never been before, no hiding, no veils, no attempting to slim your Self down in vain hopes of fitting in, no trying to contort oneself to match other people's tiny ideas of what they want you to be. Free of all of that and so much more.

Freedom.

Going deeper, the goal here is for you to fulfill your calling, the unique reason your soul chose to connect itself to a body and walk among us. Your soul had a very good reason for doing that, one that you cannot ignore and expect to experience peace of mind and heart and any shred of lasting fulfillment. Your soul is here on a one-of-a-kind mission, it has a unique reason for being. It has lives to touch. Are you in alignment and integrity with your soul? Or are you arguing for a lesser space than what you came here to fill? Are you heeding your soul's calling? Or are you somewhere wondering how you can get by until the next paycheck?

The bigger question here is: are you living your DESTINY?

This work is to inspire you to answer your soul's calling with everything

3

you've got, and then some, regardless of how uncomfortable it gets, regardless of what you may lose in the process, regardless of the opinions of others, and, most of all, regardless of your own dreaded terrors, fake as they may be.

I must warn you, choosing to surrender to the call of your soul could lead to unusual and unanticipated outcomes, including loss of family members, friends, lovers, children or even parents.

No worries.

Christ cautioned that whoever is willing to follow Him must be willing to leave father and mother and brother and sister and houses in this life, and if you are willing to do that, you'll reap them 100 fold again.

God always gives beauty for ashes.

My soul's Destiny as a Christian Witch in this lifetime cost me all that and more. Not because it had to, but because it's part of the Divine Destiny Plan, to be me, authentically me, and to stand in my authentic power, whether anyone else approves or not, while knowing I could never be alone or abandoned or out of the love I AM.

I Am One with The One.

You and I are here to be, do and have what the soul is calling for us to be, do and have. No matter what other people say. I must stress this, it's a biggie for us humans, we want so badly to fit in, but *fitting in is NOT our calling*. Never has been, never will be.

This is not easy.

Is it worth it?

Permit me to ask you a question: if you were totally fulfilled in every area of your life, happy beyond logical reason, abundant in every area of your life and life's concerns, woke up every day joyful and ready to leap out of bed to see who you could bless with your rare and divine mix of gifts, talents, skills and abilities and your life is humming like a hummingbird in every imaginable way, would it be worth it?

I don't know about you, I can only speak for me; I'm willing to pay *whatever the cost.*

And be assured, it will cost. Nothing this big, delicious, juicy and magnificent comes free. There are requirements. They're outlined in this book, even though this is really more than a book, it's a way of life.

Destiny.

Next, the goal here is for you to **LOVE YOUR SELF**, lumps and all, warts and all, beautiful imperfections and all, simply love you, through and through. A love affair with your Self, not in a narcissistic kind of way (we know what that got the Greek god), no, in a knowing you are a child of heaven sort of way, and as such, you deserve to be, do and have the very best. *Love your Self.*

Love.

That's my goal here, Divine Being of Love & Light. If you get even more from this work, oh yummy! *Let's get started...*

Who I Am

I am a witch. A born witch.

When people hear the word 'witch,' all manner of mayhem conjures in the mind.

Some are more forward thinking, and for them, Wicca may come to mind.

I am not Wiccan. I've studied it extensively in books, or at least I've studied it extensively enough to know that it isn't for me.

While there are those who practice Christo-Wicca, I'm not one of this lot.

I am not a coven leader, nor do I belong to a coven. I have nothing against covens, I'm just not called to engage in one, as of this moment.

I am not a Christo-Pagan. I understand there are Christ-loving Pagans, whom I send love to. I am not one.

I am a Christian Witch.

I was born a witch. I practice magick as a spiritual path, integrated with my love of Christ. For me it's simple, and completely common sense, although I confess it may not be common sense to some, especially Christians.

Quite simply, I love Christ and the Craft.

Who I am is Love. This is my true identity. This is my essence. Anything other than that would be a label, and labels do not always serve us on the path of the soul. Even Christian Witch is a label, of this I am well aware, yet it serves our purposes for clarity and expression. So for now, I will use it.

In my agreement with God on the truth that I am Love, I'm tasked by the divine within to do something bold and daring: to face my fears of being a witch, overcome them, and reach out to my brothers and sisters to support, teach and inspire to do the same; to dispel ignorance and fear, and, in the process, to shift the association of the word witch from something evil and dark to what it truly is: **POWER.** Pure. Raw. POWER.

I must confess, I did not want the assignment.

I feared it. It was uncomfortable. Why can't I just stay in the closet? It's stuffy, yes, and stifling…. still I'm used to these 3 walls and a door and have grown accustomed to this dank darkness.

Even when we know we've outgrown where we are, it doesn't automatically happen that we leave it. Where will we go? What will we do?

What about the people who are quite accustomed and feeling 'safe' with me being in here? The people who, when I cracked the door open and let a little of me out, freaked out and declared me of the devil? What about them?

What about all the ills that will befall me if I exit this closet?

Maybe it's safer to stay tucked inside. Be quiet. Don't make a fuss.

Not so.

Not only is it never safe to stay tucked inside, it is the worst kind of unsafe.

I heard someone wise say (who that someone is escapes me in the moment) that we think something bad's going to happen when we stand up and be true to self and serve in the way our heart and soul are calling us to serve, when the truth is, something bad's already happening if we're denying Self.

Food for freaking thought.

The essence of those words landed and made a thud in my being. *That's right Val, you think something bad is going to happen if you exit the broom closet, when, in truth, something bad is already happening.*

Is this 'bad' that's already happening a bigger 'bad' than the 'bad' that may happen when I exit?

I don't know. One thing's for sure, I can't know sitting here in this dark closet.

I must exit.

So while the human me did not want the assignment that my soul had already chosen of coming out and helping others come out, and telling the world who I really am, and standing in it in loving power, and shining my gifts, and shifting myself and others from fear to love in the process, nevertheless, I pressed on anyway.

Not without much conversation with God.

There were the begging, please can you give this job to someone else prayers... "God, there's so many other people who could do this job so much better than me.... could one of them do it?" (As if God doesn't know what God is doing.)

There were the angry prayers... "God, I'm mad! Why did you make me this way?!?!? I'm weird!!! For no good reason!!!"

There were the procrastinating prayers... "God, give me the strength to do this... tomorrow, I'll get right on it tomorrow, I promise." (Yeah, right.)

There were the they'll-never-take-me-seriously prayers... "God, they won't listen to me, I'll seem strange, I'll be marginalized, not taken seriously, then even the good stuff I say won't be respected... please God, can we just do something else?!? Something... less... scary?"

All to no avail.

It was not to no avail because there's a demanding being sitting somewhere high in the sky handing out irrevocable assignments (assignments that scare the beJesus out of you) that you must do, or else.

No.

There's no sky god making demands on us.

The reason all my begging and pleading and asking for this cup to pass didn't work was because my own heart wanted it so badly I could taste it.

I desired to be free.

I desired to exit the broom closet.

My heart was ONLY about expressing the real me.

I desired, with all of me, to do what I love, freeing myself and others from limiting and constricting beliefs of any kind... it's what I live for, it's what I love more than fresh baked warm bread with honey butter.

Wow.

So no, I wasn't talking to God really. I was talking to myself. I was trying to convince myself not to do what I really wanted to do; and the part of me that was trying to do the convincing was the little me and the part of me that was supposedly being convinced was the big me.

I was confused. Conflicted.

The little me can't talk the big me out of doing what the big me wants to do. I thought I already knew that.

Apparently I did not.

Which brings me to witches and what we're here for.

Witches are healers and teachers, way showers and guides who adhere to and master a craft. How we each practice and develop our craft is deeply personal and can differ dramatically from witch to witch.

Yet we are all working with one set of universal laws, truths that do not waver, upon which we choose to firmly build the inner adytum of the mage.

I am a Magician. This by spiritual path, my soul's calling.

I am a witch. This by birth.

I am a Christian. This by choice.

The integration of these, for me, is peace.

What is a Witch?

Let me state up front and clearly for the record that I do not speak for all witches. There are countless many of our kind, varied and various, each with his/her own one-of-a-kind strand in the tapestry of life, each on his/her own utterly unique path of the divine carved through one's own heart, each with a magickal signature unlike any other witch or wizard in the cosmos.

There is no way I could accurately put into words any definition that would fit the totality of witches. Nor will I try.

Asking 'what is a witch?' is akin to asking 'what is a Chinese person?' There is no answer to that question that would honor all Chinese people.

It is the same for witches. There is no answer to that question that would honor all the witches of the world, let alone the witches I know.

Rather than offering a pat definition for 'witch', I have a different goal: to offer my own perspective, as one among countless many; more with the view that it will add to the spectrum, to the rainbow that is magick, rather than to offer hard and fast rules that hem in and do not, nor could, encompass the wonder of every witch.

I love witches too much to attempt to define them.

Society seeks to define so it can be safe. It demands *tell me what it is, then I'll know, then I can know if you pose a threat or not. Define it! We must know what it is! Then we can know what to do with it...*

Witchcraft is much the opposite, it is mysterious, defying definition. Just as soon as we think we have a definition for 'witch' or 'witchcraft', and society thinks itself safe, for it thinks it knows what to look for, a witch will come along who smashes the definition to pieces by her very being, essence and presence, without ever saying a word. Alas, we are back at the proverbial drawing board.

Let us not do that.

In this work, I will offer you no pat definitions nor pat answers for anything. I think too much of you and the subject matter at hand. If you are looking for a summary, or a tidy little basket into which you can toss the lot of witches, so you can feel safe, you have come to the wrong place, and I cannot say that I hate to disappoint you, because I do not.

I must also state that I speak for no one save me. I do not speak for witches at large, I am not a spokesperson nor am I a representative. I do not speak for Christian witches everywhere.

I am a solitary witch, offering my solitary perspective.

Take it and make of it what you will. My concern is not what you make of my message, only that I have conveyed it with integrity. From this vantage point, agreement is not required.

For me, a witch is a wise one (I have met many witches who tend to agree with this statement, although I am okay knowing there may be plenty more who do not) — one who is wise in the ways and practice of a craft — the craft being magic (or magick for some; more on this later).

For me, witch is a **knowing**. I don't have, nor do I require, evidence that I'm a witch; I simply know I am.

Thinking of it this way keeps it simple for me, and I like simplicity.

Without defining, there are characteristics I could say I've observed in myself and witches I know... we tend to love nature, have a relationship with the whole divine as God/Goddess (both feminine and masculine aspects), have gifts that align with our walk on the planet (such as psychic abilities, empathic abilities, telepathic abilities, channeling and many other varied gifts), tend to be drawn to healing, serving and supporting fellow humans, and choose to use the healing arts as a natural extension of who we are, using many and varied methods, that could include potions, oils, herbs, incense, flowers, flower essences, feathers, stones, crystals, salts, trees, oceans, seas, lakes, rivers, mountains, and so much more. Everything on the physical plane of existence has its own nature spirits, of whom I find that many witches are in conscious commune.

I can't say that I've ever met a witch that didn't have a love and reverence for nature as an expression of the divine.

Loving nature aligns perfectly with practicing the craft. Nature follows laws, as does the craft. Many of the most potent items used in the craft come from nature. Not long ago, I received a wand from a fellow mage — quite a powerful Wizard in his own right — carved by his own hand, from the wood of a cypress tree, dressed with the essential oils of Frankincense and Myrrh. I opened the package on the beach; the wand's first induction in my hands was into sand and sea. It all felt quite natural. I could feel that the wand was just as much at home as was I. When I shared that with the mage, he told me of his connection with the ocean, thus highlighting the inherent perfection and connection.

Also integrated into the craft for many witches is the use of symbols, sigils, alchemy, astrology, numerology, wand lore, and divinatory tools such as pendulums, Tarot, Runes, tea leaves, cowry shells, pebbles and/or pennies and more... almost anything can be used for divination I've found. Our divinatory tools are not the source of the information we receive, they are conduits. One could choose to use a conduit or not. The information can still be accessed.

Many witches, as did Christ, communicate quite comfortably with beings who are not human, including 'dead' people, angels, demons, spirit guides, Archangels, Ascended Masters, ancestors, the Djinn, the Fairy Kingdom (of which many witches have a natural and necessary working relationship with due to the common care for nature), the magickal Elf Kingdom, the Vampire Kingdom, gnomes, trolls and many more not-human entities that we coexist with in this great cosmos of life.

For Christian Witches, use of the Bible, including the Apocryphal Bible, may be standard protocol, though there may be Christian Witches who never touch a Bible. To the Christian Witches who do use the Bible, we have found it to be one of the best magickal books you could ever hope to get your paws on, and the magi of the Bible are some of the most noteworthy Magicians who ever lived, including Enoch, Moses, Solomon, Elijah, Daniel and of course, Yeshua (also known as Jesus – in this work he will be addressed by his Hebrew name Yeshua, or as 'Christ' or as 'Yeshua the Christed One').

Though these are tendencies of witches I know, this, once again, is not meant to define (which is a cutting away and narrowing down). Much the opposite, I share here to broaden, enrich and deepen our spectrum of understanding.

I might also add that witches are everywhere, in churches (clutch the pearls!), at the market, in hospitals and doctors offices, in schools, in politics, in fashion and entertainment... we are *everywhere*. Case in point, as I walk through Barnes & Noble, I'm amazed at how many witches are on book covers, most frequently on books that have nothing to do with witchcraft. You'll find them on cookbook covers, home and garden book covers, novel covers... like I said, we are everywhere.

You'd be amazed at who's a witch.

I tend to recognize other witches, sort of how people of a particular tribe recognize other people of that tribe, even when it's not readily apparent to outsiders.

There's also the matter of respect of privacy; a witch gets to say whether she/he is public or private in her/his workings. There are witches in circles and covens who take oaths of secrecy and will never reveal the identity of another witch, and rightly so.

For some, secrecy is important. For others, not necessarily. I am public as a witch; not so much because I wanted to be as much as it is my soul urge. The most important thing about secrecy is that one knows why one is secret. If it is because of fear, it's time to come out the broom closet. Either way, it's a soul choice, so let the soul lead the way. It knows.

Maybe just as important as knowing what a witch is, is knowing what a witch is NOT. (See my video on Youtube: *10 Things A Witch is NOT*)

Here are my top 10:

A witch is NOT a demon. We command demons, just like Christ.

All witches are NOT cauldron stirrers nor do all witches have cauldrons.

13

All witches are NOT broom riders. I don't ride my broom every day, only when the car can't get me there fast enough.

A witch is NOT a wart-wearer. I don't have warts. If I did, I'd do a spell to get rid of them.

A witch is NOT green. I know a lot of witches; some are deep brown, some are almond skinned, some are white, some are caramel colored... not one of them is green.

All witches are NOT pagans. Pagans are pagans and witches are witches. Some pagans are witches and some witches are pagans, yet not all witches are Pagans and not all Pagans are witches.

All witches are NOT hut dwellers. None of the witches I know live in a hut in the enchanted forest. Mansions, yes. Condos, yes. Houses, yes. Apartments, yes. Huts, none that I know of, yet there could be many. Just don't toss the lot of us into a hut in the enchanted forest (which by the way sounds like a lovely way to live, it's just not the way I live).

Witches do NOT eat small children. There is one exception, when I nibble on my grand babies (I can't help it, they're irresistible.)

Witches do NOT all wear black. I prefer white most of the time.

Witches are NOT of the devil, nor do witches work for the devil, nor are witches in any way in league with the devil. Most witches, including moi, do not subscribe to the concept of the devil (as it's been perpetrated on the masses).

There you have it. What a witch is, and what a witch is not. Let us be free of misconceptions, yes?

My Assignment

My assignment, as briefly mentioned earlier, is to do all in my divine power to shift the perception, the connotation, on the word witch from something evil, dark and scary, to what it truly is for me: POWER. Pure, raw power. I choose to use the power for healing and uplifting human consciousness, yet every witch is free to use the power in any way he, she or they see fit, and will reap corresponding consequences, by Universal Law.

At first, I wanted nothing to do with shifting consciousness around the word witch.

For me, the word witch is akin to the word President, a person of immense power, yet it remains to be seen how this power will be yielded.

Contrary to the deep-seated beliefs of the mass populace, the word witch does not automatically mean 'evil, or 'scary' or 'in cahoots with the devil.' It's time we grew up and stop believing what we've been spoon fed.

One of the biggest reasons I was downright resistant to follow this soul urge of helping, along with other witches and mages, to clean up the mass consciousness by my being, bearing, words and actions is because I recall painful past lives that began magickal and ended tragically. I can recall at least 3 previous life lines in which magickal practices ended my life... I've been burned at the stake. I've been drowned. I've been killed by a demon.

I'm done with living magickal and trying to help other people. It didn't work out well for me.

That sense of foreboding led to a watered down message. I didn't want to take on talking about witchcraft. I wanted to keep it light and easy. I wanted to call myself an 'Intuitive Adviser' because it sounded softer than witch. I wanted to keep the proverbial cat in the bag and not let anyone know I was practicing magick, or studying magick, or in love with the knowing I am a witch. I didn't even want to utter the words 'occult.'

Witch, witchcraft, occult and magick were nasty swear words where I grew up (in the cult of Jehovah's Witnesses) that ended anyone who adhered to, or even touched or uttered words about these practices in the one place and one place only: complete and utter annihilation. At the hands of Jehovah God no less.

That's the brand of fear-inducing mental poison I grew up on.

Better to keep my mouth shut and take this witch secret to the grave.

My diabolical plan for keeping my mouth shut and minding my business was foiled.

The call of my soul was too strong, the gravitation to magick too irresistible. I couldn't run anymore, although I'd given it my best shot. I couldn't hide anymore, though I'd tried my darnedest.

I couldn't not live my truth any longer.

It was too hard keeping the edges tucked in, hoping no one would notice, too time consuming, too draining on my energy field.

So I decided to follow the call of my soul, yet again, into uncharted waters, not knowing where the heck I was going, not seeing more than 1 or 2 feet ahead of me, dragging my feet, shaking my head no and feeling the fear in the pit of my stomach just about the whole way.

Until something happened.

I had a YouTube channel, and one day the Voice said: *tell your story.* I knew intuitively it meant to make a video about my journey.

Uh oh! Here we go. Whenever I get seemingly little nudges like that from the Voice, it always turns into something far bigger than what I was planning, or can even conceive.

So I sat down in front of the video camera to tell my story. When I first heard the words "Christian Witch" fall out of my own mouth as I was recording, I was just as shocked and horrified as some of the YouTube viewers would soon be. *Did I just say that??!?*

NO WAY AM I PUTTING THIS OUT THERE. NO WAY.

Before I could offer too much protest, divine inspiration moved in me with such a fury such that before I knew it, said video was uploaded to YouTube. Even still, I promise you my fingers were shaking like the Dickens when I hit the 'upload' button on that video.

All that, and I did it anyway.

That video, titled *How I Became A Christian Witch*, immediately set off a firestorm that I was thoroughly unprepared for in human realms, and completely prepared for in the spirit realm. Years later, it continues to be in the top most viewed videos on my channel. It sparks incredible debate, which I love. It brings up fears. It brings up questions we feel safe and better not asking. It brings up challenges to belief systems that we don't want challenged. It brings up blood and angst and fears and ugliness and judgment and shame and guilt.

All that, from one little video.

Well, that little video, if it changed no one else, irreversibly changed me. I was out.

Outed by Spirit.

Darn. And that closet seemed so safe.

Except that it wasn't.

I was locked up on the inside, not feeling safe enough to reveal who I truly am, because of fear.

My flawed thinking: a shameful life is worse than death. At least if you're dead, you're not here anymore... the pain and suffering has ended. Besides, most dead people don't get talked about in a bad way. Just the opposite, death tends to make everybody look better than they were when they were alive; the good parts of a dead person's character are the only socially acceptable parts to talk about. You never hear that a person was a hellion at their funeral. You usually hear all the good stuff, and that's what we focus on. At least in death I would have gotten a bump up.

Living in shame, I thought, or worse yet, feeling abandoned, equates to tremendous pain. A life of shame and pain is worse than not being here. Life on the other side is a whole lot more peaceful than this human life we've chosen. That's what I told myself and that's what I believed.

Once I was outed, the game was on. Not that it wasn't on before. It was always on. The difference is now the game had elevated itself to a whole new level, the stakes got upped on me at the Poker table. I was outed on YouTube.

What are you going to do now Valerie?

See or fold? Bluff? Or go all in?

I chose to go all in.

Well, let me say that my soul chose to go all in.

The human me still wasn't quite all in, but she was considerably well along her way than she was sitting on the floor of that stuffy closet. Even still, I wasn't home free yet; the human me had a rack of residual fears to deal with; fears the soul didn't have. The human me still had to contend with the 4 horsemen of the Apocalypse: procrastination, abdication, trepidation and hesitation. Ironically, taken together, they form an acronym: P.A.T.H.

When fear is at a high, the path will be obstructed though it be the most natural path. The seeming obstruction could be blocking us from the thing we desire most.

Still, we'll find a way to be afraid of it.

That was me.

Afraid of my calling, afraid of my own heart.

Afraid of my assignment, even asking God/Goddess if She could find somebody else to do it. This I now recognize as pride and arrogance. Only ego arrogance would incite me to attempt to define or identify myself as anything but divine.

No. All these ideas are to be rejected for the falsities they are.

God as you, as me, knows what God is doing.

While I AM knows, 'I' do not. I don't have to know. God as me knows.

Since it is that way, and it ain't never going to be no other kind of way, I get to listen intently to the Voice, the inner wisdom, and follow it, with deep faith and trust, knowing that it will unerringly carry me somewhere real good. I don't know where that somewhere is, and the relief is, I know now that I don't have to.

My assignment is clear: change the word witch from evil and dark and fraught with fear, to the truth: POWER. And for me, the expression of this POWER is love and light.

And oh yeah, Valerie, you'll be starting with and in your own consciousness. This is how to change the world: by changing self.

This is my wickedly delicious divine assignment. Who better to do that than a witch?

A Witch is Born & Not Made

I was born a witch; which means I can't remember being anything other, even when I wasn't consciously aware of all 'witch' meant.

This is where the plot thickens.

Just because you don't consciously know all of what a thing means about you, doesn't mean the thing isn't true.

As a matter of interest, it appears to be that the more we fight not being a thing, the more that thing we really are. Like Shakespeare put it, "dost thou protest too much." It's a way of questioning motives, and asking self, why am I protesting whatever I'm protesting? Could it be that the thing I'm protesting about myself is true?

A story… let's go to Barnes & Noble.

So I'm standing in Barnes & Noble at the Bowie Town Center in Maryland one day in my favorite section of the book store: New Age. The sections of the book store that want me always pull me so I give in to the urge every time I go into Barnes & Noble, or any bookstore, or any store. Where am I being pulled today? *What do I want here soul?* It guides me unerringly to where I'm supposed to be. So, here I am, in the New Age section of the bookstore. I'm perusing books on the shelf like I normally do when all of a sudden, my body starts rocking, at first softly, then swaying more. Back and forth, swaying in a gentle rocking motion forward and back.

Okay, a being or something on the other side is trying to get my attention. I'm used to phenomena like this. I gave my body, mind and soul over to Spirit, and when you make that kind of deal with the Universe, bizarre and interesting things start happening to your body, which, if there be a way to consciously control when or where or how this phenomenon occurs, I haven't found that way yet. Gently swaying back and forth, I ask, *what is it? What do you want me to see?* I turn around. Behind me are vampire books and the like. I've never been into vampires, they are not my friends. Of all the beings in the spirit realms, I pretty much keep away from them. The whole blood-sucking thing doesn't seem very loving to me. I know they have to live too, but I'd like it not to be at the expense of my mortal body. Anyway, the answer was not in the vampire books behind me.

I turn back around to where I am facing. The rocking gets stronger. I close my eyes, breathe and center myself. That clicks something together for me, like a key in a lock. I get the intuitive hit to feel into where the rocking is coming from, it seems to be originating down around my feet. I look down. Yes, it's coming from down there. I bend down and look at the exact spot, as best I can pinpoint it, where the vibration is. It's a row of books on Wicca and the Craft.

I reach out my hand. It magnetized to a book on the Craft. I receive it into my hands and allow it to fall open. My eyes land on this passage:

"A witch is born and not made."

The paragraph went on to spell out that one can have all the accoutrement of a witch, yet that alone does not constitute being a witch. On the other hand, the passage went on, even if one does not have any of the accoutrement of a witch, and does not follow the path doesn't make one not a witch if that one was born a witch.

The whole passage resonated with me. Try as I might to deny, hide or not identify with witch, the truth is, none of that is doing anything to erase the witch that is me. I was born a witch. That passage gave me a deeper understanding of my path and less desire to hide, deny or run from it. What was that helping anyway? Who was it helping? Not me. And at the end of the day, it will have been the most colossal waste of time and energy ever, because nothing will have changed.

Like I said, I was born a witch.

Ain't nothing going to change that; a fact I have become quite enamored with.

My Confessions

Confession is good for the soul, if not for the reputation. To me, confession is letting go, a release of sorts that cleanses the spirit, heart, mind and soul. I poured out my confessions to clear myself of anything that in any way impedes, hinders, blocks or denies my total and complete fulfillment as Source has ordained for me. If you find these confessions line up with yours, feel free to release along with me!

Confession 1:
I confess fear.

I've harbored dreadful fears of what could happen if I 'outed' myself as a witch.

I've been fearful of what people will think of me if they knew.

I've been fearful of being outcast.

I've been fearful of not being accepted.

I've been fearful of being perceived as crazy or weird.

I've been afraid of being marginalized or not taken seriously.

I've even been fearful of the word 'witch'.

I've been fearful of being identified as a witch.

I chose to be in fear of potential detrimental effects of being 'outed' as a witch based on past life memories of being burned at the stake.

That ends now.

I choose Love.

* * *

Confession 2:

I confess deceit, dishonesty, in-authenticity and lack of integrity.
I've lied to myself about the Truth of Who I Am.
I've lied to others about the Truth of Who I Am.
Because I was afraid to be the real me, I manufactured false fronts, masks and alternate identities to hide behind, each with their set of peculiar personality traits. I created a habit of switching up masks – based on limited perceptions of reality – to what I thought would be most fitting and undetectable in any given situation.
I had a 'mask' for my marriage.
I had a 'mask' for church.
I had a 'mask' for business.
Each 'mask' was manufactured to show only what I wanted to be seen, and hopefully hide the rest. I employed the 'masks' for years on end, even though they proved woefully ineffective.
Because I spent so much time and energy trying to manufacture the perfect, undetectable 'mask' for each and every situation, I robbed myself of time and energy for creative pursuits.
I've sabotaged myself.
That ends now.
I choose Truth, Authenticity, Integrity and Honesty.

* * *

Confession 3:

I confess judgment and projection.
I've judged myself harshly.
Therefore I've judged others harshly.

I confess I've projected these judgments onto others, only to have them show up as harsh and judgmental people in my world, whom I then judged, in a vicious and seemingly endless cycle of judgment and projection.
I've judged myself by thinking I should be much further along in life than where I find myself in any given moment.
I've judged myself for being a witch, as if something was wrong with me.
That ends now.
I choose radical Self-love, Self-acceptance, Responsibility and Ownership.

* * *

Confession 4:
I confess guilt.
I've felt guilty behind the thought that I was denying what I was taught as a Christian.
I've felt guilty when I thought I somehow turned my back on my faith.
I've spent hours secretly wondering if God will punish me for being bad or for not heeding the religion of my upbringing.
That ends now.
I choose knowing and owning inherent Holiness.

* * *

Confession 5:
I confess pride and arrogance.
I've felt at times that I knew better than God, that I shouldn't have been created a witch, that there were so many others things God could have created me to be, why did God create me a witch?

I've pridefully felt better than others, while simultaneously feeling less than others.

I've felt that I knew what was best for the people in my life and didn't mind telling them so.

In error, I thought I had superior knowledge.

I've harbored self-importance and superiority – as a front for deep nagging feelings of inferiority, insecurity and unworthiness – with no supporting evidence.

That ends now.
I choose Humility and Equanimity.

* * *

Confession 6:
I confess faithlessness, reluctance and resistance.

I've fallen down in my faith, which showed up as unwillingness to go ALL THE WAY whenever Spirit asked it of me.

When asked by my soul to speak the Truth and dismiss fear around the word witch, I was faithless and wayward, instead choosing to opt for less 'offensive' terminology... terminology that I thought would be more pleasing and palatable to other people, and hence not get me into 'trouble'.

I've been reluctant to take big leaps of faith because I didn't know what was on the other side.

I've attempted to demand that God show me His hand first, before I agreed to align and follow the Shepherd into and through where He was leading me.

That ends now.
I choose Faith and Alignment.

* * *

Confession 7:

I confess doubt.

I've doubted my ability to do what my soul is here to do.

I've doubted if I could fulfill my Destiny.

I've doubted if I could have success doing what I love, following my path of magick.

I've doubted God's promises to me.

I've doubted if I was good enough to get the job done that God was asking me to do.

I've doubted if I was woman enough for what I was facing.

I've doubted if I could ever find and keep love.

I've doubted if I would ever experience lasting prosperity.

I've doubted my big dreams and if they would come true.

I've doubted my deservedness.

That ends now.

I choose Trust.

Magick & Magic

For me, there are 3 kinds of magic.

First, there's earth magic – magic to effect a change in the outer conditions or environment of the one practicing the magic, by means of spells, incantations, crystals, candles, prayers, magical implements, rituals, rites and more.

It is conscious creative power and ability, and even re-creative ability: if we don't like what we've created, we can always create anew.

Everyone, I believe, is born with magic, and learning to practice earth magic effectively brings out our creative abilities to effect change in our environment, a divine gift, right, ability and responsibility. In earth magic, we learn the depth and breadth of our powers of reality creation, and that through the effective channeling of energy – through our thoughts, feelings, words and actions – we can create powerful and fast change, at will. We can do magic. That's the power of being human and divine at the same time. Kabbalah reveals that we are 1% human and 99% divine; so your magic is always working, even when you're not consciously aware of it. The God in you is the creative power and It's always creating something through you, by Law.

You can't not create.

Most of us don't explore our earth magic because we're either afraid of our own power, and/or ignorant of it, which means we get locked in patterns of victim consciousness, where the prevailing belief is that we are somehow being acted upon and not the powerful ones who act. In victim consciousness, it's unclear that we're creating our own reality, every bit of it, with the thoughts we think, the feelings we feel, the words we speak and the actions we take. It's also unclear how or why we do this, so most of us learned to take the easy way out: blame someone else.

After a while, that gets tiring, especially when we land at the wholly unpleasant realization that we are the ones who keep creating the same experiences over and over again for ourselves – the very experiences we don't want – only with different characters in the play. Why does each boyfriend cheat on me? Why do I keep having the same financial problem over and over again, no matter how hard I try to change things? Why does my husband/wife/lover keep doing the same things? And why do those same things they keep doing send me through the roof every time they do them? Or, why do I still have this health concern after years and years of trying to get rid of it?

You start waking up when you honestly look at your life and see that you were the only common denominator in it all, which makes it near impossible for you, if you have any level of sanity, to still try to pin it all (or any part of it) on someone else.

When you wake up, you remember.

You remember who you are.

You remember your magic.

And you promptly get to changing whole blocks of your life, by thinking differently, feeling differently, speaking differently and doing things differently than you used to.

Then you start getting different results, results you like better. Spurred on by your new success, you want more, so you dive in more to mind control, mastery of your feelings and emotions, being Lord of your tongue and watching closely what you do so that your actions are aligned with Love.

You are using your earth magic, and it's working!

Earth magic is a gift of the universe to all, as we all have the magical ability to change conditions in our lives at any point in time.

Anyone can learn to consciously master earth magic, and like I said, my personal feeling is that everyone is born with earth magic. Like any gift you're born with, it gets better and better the more you shape and hone it. You can shape and hone yourself into a powerful earth magician.

If you want to.

That's the key.

Not everybody is called to work with their creative powers in the form of earth magic, and not everyone should. You get to choose. We all do.

If you're a Christian reading this, you may choose to channel your creative power by using prayers, or Psalms, or praise. I do the same. Some of my most potent and quick manifestations came as a result of intense prayer.

If you're a magickal person reading this, you may choose to channel your creative power using spells, or incantations, or rituals or incense or meditation. I do that too.

The important thing to understand here, and please understand what's important in this life and what's not: method and mode are NOT all important.

INTENTION is all important.

There's no law in the universe that says you can, or can't use magic. You get to choose. There's no law in the universe that says what kind of magic you have to use, or what kind of cauldron you have to have.

I get questions like this from time to time: "should I have a natural wood wand? I heard it only works if it's natural wood..."

Once again, method and mode are not all important.

All important is your INTENTION, which emanates from the mind and heart of the magician.

I can pick up a stick on the street and make it the most powerful magic wand to me. Why? Because I believe it to be so. My beliefs create my reality. As do yours.

This is why it's a pointless and silly waste of time for Christians and witches, or any other magickal folks, to argue about anything, or judge anything.

Method and mode are not all important.

Intention is all important.

Is love your intention? Are your intentions pure? Are your intentions for the highest good of all? These are questions I ask myself.

Only you get to answer these questions, or other questions, for you. No one can answer them for you. And you can't answer them for anyone else.

A word to Christians and Magicians: there's no right and no wrong. Only what aligns with your Inner Knowing, the bigger part of you, let's call it God, and what does not. How do you know what aligns with God? By Law and Principle. Universal Law (recapped later in this work) is the way God operates. Principle is the way you align with Law. Test whatever you're doing by Universal Law and Principle. If it's aligned, and you feel the calling from deep within your heart, from your Highest Most Holy Self, go forward. If not, beware.

Which brings me to the next kind of magic: black magic, which is magic to harm. I never touch it, never have, don't recommend it, never have, don't speak of it and as a matter of fact. That's me. You choose for you.

One of the first commands to an initiate of ceremonial magick is:

"Quit the night and seek the day."

I made the conscious choice to walk in the Light.

While I don't subscribe to the 3-fold rule (what you put out comes back to you 3-fold) I do seek to align with Law in all my dealings. The Law of Cause and Effect is clear. I am cause, effect is what shows up. That applies to everyone everywhere, not just witches and magicians.

I have a saying that karma is a mother and her name is bitch.

It's my way of stating what grandma used to say in her own wordology: "what goes around comes around."

Then there's magick, with a 'k', also known as High Magick, or Ceremonial Magick, that has no goal to change anything other than the Magician. In changing something within the Magician, the results of that inner change are reflected in the outer world, by Law. The Law of Correspondence applies here: "as within, so without, as above, so below."

Magick, for me, is a spiritual path of alchemacalizing oneself in order to transform the baser nature of lead into pure gold.

There are Magicians of the High Order who practice ceremonially, and because the consciousness has been elevated and purified to such a degree, and the Alchemy of the Soul has been accomplished in such great dimension, the Magician has the power and presence of a Christ on earth, an Avatar, literally able to move mountains, walk on water and manifest anything at any time on the physical plane instantaneously.

Christ was such a one, as was Enoch, Abraham, Moses, Elijah, Elisha, Daniel and Solomon, to name a few from the Bible.

These Magicians spend a good amount of time in meditation, prayer, reflection, contemplation and study and practice of the Magickal Arts and Sciences, including divination, astrology, geomancy, Alchemy, cartography, Angelology, Kabbalah, Hermeticism, Egyptology. Egypt (aka Kemet) being the birthplace of the Ancient Hermetic Arts & Sciences and the Western Esoteric tradition.

Magick of this order is a calling. It is my calling. No one happens onto this path, it is a soul decision one makes before crossing the veil from life in spirit realms to incarnating as a human.

There are Magicians of this order who choose not to die. They know full well, on all levels of being and consciousness, as Enoch did, that death is a choice, one we are all free to make or not make.

You don't ever have to have a physical death. You can be 'transferred' (or 'translated') into a spirit being without ever having to experience physical death.

On the contrary, some of us were told death is inevitable. This is not true. You will keep on living after your body is given up, if you choose to give it up. If you choose to keep it, you can keep it for as long as you like, as long as you develop your consciousness to that level, as in the case of St. Germain, who kept his body for far longer than anyone of his age even thought possible. Many Masters have kept a body for hundreds of years, because they chose to for a particular kind of service to humanity (not because they didn't want to go).

Magicians of the High Order know – as many Masters and Avatars on their respective spiritual paths know – physical death is a choice.

Enoch of the Holy Bible did not experience physical death, nor did Elijah. There was no pause. They were translated, which means they took the same body they were in, and through stages of refinement and transcendence, ascended in that body, which ultimately turned into a spirit body.

No death.

It's really a simple process, and is the exact opposite of how you got here. When you descended the ladder in spirit realms to be born as a human, you stepped yourself down in density, becoming denser and denser, until you could be ascertained on the physical plane.

With the appropriate consciousness training, you can do the opposite when you choose to ascend up the ladder in spirit realms, only this time, you continue to step your body up, becoming less and less dense, until you're a wholly spirit being again.

There are different kinds of bodies for different dimensions of consciousness. Currently, we only have knowledge of 13 or 14 dimensions of consciousness that scientists are able to clearly identify, quantify and categorize.

There are infinite of dimensions of consciousness, yet we tend to operate in a narrow range in an earth bound incarnation, when we are clearly identified with the 3rd dimension (the world of form ascertained by the 5 senses). We may sometimes jump to the 4th or 5th dimensions if we really get to praying and praise or hallucinogenic drugs or other consciousness raising activities and/or practices.

It behooves us to go as high as we can. The higher we raise our consciousness, the more we have access to in the way of universal support, communication, wisdom and guidance.

That's why we're here: to choose to ascend consciousness such that we attain Enlightenment, oneness with The One. And none of us is home until all of us are home. That's the only destination: Spirit. And you will reach your destination, no matter how many lifetimes it takes; God is inevitable.

I'm here to support you in returning home to Spirit, your true abode, sooner rather than later.

Souls who choose the path of High Magick choose it for very definite reasons. It doesn't seem to be for young souls, as this path appears, to me, to require aeons, or thousands of lifetimes of practice to master. I've been at this for a very long time, by earth years. And still, I can't say I have it mastered, though I do have the sense that it will be.

I now have remembrance of incarnating several other times as a Magician, as I did this time. On more than one occasion, I was killed in connection with magic and/or magick. It was par for the course, practice really. One earth lifetime ended when I was burned at the stake for being a witch, and once I remember doing a form of High Magick and being killed by a demon. I remember practicing as a magician and priest in ancient Egypt, in a temple devoted to Isis.

No matter how many times I've done this before, I'm back now, and in actuality, I never left.

This is the path of the ones among us who choose to practice High Magick, as a soul choice and calling.

You don't have to be a witch to practice High Magick. Anyone can practice High Magick. It seems that being a witch and being called to High Magick are closely aligned, yet High Magick is open to anyone who chooses it.

I must issue a warning here: choose wisely. This path requires the greatest of care, attention and patience, lest some untoward results manifest. Choose, as a way of being and living, if you're feeling called to practice High Magick, to be responsible, to learn well and to take heed, to grow and deepen in wisdom and to do it from a heart of love and compassion.

With regard to magick, there are 3 steps that seemed to unfold very naturally for me:

Choice – I made a conscious choice to practice magick, to answer the irresistible call. For me, this means living a life of magick, not just doing magick. It's becoming magick. What it means for you, you get to decide. You also get to choose how far down this rabbit hole you're willing (or able) to go. I decided I'm ALL IN.

Initiation – I've had several initiations over the years. I've found that there's never a need to ask an inordinate amount of questions about initiation. It becomes crystal clear when it's time for an initiation. And if you're a prayerful Magician – which is the route I take – you'll know when it's time for an initiation, and you'll know where to go, and as important, who to go to (if others are involved, which may or may not be the case) and how to unfold it. All elements of my initiations have come together, as if by magick. Indeed it is. My first initiation was solitary, in which I received a new magickal name for my use only. For a long time, no one had ever heard my magickal name, conferred upon me at initiation by the Powers that be. Since then, I've received more sacred names, with the most recent magickal name being KAISI, which was given to me by Mother Ayahuasca through my consciousness in concert with a shaman in the mountains of Peru in yet another initiation into the healing arts. This name was to be in use, and was not a secret magickal name, as my first was. The name's meaning is distinctly why I am on the planet. By the time it's all said and done, I confess I do not know how many magickal names and/or titles will have been conferred upon me by God/Goddess. With regard to passing the initiation gates, I've found that I was 'tested' at each initiation. I almost refrain from using the word 'tested' here because of the image it may conjure. For certain, the Universe is not testing us in a 'let's-see-if-we-can-trip-her-up' kind of way. It's more of a 'proving', so that the ground I do gain is maintained. You may find, as I did, that you will be initiated at many levels. You will pass through successive gates in order to attain deeper and deeper knowledge, understanding and – after successfully passing the requisite initiations – mastery. Each gate you pass holds keys for the next, and the next, and so on. Each gate you pass strengthens you for the next. The wisdom gained is cumulative. The initiation gates fly open ONLY after you demonstrate mastery of what's before you. You cannot go to initiation gate 2 if you haven't mastered initiation gate 1. This is where your practices are proved. Do you *know* what you've studied or is it only theory? Have you actualized it, realized it? Have you put your learning into practical application and gained the desired results? Over and over again? Have you achieved a level of mastery with what's before you, even if it's the simplest of magickal operations? Only after proving that you can demonstrate will you be allowed to pass through each initiation gate. Again, these initiations are not self-imposed, or by humans. There is a great universal Force that is always at our back and making us better. That is my experience. You get to experience this life as you will.

Study & Practice – Study is required; we get to actively seek wisdom as it's not lying around on the streets. If you're COMMITTED to a life of magick, you'll make a search for what's real and true (especially in this internet age with its plethora of information on magick readily available online, some of it of questionable quality). I was, and am, diligent about finding truth, In a word: Relentless. I was willing to read, study, assimilate, grow, read and study more. When my soul first woke from its decades long slumber, my appetite for metaphysical and magickal information was voracious! I couldn't stop searching, researching and devouring any and all information I could get my paws on. Christ gave us the key in his story about the woman who loses a pearl of high value. She sweeps her house meticulously until she finds it. She does not miss an inch. She overturns every bit of furniture and every item in the house, seeking her precious pearl. An identical intensity of search is required for mastering High Magick. A question for you: if you were to learn the secrets of the universe, secrets that could set you and the whole world free, wouldn't that be worth any search? I say yes. It's like a person with a treasure map searching for the hidden treasure. They don't rest until they find it, even if it takes years. They travel far and wide with one thing on their mind: the insatiable urge to find the treasure. Why? Because they believe that upon finding it, they will be rich. For me, the same is true of magick. A scripture that always rings true for me is the passage that reads "study to show yourself approved." I don't take this verse to mean that there's some approval required from outside myself. I LOVE studying magick and the occult, and could spend all day doing it. Yet it's not enough to study only. I get to practice magick, to actually do it. I've given my inner life to the study and practice of High Magick, the ultimate great work of Alchemy of the Soul. Magick therefore became part and parcel of everything I do and WHO I AM. STUDY. STUDY. STUDY. And PRACTICE. PRACTICE. PRACTICE.

I aspire to join the circle of powerful masters of magick, including Enoch, Abraham, Moses, Solomon, Elijah, Elisha, Isaiah, Ezekiel, Daniel, Merlin, St. Germain, Aleister Crowley and to me, the greatest Kabbalist who ever lived: Yeshua.

Let me conclude this chapter with this: there are witches who don't practice earth magick or High Magick. There are Wiccans who practice earth magick. There are magicians who are not witches or Wiccan, who practice ceremonial magick, and on and on. The terms witch, Wiccan, magician and Pagan are not interchangeable. They mean very different things to the people who practice and walk these paths. I am a Christian Witch, and I choose to practice High Magick.

Note: In this work, to distinguish High Magick from other forms of magic, the word will appear with a 'k' at the end.

Why Be Magick?

If you're going to *be* magick (not just do magick), if that's your soul choice, and it's real for you, authentic and true through and through, and not an exercise in curiosity, for curiosity will never do, and is certain to undo, if this be your soul choice, your Destiny, then let us now give attention to motive.

Why be, or do, magick? Why are we, who are led by soul choice to this path, by Destiny's hand, here, when there are so many easier paths we could choose? So many more simpler ways to skin the cat, and many more less objectionable to the people around us? Why would anyone choose to be on this path when it is such not the easy one? Why risk so much, when not aware of what the path costs? Why choose to give up so much, when well aware of what the path costs? Why?

It's so much easier to do nothing, or to pick an easier road, like picking a smaller cross.

What's the intention in all this?

A word to the wise: know your intention clearly before you start out on this un-turn-aroundable road, and if you're already a Mage, examine your intentions continually, sweeping like radar over anything and everything you think, say and do, checking for motive.

Let's talk about why your soul would have you on this path. For that, we must have a firm understanding of the nature and motives of the soul.

The soul cares about one thing: evolution. Going home. Home to God. Everything it sets up is to get to God. Everything it does and is, over aeons of time, lifetime over lifetime, is for one purpose and one purpose only:

Oneness with the One.

Christ ascended, and when He did, He told us, so purely and simply, with no reservation, no doubt, no wondering, no hesitation, and more importantly no apology, no shrinking and no hiding, "I and the Father are one."

Wow. Powerful. These 6 seemingly tiny words form a great bridge between heaven and hell.

The soul who knows and experiences oneness with its Source, God, is a soul that is ascended, and is home, free. We call the experience different things... Born Again, Enlightenment, Ascension. They all mean the same thing, you've realized fully your divinity. In essence, you ain't human no more, though you may still have a body, and you don't have to do this human thing anymore, ever, if you don't want to.

You've joined the ranks as an Ascended Master, like Enoch, Elijah, Melchizedek, St. Germain, Kuan Yin, Christ, Buddha, Arcturus and many, many more souls who've walked this path and made it. They are all, every one of the Ascended Masters, dedicated, devoted and deeply engaged in the work of evolution for all souls everywhere, out of compassion. Enlightenment has many children, sired by the Father, compassion being the firstborn. Or, you may become a spirit guide to those still seeking ascension.

You can call on any or all of them for your soul evolution, and you will get a response (more on this in another chapter).

For the soul who has yet to experience Enlightenment, and is somewhere on its journey of intensely seeking it, and will indeed stop at nothing, lifetime over lifetime, to be it, is the soul who could look, at times, like it's having a 'hellish' journey.

You see them every day, people who are not in alignment with their soul and its main and only impulse: going home to God. The soul is singular in its mission and purpose. Its "eye is simple."

Like Dorothy. Her aim was simple: home. Even in the face of meeting strange and wonderful characters – all representing some aspect of herself – she never once lost clear sight of her vision while on her enchanted and most unusual, sometimes bizarre, visit to Oz. She was only visiting, and *she never forgot it*. She didn't get comfy, she didn't set up shop, or a get a new condo in Oz. No; everything she did, everyone she met, every choice she made, was to go **home**.

Your soul is Dorothy.

Is it any surprise she made it?

No.

God is inevitable.

All souls reach home. How long it takes is the question.

What about you? Are you in alignment with your soul?

I believe soul food was invented by people who knew they weren't home, knew they had to get back, and were trying, by every means possible, recipe by recipe, to make it there.

Soul alignment.

Get there. In full on alignment with your soul.

Your soul only wants God, only ever has, and only ever will. That's why nothing else satisfies for very long. All the trinkets offered in Oz (aka planet earth) lose their shine in very short order without God. That's why the dope fiend always needs another hit, the shopaholic always needs another mall, and the lustful one always needs another bed partner.

We're not searching for different things. We're searching for the same thing, one thing and one thing only: Love.

Aka God.

Aka Goddess.

Aka Spirit.

Aka Infinite Intelligence.

Aka Allah.

Aka Buddha.

Aka Krishna.

Aka Jehovah.

We've been sublimely inventive in the names we've made up for Love, and we have made them all up, because God is un-namable, we were just trying, the best we knew how, to wrap our tiny feeble minds around God, and what It might mean for us, or be to us, or do to us, or for us.

We've made up all these names for Love, and then we started fighting over them. Weird. But humans are weird.

No matter, the soul wants one thing, Oneness with Source, to go **home**.

Now that we know the call of the soul, how is it achieved? If you want to go home, how do you get there?

Love, Wisdom and Power. This triune flame, burning in every heart, guides you home. Yes, your HEART guides you home.

Once you're sufficiently drenched in love, you'll naturally move into service, which is where and how you make a difference on this planet with the life incarnation you are gifted with right now, fully utilizing the divine power coursing through you.

And if your desire be to really make a difference on this planet, bringing souls to the understanding of who we are, Divine Beings of Love and Light on a most miraculous journey home, you will have to make a desperate, near obsessive search for Truth, and her beautiful daughter, Wisdom, born of the marriage of Truth and conscious, practical application of the same. We're not here to simply know the truth… we're here to live it.

What you obsess over night and day will reveal its secrets to you. If you obsess over God, the Spirit within, night and day, praying and asking and seeking for truth, the secrets of the universe, the wisdom of the ages, with a pure and clean heart, motivated only by love, with the intention to apply that truth so that it blossoms into wisdom, you cannot be denied. Eventually, the Inner Being will take you up on your incessant requests -- which have only proven your commitment to the path – and bring you into higher awareness. You'll have more information than the average bear. Not for the sake of information; who cares about knowing more? No one, You'll have knowledge for the sake of saving lives, first and foremost, your own. Once you're free, by the path of Wisdom, you can free others. You can only free others to the extent that you're free. You can't give something you don't have. Get free. Put your oxygen mask on first. Then go about the all-important and only real and true mission, setting all souls free, whatever that means for you, and however God guides you in your very vital and indispensable part in so doing. There is a clear plan on your role in this whole scheme of things. It's for you to know it, be it, and live it.

This is what Yeshua ben Joseph means when he says, "wist ye not that I must be about my Father's business?" According to the account we have, he was only 12 when he asked this question. What is the Father's business? Well, what is the Father? God is Love. Love is the Father's business, love for every being everywhere, in all dimensions.

Love says that none are shackled by ignorance. Love says that all can and will be free, by means of the Inner Holy Light that shineth in one direction: the God direction. Love says that God is inevitable, and every soul will surely find its way to Her. Love says there are unlimited opportunities to do it over, better and better each time. Love says that no one's home until everyone's home, that it's not enough for you to be free; compassion says that once you wake up, you get to participate in, with joy and gladness, freeing those who are still enslaved.

Harriett Tubman style.

She could have gotten free, and chose to enjoy her new life in New York, never giving a thought to anyone else, least of all anyone else who was still a slave. It's too easy to forget. Who wants to remember a painful past, or anyone associated with it? *No, let's just forget. That's so easy and comfy.* But she didn't do that. Thank God, she didn't think that way. She had a dream, in which the divine appeared to her with an assurance that if she took up the soul work of freeing those who were still enslaved, she would be protected at every turn and no harm would come to her or the ones she escorted. She was about her Father's business. Even though she was free, done with slavery forever, that wasn't enough for her. It's not enough for me either. I pray that compassion runs so deep in you and reverberates so strongly through your being that it's not enough for you either.

Once we are free, our main business, the Father's business, is to free other minds.

Morpheus style. He kept searching the Matrix, in a magnificent obsession to find "The One", "The One" who was prophesied to free all by ending the war. Think about it, Morpheus was free, unplugged from the Matrix. He could have chosen to stay in Zion, live his wonderful life with his lover, dance in the temple and that would be that. Except that wasn't enough for him. He HAD to search the Matrix, he was compelled to. Compelled by what?

LOVE.

I sense this is why you're reading these words in this very moment, because I was supernaturally compelled to write them. I couldn't not write them and hope to stay sane or vibrantly alive for very long. I feel like Jeremiah, who said that the Lord's word was like a fire shut up in his bones. If he didn't speak the message in him – the message entrusted to him – he felt as if he would literally burst into flames. Michael Jackson style. Spontaneous combustion. It's when so much energy is built up that it can no longer be contained, then POOF!

Yes, your soul is clear, it is on a journey of and to Love.

What we don't always remember is that the Love is right here, right now, right where we are, in all its everything-ness. We can't be out of the love, but we don't always remember that.

That's where magick comes in. That's where any path the soul chooses comes in. A path, and everything on it, has a beautiful, cosmic design, according to exact divine specifications, for one purpose: to help us remember. Magick is a soul technology for remembering.

When you remember who you are, why you're here, what your soul came here to be, do and have, when you remember your unique Divine Destiny Plan, the plan you made in heaven with your Spirit team before you came here, the *real* magick unfolds!

When you remember, everything changes.

When you don't remember, everything's painful.

Your joy and pleasure on the path of Destiny are directly correlated to your level of remembrance.

Remember a lot = enjoy a lot.

Real forgetful = real painful.

It's your choice.

When I was real forgetful on the path, I was in a bed depressed, and the most painful part about it is was, I didn't know why. It seemed that my life should have been happy, I had a great husband, a beautiful healthy 3-year-old smart son, a beautiful healthy brand new baby daughter, a loving family, a whole community of Jehovah's Witnesses who loved me, the home we wanted, in the neighborhood we wanted, with great health.

And still, I was deeply depressed and near ready to take myself out with a bottle of pills.

Why?

Because I had amnesia.

I didn't remember who I was, or why I was here.

Very forgetful, hence very painful.

Pain isn't God's judgment or vengeance.

Pain is the natural by-product of forgetting.

As humans, we all forget, so we all have pain. It's a very useful thing to get our attention. How else would you snatch your hand back from a hot stove? Pain. If you didn't have it, your hand would stay on the stove and get burned. Pain is just an early – and quite beautifully loving – warning mechanism to urge us to give attention. How long you choose to stay in that pain, and how deep you choose to take it, and how attached and loyal you choose to be to it, and how willing you are to make excuses for it, are all up to you. Long lasting and deep pain that we're attached and loyal to goes by the code word 'suffering.'

You can choose to come out of the pain (and suffering) anytime you want, by remembering.

We could put it this way: pain is unavoidable, suffering is not.

Pain will happen, to all of us, at some periods more frequently and intensely than others. That's all par for the human course. No Magician concerns him or herself with that, we know too many ways to shift the energy rather than wallow in it for very long and let it turn into something else.

Suffering, unlike pain, is not a requirement for life on this planet, contrary to popular stupidity. We just keep choosing so much of it, suffering, that is, (prolonged and deep attachment and loyalty to pain with excuses for why we're holding on to it) because so many of us have forgotten, and refuse to wake up. I've observed the phenomena of human suffering up close in my spiritual life coaching practice. I can't tell you how many people I've listened to, who've offered countless excuses to hold onto pain they've long outgrown, and has morphed into suffering, and as such, has them by the jugular, slowly squeezing them dry of their vital life force energy.

Once pain taps you on the shoulder, it's present to be a wake up call, not to be a trigger deeper into the coma of unconscious living, nor is it a go numb opportunity.

Now that you've clearly sensed your soul's calling, if for no other reason, choose to be magick to FREE yourself from any and all unnecessary pain and suffering.

Remember.

We Forgot

T hanks to the mass conditioning affected by Disney, the early church, the Roman government and many more entities and influences than I can name here, many of us have come to despise witches, Pagans, and magical beings of all sorts.

We forgot our magical roots.

It was not always so.

Magical beings, including witches, root doctors, shamans, magic practicing priests, oracles, dream interpreters, since antiquity, have been sought out for the wisdom of the ages and help with all manner of common problems, from crops to health, as well as all manner of uncommon problems, such as causing a man's private parts to not function if he leaves his woman for another woman. When I was in Jamaica, they told me of the Obeah man, who has every potion and oil you could imagine, or ask him to whip up for you, including "Oil of Don't Leave Me". Would I really want that oil if I was with a crazy person?

Anyway, the point is, magical people have been sought out for help, wisdom, healing and guidance ever since we've been on the planet and came to know that there were gifts and powers that seemed to be beyond human capabilities, that, if honed, could change things and people, and heal us and others. The ones who developed these innate gifts and abilities, and were gifted in magical ways, and who learned further to tap into the healing properties of the earth and nature, including stones and crystals, oils, flower essences, herbs, animal feathers and more, were asked to help and assist their fellow brethren, and most often did. Instinctively, they must have known that their gifts and abilities were for the greater good, or for cursing, if need be. Either way the powers were used — for blessing or for cursing — we knew the powers were effective. They worked.

Throughout the ages, it was easy as pie to procure an ointment or magical brew for just about anything. It wasn't considered taboo. It was the way we lived.

We lived magical. Not just some of us. All of us. We knew there was magic all around us. We knew there was magic in the trees and the earth and the flowers and in the dance of the fires we sat around at night and in the sky over our heads. We knew, and we practiced. Those who didn't practice — either because they didn't know how or didn't believe they could — visited upon someone who did.

Whether you lived in ancient Egypt and visited the temple of Isis to consult with a high priestess about your dream and its interpretation, or went to one who reads the sky in the orient to discover your lucky stars, or visited the root doctor in your village for a reading on what crops to plant and how the weather of the coming year would affect them, or visited a Tarot card reader about whether your mate is cheating, we believed in magic.

More than believing in it, we lived by it.

Then something happened.

As far as I can ascertain, and I'm open to seeing it differently, It all seemed to go awry once Christ came and left. After Christ was crucified, there were many sects, or tiny groups, teaching what they felt he said and did. The group, I believe, that was closest to what he truly taught and lived were the Gnostics. (Some say Christ himself was Essene. This may be so, though I must confess I do not know.)

Gnosticism springs from the Greek word meaning 'to know'. After having read goodly portions of the Gnostic Gospels, I believe the Gnostics were the closest to preserving the true essence of what Christ lived, taught and demonstrated. I do not have proof of this belief, it's simply an inner knowing that seems right to me.

I also believe the current Christian church, as we know it in this twenty-first century, is very far off the mark of the essence of Christ.

Some of us forgot how to love.

The Gnostics were suppressed, and many of their books destroyed. Because truth cannot be forever hidden, the Gnostics continue to this day, sharing with us the true essence of Christ's life and teachings. The Gnostic Gospels make more sense to me and hold as much meaning for me as the 4 Gospels we find in the Bible canon.

Centuries after Christ died, the church and the government (almost one and the same at the time) decided to not allow the varying factions of 'Christianity.' It wanted a unified approach, one that would unite and solidify the Roman empire. Factions are splinters in the heel of government. The decision having been made, anything and everything not aligned with the Church's official take on Christianity was labeled of the devil and declared heresy.

What ensued over the ages has been nothing short of a mass suppression and demonization of magic. By the time the *Hammer of the Witch* was written, the tide of history was further altered away from our magical roots and deeper into fear and darkness. In the darkness, the masses of society came to believe many things that were not true, including the lie that witches (and all magical folks) are somehow in cahoots with the devil.

It was convenient, as all lies are.

With the descent into fear and darkness, the death knell to many witches, and magical folks of all sorts, had fallen.

No longer did we live magical. It was too dangerous. No longer did we consult magic books or oracles or root doctors. It wasn't safe. No longer did we visit soothsayers or necromancers or dream interpreters. Those folks were being demonized and wiped out en masse.

Humanity fell into the dark ages, when fear enveloped us for centuries. We forgot our magic. We would not see the light of day until after the 15th and 16th centuries, in the wake of more witch blood being shed in the name of religion than we can fathom.

Witches call it 'the burning times.'

The times when it was heresy to use your magical power. The times when anyone could point the finger at you, call you a witch, and you'd be tried, and possibly hung, burned at the stake, beheaded or drowned.

The times when we also scoured our lineage of any signs of the Sacred Feminine and decided to turn God into a male. The Goddess was nearly submerged into oblivion.

It is not unrelated that the witch and the Goddess were seemingly attacked and wiped out at the same time. There is an sacred and unbreakable kinship between the witch and the Goddess, and the ruling entities at the time wanted no parts of either.

All ideas of Christ having a consort were also erased from history, or at least attempted to be erased. All ideas of a Divine Feminine were eradicated, or at least attempted to be eradicated. It didn't work. Thank Goddess.

Where love is in any of that is beyond me.

Yet it was all claimed to be done in the name of God.

I do not worship that God.

The God/Goddess I know is Love. The God/Goddess I know takes over one's mind and transforms every inch of it from fear to love, if the subject be ready, open, pliable. The God/Goddess I love, serve, worship and live, breathe, move and have my being in is pure, unconditional love; never pushy, never demanding, never takes away, never kills.

God/Goddess only loves.

In this pure, unconditional love, all is healed, all is made right. In God/Goddess, truth shines brilliantly.

Because of our errant thoughts and the human ego tendency to judge, humans have created large sectors of people to hate. We point accusing fingers at each other and say "you're wrong!" or "you're of the devil" or "God doesn't approve of you." Who are we to say any of it? Who are we to judge? Who are we to set ourselves pridefully and arrogantly in a holy place, the place only God/Goddess resides? Just who are we to do that?

Yet, we do it every day. We judge. Self and others. We say what's bad, who's bad, and what they should do to be right. Who made that up? We did. Then we apply our standard to everybody, and who doesn't fit it, we call evil.

Enough.

This is not love.

As a practicing Christian Witch, I have heard the most hateful, hurtful comments from Christians. How can this be? How can the group who says they are blessed by and favored of God, and have love as their abiding principle, and say they are 'saved', and say they follow Christ, judge so harshly and hatefully?

How?

Best not to ask that question. I haven't had it answered yet. What I have received, in my innermost sanctuary, as my path is LOVE.

Once, I was in fervent prayer asking God/Goddess, 'what do you want me to do?!?' I was in a place in my life where I was asking the divine to show me the way. I wanted a word from God. I was hungry for it. I knocked incessantly on the doors of heaven til an angel swung the door wide open and I received my answer:

"LOVE EVERYONE, ALL THE TIME,
REGARDLESS OF WHAT THEY DO."

That's it? That's what you want me to do God? That's my life purpose? What kind of answer is that?

"LOVE EVERYONE, ALL THE TIME, REGARDLESS OF WHAT THEY DO."

I was stunned.

I will never forget that day. The lights went on. I thought there was some high and lofty thing I was here to do. Maybe there'd be angels and trumpet blasts from heaven revealing some great and noble truth to me that had never been revealed to anyone on the planet.

How prideful.

No, Valerie. There's nothing new you're getting that hasn't been revealed before. You're not special.

The only thing that's ever going on in the universe is love.

And because love is so beautiful, if we cling to it, we will not forget.

A Word of Caution

If you're a casual questioner, let's talk.

What is meant by 'casual questioner' is that you're somewhat curious about magick. By nature, casual questioners who are simply curious are not committed.

There's no harm in being casual or curious, yet there is something you must know: as long as you are simply casual and/or only curious, you will not be granted the secrets of High Magick.

True understanding in the Mystery Schools – and of the ancient wisdom they are custodians of – is hidden from casual questioners. No mighty mage is casual about his/her search for wisdom, truth, understanding and ultimately, enlightenment. Though some may have begun their search in curiosity, somewhere along the road, the continuously fed curiosity was fanned into a thirsty flame and then a raging bonfire.

Only the ones compelled by this burning desire, searching diligently for the secrets of High Magick, with pure intention, persisting in the search for years that roll into decades, are granted access.

High Magick is not a quick fix.

It is not an instant success, nor does it cause it.

I remember doing a reading for a client who asked me for a spell for fame and fortune. If such a spell did exist, I would not perform it. It actually may be detrimental to anyone who's unprepared for the results. I have found that there's no such thing as waving a magick wand and having fame and fortune.

There is a process of becoming schooled in the High Magickal Arts and

Sciences, and that process, for me, has not been fast.

It's taken years, dedication and devotion.

With that said, I offer you an emphatic NO... this path is NOT for you if you are a simply a curious and casual questioner.

If you're an earnest truth-seeker with pure intention to become enlightened, ascend and serve, and you're willing, ready and able to persevere in your practices in order to master your craft, you will be richly rewarded.

If you are simply casual and curious, the secrets of the Universe will remain hidden from you.

You now have a choice: you can stay curious, and not expect much.

Or, if you know you're called to this path, you can answer the call of your soul, commit your mind and heart to whatever is required, with all you have and all you are and experience true magick. If this is your commitment, and you stay the course, you will be richly rewarded.

As always, the choice is yours.

Choose wisely.

Genesis

I confess my genesis as a Christian Witch emerged under a set of circumstances which could be deemed bizarre.

I was the first born child of 4 to a beautiful and bright woman, who was 19 years of age at the time of my birth, single and living in Harlem, New York City with her parents in 1961.

My mother was no ordinary woman. I must confess I have no idea how she managed to avoid being completely ostracized by family and friends for having a baby out of wedlock as a teen in 1961, when Ricky and Lucy were still sleeping in twin beds (even though, for a stretch, Lucy was very pregnant on the TV show). These were the days when a toilet couldn't be shown on television.

I was born in Sydenham Hospital on 125th Street, smack dab in the middle of Harlem. The hospital is no longer there, a little fact I find amusing.

She named me Valerie, after her favorite soap opera character, and brought me home to my maternal grandparents 'railroad' apartment on what was then 8th Avenue in Harlem (the street having since been renamed Frederick Douglass Boulevard). That style of apartment was nicknamed 'railroad' because of its design, it was straight through, like railroad tracks. You had to pass through one room to get to the next. Our home was shared with the usual rats, mice and roaches of New York City tenement living, and I didn't know any better at that juncture.

They say I slept in a drawer when I first came home from the hospital, a not uncommon experience for a baby in those days, though they must have gotten me a crib at some point, as I've seen pictures of baby Valerie in a crib wearing all white, or perhaps it looked that way because all the photos are black and white.

There always seemed to be a lot of people coming and going in that little railroad apartment. My grandmother had 4 children, my mom and 3 sons.

There was Uncle Gary, funny, smart, and definitely, in the 60's when I was born, a Black Panther kind of dude. The Black Panthers were considered dangerous to common black folk, or at least to the ones I was around. The Panthers seemed angry to me, albeit justifiably so. Too angry... and a black person in those days who was too angry at what white people did never had a good life, and, at worst, could be expected to meet with injury or death, even in the liberated North.

As I got the story, Uncle Gary's walk with the Panthers lasted until he went into the military, and I guess upon seeing all manner of colors, shapes and sizes of people in his world travels, had a mind reversal and came out only to marry my aunt, our beloved Aunt Sarah, a white woman. A mind reversal is a good thing.

Then there was Uncle Algie, short for Algernon, (named after an older relative) who was the uncle I loved the best; he was so young and vibrant and handsome and fun, until we got the news he was killed in a drunk driving car accident, only a few years after he and my other uncle, Uncle Vaness, were driving in a car, drunk, and got into an accident that killed Uncle Vaness.

Maybe my uncle Algie got a little more reckless with his life after being the driver in the accident that killed his brother on the Brooklyn Bridge one dark and tragic night our family will never forget. Two down. Two left.

Now there were two of the four siblings remaining: my mom and my Uncle Gary. It is most ironic that Gary seemed to be in a dangerous place, in the war, yet was safe, and the two brothers who were deemed safe at home were the ones killed.

I wonder from time to time if my Uncle Algie ever got over the pain of thinking he may have been the one who killed his brother. Even if he wasn't guilty of killing his brother, it's a hard thing to live with if you're the driver of the car when the car gets into an accident and the outcome is that the person on the passenger side, your brother, is dead. I would imagine that the wish is to have been the one taken if it would save the other.

That must have been a lot to live with.

We didn't blame him. We were just all sad. Really sad. When Algie died, I was really sad.

My favorite uncle was gone.

The 60's were a strange period of no seat belts or car seats or helmets or anything that helped protect you from life, and seemed, to my young mind, full of accidents and assassinations.

I remember gazing through a store window, holding my mom's hand, at multiple black and white TV screens of all sizes showing one thing: pictures of that wonderful man who almost everybody loved, riding in a car, when out of nowhere, somebody pulled a trigger and blew his head off.

His wife looked utterly distraught.

Then there was that other man, who seemed to be doing some kind of good work, 'down south,' where they must not have tolerated people with suntans. Edgar was his name.

They shot him dead too. I heard the grown folks talking about him with tsk tsk while shaking their heads.

And that other negro man, the one who had a dream, the preacher. I liked him.

They shot him dead too.

And that man who went to Mecca and back. He was up at the Audubon Ballroom where Rev. Ike saved souls and preached prosperity. That young man was getting ready to say something to the audience that somebody didn't want him to say.

They shot him dead too. One soul Rev. Ike couldn't save that day.

Then there was the brother of the nice man who was riding in the car.

He got shot too.

Why do people get shot, was one of many lingering queries hanging around the edges of my mind in the 60's, along with *who makes guns?* and *why do we use them on each other?* And the granddaddy of them all: *are we safe/am I safe?*

When I was 4, everything changed.

I don't know if – when we wake up in the morning on the day when everything in our world is about to change – we get any warning. I wonder if we know something's coming. Something big. A warning would be nice, because then the human could prepare itself. Maybe a message that says: *life as you know it is about to end... you will never be the same.*

Yes, that would be nice.

Unfortunately – or maybe it's the best kind of fortune – we don't get any warning when life is about to change. Maybe the lack of fair warning is part of the process. The shock factor has to be there, so we can really grow. I guess that's why we call those happenings 'out of the blue', as if the universe had nothing better to do that day than send us a jolting, life-altering, and potentially life-shattering, surprise.

That day was one of those days. My life was about to change, big time. No fair warning. No messages. At least not to my little mind.

Pause for a moment and consider this: there's a trajectory every life is on, a direction, even if it's not the direction we think we chose, or even if we seem rudderless, nevertheless, there is a trajectory, even if unclear.

Then something happens, some west wind shifts east, or some 'random' influence steps onto the scene, or some event splatters across our path. That's the precise moment when everything changes. The trajectory completely shifts, and instead of going west, that life is now clearly headed east.

Did the soul call for the trajectory change?

YES.

This is a message about empowerment, and we know, as empowered beings, that there are no victims, even when it looks like it, so yes, absolutely, your soul calls for the trajectory change, every time, no exceptions. Even if you're 4 years old and don't understand or expect it. Even when you got older and wished you had not met up with that particular trajectory change, like a divorce, or a car accident, or a difficult diagnosis. No matter. If we do not know, the soul knows.

We always know when we've had a trajectory change after the fact, because we can look back at that precise fork in the road and say, there was a pre-event life that I was living, and there's the way I live after the fact.

The trajectory change, while shocking, is always necessary (or they wouldn't happen) and called for, by your own soul.

Like Saul on the road to Damascus, blinded by the light.

Trajectory change.

Or Malcolm X on his pilgrimage to Mecca.

Trajectory change.

Or Moses murdering the Egyptian.

Trajectory change.

Or mom and me, meeting a man on the street.

Trajectory change. That particular trajectory change would take me decades to figure out.

Back to the story.

That life-altering day, my mom and me went to the grocery store. Nothing sensational there, it looked like any other ordinary grocery-making, hot summer day in Harlem.

On the way back from the store is where the story gets interesting, when we meet, by synchronicity, a man, standing on the street corner, bearing the Watchtower and Awake magazines.

No, this was not going to be just another grocery-making, hot summer day in Harlem. The earth was about to move under my feet.

The man with the magazines sports a dapper suit and Fedora. He has books too, one of them is really big, and bears a strange resemblance to the one Grandma has on the table at home. That big book in our railroad apartment doesn't get used much, what with all those words, but we do have one. It seemed necessary to have one. I saw the book in almost every home I went to. *Who could read all those words though?*

No, I decided, *that book is definitely not for reading. It's for having, but not for reading.*

It's more of a statement than a thing to be picked up and handled... a statement of who we are, and what we believe about life. It's a protection.

It's a reminder. It stays open at about the middle, to a word that starts with P. Maybe it's open in the middle because no one really knew where to open it to, and the middle was fair. Even pages on this side and that.

The book just lies there, without doing anything, and without anything being done to it, as if it had some magical power over the people who had it, whether they read it or not.

Yes, this man has the same kind of book, I'm sure of it. The thin pages give it away. None of my story books have thin pages like that. But that big book on the table, opened to the middle, with a word at the top that starts with a P, that book has thin pages, just like his.

I hear him call it a Bible. *Yep, that's what they call it alright, a Bible.*

The man starts the conversation with my mom by asking a question regarding the destiny of her soul, a strange question to ask a strange person on any random street corner, especially on the way home from the market with ice cream in the shopping cart.

Religious people do not seem to have protocols around when and where they ought to ask these sorts of questions, so asking them right here and now, in between the hobo on the street and the bus passing by is as good a place and time as any.

"Would you like to live on a paradise earth forever?"

What kind of question is that? Who wouldn't? In all the history of the people who stand on street corners asking that question, I don't think one sane person yet has answered "no."

"Do you have a relationship with the King of Kings?"

Who's that? I wonder. I've never heard questions like this before, and what's more, now I'm confused.

Who is this man?

And why is it so hot out here?

And besides, we're not supposed to talk to strangers.

I don't like him.

He has my mom's attention. All of it. Not good for a kid.

She, unlike me, was intrigued; intrigued enough to pummel him with not a few questions of her own, questions she'd obviously been saving up, churning over in her sleep, though we never caught wind of it.

I had no idea my mom was questioning life like this.

Isn't it funny how you can sleep right next to somebody and not know the deepest questions they ask, or the urging of their heart, or the longing of their soul? I slept with my mother almost every night, and never had an inkling about all these questions she was obviously piling up to ask God knows who. For the time being, this stranger on the street would do, melting ice cream and all.

Thank you very much Bible man.

Every question she asks he answers from that big book, furiously flipping pages, generously sharing the book with her so she can see it for herself.

Looking up at his kind, old face, I wonder if that man had read all the words in that big book, and if he had, how long did it take him? *I don't know anybody who can read all those words.* He even had parts of it memorized.

The conversation goes on for 4 hours, and, as they say, the rest is history.

The man was one of Jehovah's Witnesses.

When we adjourned our synchronistic – albeit humanly unplanned – gathering on that Harlem sidewalk, two things were decided in my mother's mind:

1. *This just might be the answer to my prayers*, and

2. *I have to know more.*

The Bible man invites my mom to take the next step: attend the local Kingdom Hall of Jehovah's Witnesses. Along with it, he offers her a home Bible study, to be conducted by one of the female Witnesses and another 'sister' from the Kingdom Hall who would accompany her. It wasn't appropriate then, and still isn't now, as far as I know, for a male Jehovah's Witness to conduct a home Bible study with a single female, especially one as young, attractive and shapely as my mother.

My mom's YES to the invitation was more than enthusiastic, so off we go to the Kingdom Hall the following Sunday, all dressed up in Sunday-go-to-meeting clothes; my mom, me and my brother, who is 2 years my junior. (Yes, my mom got pregnant again, 'out of wedlock', and had her 2nd baby in 1963, a bouncing baby boy. As I write this, I'm getting the sense that my mother was somewhat of a rebel, or at least a renegade.)

When we arrive at the Kingdom Hall, there wasn't much unusual, especially because I didn't have much to compare it to, we weren't the church going kind of folk, so this Kingdom Hall place was probably, from what I can tell, pretty benign and not much different from any other place people dress up and go to on Sunday mornings.

Little did I know that the cult was sinking its teeth in.

The people were nice and kind and welcoming. My mother loved it, so we came back, and back and back, and well, here it is, as of the writing of these words in the year 2018, more than 50 years later. My mother, having been faithful to the Jehovah's Witness walk from that day on the streets of Harlem in 1965, until her exit from this physical life on January 19, 2013, had truly found her soul's calling. For nearly 5 decades, she held undeviatingly true, as best she could, to what she had discovered on the street corner on that trajectory changing day.

Me, on the other hand, well, that's where the plot thickens.

You see, while I later grew to like the Bible Man, he was a member of the congregation we attended, I wasn't really *feeling* him when we first met on the street corner. I didn't consciously know Universal Law back then, but had I, I would have known that I was not resonating with him like my mom was. He and mom were on the same vibration, I was on a different vibration.

I didn't know then that I was on a different vibration, I just knew how it felt. It felt *okay* to be at the Kingdom Hall, but not great. It was more of a flat experience than anything else, at first, like eating plain white potatoes with nothing on them, not really pleasing, and not repulsive either, just sort of blandly in the middle. As my mom used to say, 'nothing to write home to mama about.'

What I know now is that my soul wasn't singing there, it would not be the destination for me, like it was for my mother, although it took me over two decades to figure that out and make my exit. My experience with the Witnesses can be described, at its very best points, plain vanilla and at its very worst, debilitating, psychologically damaging, emotionally repressive and painfully restrictive. While it was not the destination for me, I deem it a worthy stretch of road that shaped and molded parts of me into who I am today. On some level, I required the experience of being in a cult, for all it would teach me and for all the ways it would grow me.

For that, I am grateful.

Because mom took to it like a fish in water, and I was only 4 and my brother was only 2, it was her responsibility to thoroughly condition us to the new-found religion, and she took her job on with vigor.

A word about religion.

Religion needs converts, zealots, people who will spread the word with the aim of making more converts. Religion needs to be spread. Because its main need is to spread, the methods of doing that have become questionable, the end being so compelling. Hence we (I include myself as I am a former religious zealot) say means justifies ends. Its okay to invade another country, knock the people who live there in the head, hold a Bible in front of them and tell them this is their new religion. If they convert easily, all the better. If not, we're prepared to make the conversion any way we have to. Because religious zealots are set on converting, we don't need your permission, or agreement, to convert you.

Conversion can be done by force, we have mistakenly thought. We mass enforced that mistaken belief.

That was my party line for years.

I'll convert you one way or the other, it can be hard, or it can be easy, but you're getting converted.

Why?

Because I say this is the best thing for you, and you ought to accept that. You ought to know, that because I read this big book, and I believe this big book says I'm right and you're wrong, therefore you should believe the way I do, and if you don't you'll die, but if you do, you'll live eternally, then it's my aim in life to help you see that if you don't do what I say, you'll die, either now or later. However If you go along with what I say, you'll live forever and you'll even thank me for saving your life.

That's what religion was to me. I was a zealot.

A card-carrying cult member.

Now, religious zealots scare me, they are the worst kind of fanatical. I say this not from a space of judgment, but from a space of self-contemplation; whenever I have been fanatical, I have been dangerous.

If given the choice, I'd rather meet up with an atheist on a 'random' street corner than a fanatical Christian. I'd prefer a person with no beliefs than one with uber compelling beliefs. Compelling beliefs have proven themselves, time and again, to be detrimental to both the people who own and espouse them, and to the people who the beliefs are being foisted upon.

I don't want to have any beliefs.

Only knowing.

Knowing God/Goddess, experientially.

Knowing who I am, experientially.

Knowing the universe and my place in it, experientially.

I don't want anyone to tell me what my beliefs are. I want to experience life for myself and draw my own conclusions. I want to explore. Life is a grand adventure.

So you can see why, on a soul level, me and religion never got along, even though there was the radical and thorough attempt to condition me in its ways.

On a head level, because my mother and her new found religion did a superb job of mind conditioning, carefully instructing me in all the Witness ways, I was a convert, albeit a reluctant convert.

A 4-year-old convert, who, in a trajectory change like my little self had never seen, or experienced, no longer celebrated Christmas, or my birthday or anyone else's, or the coming of the Easter Bunny or the Tooth Fairy.

Santa had to go too.

Along with fairy tales. My beloved stories had to go, replaced by Bible stories. When I protested, "Not my storybooks! Why?" mom made her point clearly: "tale means lie, Valerie, so fairy tales are really lies. Why would you want to read a book of lies? They're going in the trash."

Tearful goodbye to Cinderella and all her make-believe, or not-so-make-believe friends.

While it made perfect sense on a head level, it did not at all resonate with my little heart.

What if there is an Easter Bunny? And what if I should know him?

And what if the Tooth Fairy really has my teeth piling up somewhere, carefully tending to them? They're my teeth, shouldn't I want to know about the caretaker of them?

And what about Santa? Does he like it if people just up and stop believing in him? Are there repercussions?

It was all too much for my little 4-year-old mind to digest, so I did what any self-respecting 4-year-old would do: I went along with the program, seeing as how my options were pretty much nil at that point. What mom says goes, and even grandma can't save me from the madness (notwithstanding her many valiant attempts).

Too late. I was now a convert. Albeit a 4-year-old convert; the people who do the converting aren't picky and never disparage age. More souls. The younger the better, they're more malleable. With new converts, our religion can keep growing. That's all we care about, world domination, and right now, this 4-year-old is our newest recruit in the war on who gets to take over the world with their religion.

They put a Watchtower and Awake in my hands and sent me out on the front lines. Of course I was accompanied by my mother, my brother, and all the other Witnesses in the world who were doing the same thing, whether they wanted to or not.

Where's the joy?

Where's the elation?

Where's the bliss?

Where's the soul satisfaction?

Not much of that, just do as you're told for now. There'll be plenty of time for joy and elation later, after it's all said and done. This life, in the here and now, is about the war on the world, and the one who rules it, Satan the devil. The next life, the one we get as a reward for fighting the good fight now, is all about reward. But you can't get that life until you trudge through this one.

That made absolutely no sense to me, but since the people who were largely responsible for feeding, housing and clothing me were the ones espousing the new beliefs, and with my child's mind completely open and receptive, I had little choice other than to swallow the dogma whole.

Never mind that what I was hearing didn't match what I was experiencing. I experienced spirits in our railroad apartment in New York City, old spirits, untoward spirits, all kinds of spirits. I didn't know what I was looking at, still, I wasn't afraid. I thought it was normal to see spirits.

Until I heard the belief-shovers say that there are 2 sides, good and evil. Anything we see that's not a human being or animal or explainable, is on the evil side, it's a demon, or from the devil.

Hmmmmmmmm.

I didn't feel that way. Some spirits seemed lost, not evil. Other spirits seemed happy, and only wanted to play. Some spirits were sad, others were looking for people. I didn't feel like they were all of the devil, even though, at that age, I wasn't altogether clear on the devil either, I only knew he wasn't a very savory character. Every time I heard mention of him, it was in a negative connotation, so that had to mean he was to be avoided at all costs. I made up in my mind that if I'd ever met him, I would explain that it's probably best that we don't talk, and then I would just walk away.

Yep, that was my plan.

I haven't met the devil yet.

And in all these years, I have yet to discover even a shred of evidence that a devil exists.

After all these years, I still have no evidence for a devil.

Maybe I'm like the atheists on that one. They say they have no evidence for God, so they don't believe in God. I, too, have no evidence for the existence of a devil.

What I do have is evidence for an inner enemy we call the negative ego, steeped and wallowing in fear and separation. All the thoughts that urge us to do something unkind or unloving or wretched or horrifying to anyone else come from inside our own heads. Not from an outside devil.

He is an easy scapegoat, so I can understand why believing in him would be seductive.

Who wouldn't want someone you could pin all your unloving stuff on, someone who could take blanket blame, releasing you of responsibility? Sounds like the perfect alibi for everything.

While a devil may be convenient, belief in him is not empowering.

I remember a conversation I was party to as an adult Jehovah's Witness. I was about 28 or so, newly married, with my first baby. Two sisters in the congregation and I were talking about having a family and full-time ministry (at the time I was affiliated, full-time ministers were called Pioneers, devoting 90 hours per month, an average of 3 hours per day, to 'field service' or getting more Witnesses by proselytizing). In the conversation, one sister said to the other that she wanted to become a Pioneer, and as soon as she put her application in, she got pregnant. She said "the devil sure is busy."

I remember thinking, *maybe you and your husband were busy*, though it would have been the height of inappropriateness to add my two cents to the conversation, especially since she seemed so bent on making the devil take the rap for her getting pregnant.

Back to my 4-year-old converted self.

The mind conditioning of my 2-year-old brother and I is well underway, much to the chagrin of my grandmother, whom we still live with in our railroad apartment, and who is thoroughly appalled at the sudden announcements from my mother that she and her two kids will no longer be celebrating birthdays or holidays, they being the work of satan the devil and pagan in origin.

What?!?!?

My grandmother is NOT happy.

I don't think she ever got happy, in her 94 years of living on this planet, about my mom's soul choice. After a while my grandmother worked her way to being able to tolerate my mom's religion, but it was never anything she celebrated. Grandma looked sideways at Witnesses, never really trusting and never really falling into being okay with her daughter's soul choice. Yes, she tolerated it. At times better than others, but I felt my mom never really had her mom's approval. Therefore, it's no surprise I feel I never really had my mom's approval when I decided to make my soul choice.

But then again, my grandmother didn't have to be happy with the whole affair. It wasn't her choice to make, my mom's life here was my mom's and not her mom's, as my life here is mine, not my mom's.

So the three of us played out the generational pattern of mothers who aren't happy with their daughter's soul choices, and who aren't shy about speaking to their discontent, or worse yet, not speaking to their daughters; as my mom had chosen to do for years with me in reaction to my scandalous break away from the Witnesses when I was disfellowshipped (more on that coming up).

Such is the price we pay for soul choices. If we make the choice for the soul, for enlightenment, for happiness, for joy, for the Creator and all the Creator has for us in our divinely designed journey here, which will be, by its very nature, unlike any other soul's journey here, what we are indeed doing is risking the approval (or disapproval) of the people we love most.

We think we need their approval.

In reality, we do not.

Baffled

I confess I'm convinced the Witnesses saved my mother's life. It was the best thing that could have happened for her. We do not know, considering the path she was on, what would have happened if divine destiny had not stepped in with the trajectory change that hot summer afternoon on a street corner in Harlem.

Notwithstanding grandma, a strong argument could be made in favor of the new-found religion. It did my mom good. Immense good. There is little question her soul knew what it was doing.

She's suddenly found everything she was looking for, even without knowing she was looking, or what she was looking for. Her questions having been thoroughly and dutifully answered, one by one, to her satisfaction, gives her life new meaning. It fit her world and all its fragmented pieces together in a giant and glorious finished jigsaw puzzle. No loose pieces. No missing pieces.

The religion was what she wanted, better still, it was what she needed. The divine always gives us what we need, when we need it, and was poised to give her another piece of the puzzle: a husband.

It's 1968 and mom has dedicated her life to Jehovah a few years ago and symbolized it by water baptism and is fully indoctrinated into Witness life. On that note, she would not hear of or engage in dating a man who's not a Witness. That's a tall order. She had quite a few suitors to turn down, being curvaceous with a thick, full head of long dark hair, and an easy, fabulous smile. She was, as they say, 'quite the looker.' Being naturally gregarious, mom had the uncanny ability to turn almost everyone into a friend instantly.

I see her as a stunningly beautiful woman. She stayed that way up until the day she gave up her form and left the earth.

In 1968, she is undoubtedly the subject of many men's dreams at night. To focus exclusively on Witnesses was both a test of will and a point of determination if you're getting offers on almost a daily basis. If you're not getting offers, it may be easier to look exclusively at Witnesses for potential partners.

As 'fate' would have it, she didn't have to look far. Right downstairs was a butcher shop, where a quietly and intensely focused young meat cutter named Jimmy carved pigs into pork chops and cows into roasts.

My mom goes into the butcher shop at least weekly, to buy the family's meat. Jimmy always smiles, but doesn't take his eyes off his job. Fingers and knives don't get along when they come to cross purposes. The knives Jimmy works with are long and sharp. He makes them sharper by scraping them swiftly across a long iron pole, back and forth. I don't know what it means, but his little ritual helps get the meat off the bone, or slice through the bone.

Jimmy gives mom the best pork chops, the best bacon, the best roasts. Grandma, who sends mom to the store, knows something's up. The same money is buying better and better meat.

Let us pause the story for a moment to engage the backdrop that is Harlem circa 1968, before the days when humans got the bright idea to pile everything up in the same store, tires and dresses and chickens and loaves of bread and all.

It is 1968. If you want a loaf of bread, you go to the bakery, where the people who tend the bakery came in early that morning to create and knead the dough that will make its way into the oven, which you will get a heavenly whiff of. When your mother or grandmother sends you to the bakery, the baker will smile at you, give you the bread he knows your family eats, and receive the money grandma tucked into your skirt pocket, tightly wrapped in a note. Grandmas love making notes. I don't read the notes; it's not allowed for the one carrying the note to read the note. It's rude. Nosy. I don't do it. I dare not.

If you want a dress, you go to a dressmaker.

If you want meat, you go to the butcher shop.

It's a simple way to live, so very uncomplicated, so quite clear. You always know where you are and what you are getting.

Later, life sped up and we didn't have time to make errands all over town to buy this here and that there, so we mutually agreed to pile up great hoards of items in one place and buy them all together in ginormous shopping centers.

Shopping was no longer a social staple, a time to catch up on neighborhood gossip and generally see how everyone was doing. Instead, it was downgraded to the level of necessity, to be handled in the fastest and most efficient way one could manage without knowing any of the people who were pushing the big shopping carts next to yours.

I don't know if I like the modern idea.

There's a pristine beauty to eating bread touched by someone that very morning, the one who cares deeply enough to arise early, while we are yet slumbering, to knead the dough well, who's name we know and who never fails to greet us warmly when we enter the bakery; something wonderful about being wrapped in clothes sewn by someone we know, who lives right down the street and gets quite the subtle enjoyment out of seeing her wares sashay about the neighborhood on backs and bodies of people she knows.

In its own weird and wonderful way, 1968 in Harlem is a beautiful place to be.

This is how Jimmy and Jackie meet; at the butcher shop on the corner. After awhile it comes out in conversation between my mom and Jimmy that they are both Witnesses.

Talk about synchronicity.

They are elated. It means they can move forward on the mutual attraction they're experiencing.

If one was a Witness, and the other was not, no matter that the mutual attraction exists, nor how strong its pull, they could never, and would never, in integrity to the Witness promise, indulge it.

Yet, these 2 have the synchronicity green light. They're both Witnesses. They converse more.

Trips to the butcher shop are more about Jimmy and Jackie than pork chops and bacon.

They decide to go on a date. He comes to our railroad apartment upstairs on the 2nd floor. Grandma is there, and me and my brother. My brother doesn't seem interested in the visitor, but I am. Intensely interested.

I decide I'm going to find out more about him, that I'm going to conduct my own personal investigation. I don't know what told my 7-year-young self to do that, but something in me informed me that this man was meaningful, important, that he'll be around for a while.

If that be the case, I have a few questions of my own.

So I put them to paper in a questionnaire I concocted and conducted my first investigative interview whilst sitting on grandma's couch one evening before Jimmy and Jackie went on a date. Notwithstanding the embarrassing hue of not a few of the questions (including the infamous question kids love to ask, "How old are you?") he answered every one, patiently and humbly, with a touch of humor, a wholly voluntary act of valor on his part that made me feel particularly important, noticed and acknowledged. It still warms my heart to this day that one such as my soon-to-be father would take the time and interest to allow himself to be subjected to the queries of a 7-year-old in an age when children were 'seen and not heard.'

Yes, my little mind was made up, *I like him*. That love affair with my father continues to this day.

My mom and soon-to-be dad continue down the path of mutual attraction all the way to holy matrimony on Saturday, June 14, 1969 at the Kingdom Hall of Jehovah's Witnesses on Bradhurst Avenue in Harlem where my mother had been a faithful member of the Bradhurst Congregation of Jehovah's Witnesses for the past 3 years.

We immediately move into a 5th floor 3-bedroom apartment in a walk-up tenement building on St. Nicholas Place — called 'Sugar Hill' — in Harlem, where the 4 of us, my mom, new dad, brother and me take up happy residence and where I was soon to witness one of the strangest sights

I'd ever seen in my 8 years of life on planet earth...

Mom and dad sorted through piles of wedding gifts. They were well liked and well known, and mom was moving into her first new home with dad, so they were flooded with gifts, from Witnesses and non-Witnesses alike, including family, friends and neighbors.

One of the gifts, obviously from a non-Witness, was a wooden statue of praying hands. It was adorned with a beautiful engraving of what I believe to be the "Our Father" prayer, though mom and dad never let me get close enough to read it.

I watched my father take a hammer to those wooden praying hands.

He sat on a workbench in our new apartment, surrounded by wedding gifts, and hammered the praying hands to smithereens.

I don't understand.

Don't we pray?

The hands are so beautiful, they make me think of God... they make me want to be with God.

My parents make us watch the demolition.

They explain to me and my brother that the praying hands are dangerous, an idol, and comprise worship of Satan the devil. They further explain that we do not worship or idolize anything except God; idols, or anything like an idol, could bring us in contact with the devil or his demons.

The praying hands must go. These kinds of things must be destroyed, lest they become a snare. Considering their particularly dangerous nature, they must be destroyed, decimated, lest someone else see them in the trash and pick them up, and bring the demons into their own home.

I confess I am thoroughly baffled. I cannot come to terms with the deliberate and willful smashing of the beautiful wooden praying hands, a gift at that.

If we have praying hands on the mantelpiece, are we idol worshipers? Are idols this beautiful? How can something of the devil feel so good in my soul and spirit? I loved those praying hands...

No matter how I try, it does not fit together in my 8-year-young mind. My puzzle pieces are all over the place, and the colors do not match.

But mom and dad are convinced, so for now, that will have to be good enough for me.

Unbridled Judgment

In a few short years, my mom's new religion elevated her from the lot of a young, rebellious, inexperienced, unwed mother of 2 living at home with her parents, in an uncertain world, to the respectable plane of being a married woman of faith with a family, a home of her own, a bevy of new friends and a strong religious community to go along with it. Total life transformation. According to my mom, it was all for the better.

Like it or not, I must go along with the program, even though something in me is not well.

We are deep in the clutches of the cult.

Because of the move to our new apartment, we change congregations and begin attending the Kingdom Hall on 151st Street and Broadway because my father had been serving there as a 'ministerial servant,' He was formerly in the territory of Manhattanville Congregation of Jehovah's Witnesses when he lived at home with his mother (on 146th Street between Broadway and Amsterdam). Witnesses are strongly encouraged to attend the Kingdom Hall in their 'territory'. A territory is a plot of land assigned to a particular congregation of Jehovah's Witnesses to 'work' by knocking on doors (with the goal of gaining more Witnesses). In our case, there was a Kingdom Hall closer to us, the Edgecomb Congregation of Jehovah's Witnesses, which was on St. Nicholas Avenue, yet since my dad was in the Manhattanville congregation, that's where we went.

He must have gotten approval from the elders to pull that off, or maybe the congregation needed ministerial servants like my father, hard workers who would tow the line without question, so they allowed him to stay, and bring along his new family.

A little bit about how my mom ran our Witness family is in order...

Because unbridled judgment knows no limits, even among Witnesses there were favorites. In order for my mom to be convinced that a person had any business around her kids on a continual and close-knit basis, the individual had to be a practicing Witness who demonstrates strong zeal by near perfect meeting attendance, weekly participation in field ministry, commenting at meetings, as well as be 'in good standing' with the Witnesses. 'In good standing' means there are no offenses on one's record, like fornication, or adultery, or sexual misconduct, which runs the gamut from kissing someone you're not married to, or engaged to, all the way up to what Witnesses call 'heavy petting' which means feeling each other up. Homosexuality is also on the list of 'sins', as well as the obligatory lying, cheating, stealing and other general offenses of the 10 commandments and Paul's writings.

Other Witnesses, who didn't fit my mom's, and by extension, the religion's standards, or who were not as zealous as the religion thought they should be (and I will use the word 'fanatical' here) were considered 'weak in the truth'. They were there, but they had one foot in and the other on a banana peel. My mom wasn't keen on those kinds of Witnesses either. She could spot the outliers in a second, and she wasn't having it. Witnesses viewed those kind as dangerous to themselves and other members of the 'flock'. The emphasis was on strengthening these in the 'truth' before socializing with them could be approved.

Witnesses don't mix with 'worldly' people. A 'worldly' person is anyone who's not a Witness. They are considered to be of this 'world'. It is taught that Christ said we are 'in this world, yet not of it.' Anyone who didn't get that memo and hadn't yet joined up with the Witnesses is considered 'worldly' by the cult's standards.

The exception to this rule of making sure we were only surrounded by like-minded, behavior matching religious zealots who were solidly pledging allegiance to the cult, not unlike ourselves, was family, even if they weren't Witnesses. Though socializing with non-Witness family members was allowed, it came with a warning: BEWARE. And if they were extended family, and we didn't absolutely have to be in their presence, to hell with them.

My grandparents were different though. First off, they were not about to allow my mother's new religious fanaticism curb their relationship with their grand kids. That they made clear and never wavered on. They agreed to give up buying us holiday and birthday gifts, out of respect for my mom, but they were not backing down on family bonding across the generations, regardless of the cult's teachings.

From the time I was born until my mom and dad moved us into their own apartment in the year 1969 to a neighborhood nicknamed 'Sugar Hill', we lived with my maternal grandparents. So it wasn't like we could live with them and actually not speak to them.

My mom had to tow the line with her mother, and since there was no Witness mandate not to see your parents or grandparents, off we went to grandma and grandpa's house pretty regularly after my mom married and moved us into her and dad's new apartment.

Before embarking upon visits to grandma and grandpa's house, mom made sure to remind us that they were 'worldly', hence, be watchful. She had us on alert for grandma's house, even though I never got the impression grandma was the culprit. She seemed pretty innocuous to me, always the sensible, wise one.

If anybody was the culprit, it was surely my renegade grandpa, who yelled obscenities at the television when the players in the baseball game didn't do what he thought they should, smoked "like a smokestack" indoors with all of us around (we hadn't yet discovered the dangers of 2nd hand smoke), had questionable 'buddies', played numbers, told dirty jokes and sipped interesting smelling drinks out of mugs shaped like naked women with slogans printed on them, like 'bottoms up'. My mom's disapproval and downright disdain for some of my grandfather's ways was more than apparent.

I don't think he cared. Renegades certainly don't let their children tell them what to do.

Yes, grandpa was the cult's culprit, if there be one, the negative influence warned about in 1 Corinthians 15:33 – where the Witness Bible states: 'bad associations spoil useful habits.'

I adored him. Children know hearts. My heart knew grandpa was not a culprit, no matter how much his behavior seemed not to line up with the religious definition of a 'good' and 'righteous' man.

Which, for me now, begs the question, how do we throw away parts of people as unusable or unacceptable because they don't agree with our religious or moral sensibilities? Where did we get that right? It lands on me now as the height of religious arrogance.

Ever since I can remember, my grandpa was a sweet spot in my world. He gave us 'cluck-clucks', a strange combination of a kiss on the cheek with a clucking sound. I don't know if he invented cluck-clucks, or if he got them from his grandfather, or somewhere beyond that. I say his grandfather because cluck-clucks don't seem so much a parent thing to do as they seem a grandparent thing to do.

After he taught me how to give 'cluck-clucks', one of his requests whenever we met up was, "hey, there's my girl, give me a cluck-cluck!" That was one of me and grandpa's favorite things to do, cluck-clucks.

Until the day he left. We sung Amazing Grace at his funeral. I cried like tomorrow would never come.

Grandma, conservative, poised, controlled and witty, by contrast to her husband, was never an issue. I didn't ever see her drink, much less get drunk and lose control, though that was my grandfather's practice, and my uncles' as well, and for a good part of my life, it became my mother's practice too, though she drank, held and carried her liquor differently than the men in our family. We were clearly from a family of alcoholics. More on that later.

Though my mom was almost zealous about taking us to museums and cultural events to expose us to the vast and varied culture of New York City, she was equally good at shielding us from any direct contact with people who weren't Witnesses outside of immediate family, and from Witnesses she believed were not totally on board with the religion's teachings.

Please also remember that I am referring to a time that was pre-internet, pre-cable TV, pre-mobile devices and pre-mass media.

The only phone we had was nailed to the wall in the kitchen, with a long curly cord attached, and could only be used after having secured the necessary parental permissions. When we were granted permission, our parents rushed us off it really fast, because back then the phone company charged by the minute. "Valerie, you're not running the phone bill up!" was the oft-yelled warning about the telephone and how quickly I'd better get off it.

Throw into the mix that I grew up with 3 television stations, CBS, NBC and ABC. There was the public television station too, if you could count that, PBS, on channel 11 or 13, when it was on, and only viewable if you could get the TV antennae to cooperate.

Mind you, that was only for the people who had the wherewithal to buy a TV in the first place. TV was still a somewhat new and rising phenomenon, quickly taking the place of radio. Everyone who couldn't afford a TV set either gathered at people's houses who could, watched it through the windows of storefronts that sold TV's or listened to the radio.

So we are not talking about a time that would render it near impossible, as it is now, to shield your kids.

It is the 60's, and with unbridled judgment in the driver's seat, it's easy to shield your kids. You just didn't let them see anything you didn't want them to see. You didn't let them associate with anyone you didn't want them to associate with. And with that very sanitized, small, controlled world, you could almost convince a kid of anything.

You could get them to believe that the world is precisely as you are presenting it.

Corn Starch

My new dad came with a new grandma.

And a whole new family.

My dad is originally from Georgia, deep in the heart of the south. Once he and my mom got together, and got the okay from both sets of parents that they could be together, we started to get to know my new dad's side of the family.

His mother ate corn starch.

Why does she eat white powder out of a yellow box with an ear of corn painted on the outside?

Some questions never get answered. I'm okay with that.

Her name is Mary, but we all call her Mae, a name imbued with love. She had 6 children and loved us immediately, me and my brother, her two new grandchildren from the union of her son and my mother, and I loved her until the day we said goodbye to her, and still do. She had a great big heart, big as all outdoors, as they say, missing teeth, a smile that went on for days and a dog named Poopsie. Poopsie didn't eat dog food. Poopsie got all the food we didn't eat, scraps, put into a heap in a bowl and placed in the corner of the back yard. Poopsie was happy, as far as I could tell.

Mae lived in the kitchen. From there, she baked the most mouth melting biscuits I had ever wrapped my lips around. Once I got to know what that smell meant, it never failed to make my mouth water. We got excited when we saw flour on the table with dough and her wooden rolling pin. We knew the cup was coming, the ideal kitchen utensil for cutting out perfectly round biscuits. Next she placed them ever so gently on her well worn, greased and floured baking sheet and slid the whole contrivance into the oven. Pure perfection.

After that perfectly orchestrated ritual, it was only a matter of time before we were moaning. Hot buttered biscuits make people moan. I discovered that at Mae's. If you add a bit of Karo syrup, for dipping the biscuits in, the whole affair becomes intoxicating to the point that we can barely speak.

Mae was in her second marriage when I met her. She had 4 children from her first union, the youngest of which was a girl, about 13 when we first met. This child would change my life forever.

She had two younger children from her new marriage. A toddler, and a baby. Back then, it wasn't strange for a grandma to have children at the same time one or more of her children was having children, and that's exactly what happened in our family. Around the same time Mae had her youngest two children, a boy and a girl, her eldest daughter also had two children, which Mae took care of, since the mom was 'out of sorts.' The 4 of those children grew up like brothers and sisters (Mae's 2 children and her 2 grandchildren) even though they were really aunt, uncle, niece and nephew. In a close-knit extended family, title does not matter so much as position in the family. I eventually became the eldest of 4, so when my mom bought home by baby brother (the 3rd in the brood) when I was 13, and my baby sister (the 4th and final of the bunch) when I was 15, from her new marriage, I became the 2nd mom. That was my position, because I was the oldest. By biology, I was big sister. By position, I was 2nd mom.

Mae's house was always full. Full of kids, full of activity, full of food, full of life. She was a full woman. The one thing I can say Mae's house was full of was love. No one was able to hold that together in her home when that matriarch passed. There was no Mae heir apparent.

In all fairness and honesty, those were big shoes to fill. Who could do cooking, cleaning, kid-watching, baby-nursing, diaper-changing, husband-loving, gardening, dog-caring, all while Jehovah's Witnessing? It wasn't easy. Her life looked like a lot of work. To her, it was a breeze, especially when we heard her talk about working in the fields when she was a little girl in Georgia. It still strikes me as strange how close my family is to the slave and sharecropper era. Mae was born and brought up just a tad after sharecropping, and well within Jim Crow, with its signs of WHITES and COLORED. It must be hard to live in a time and place in which signs have such the prominent role in everyday life. Defy a sign and you likely risk bodily injury or death or both.

So she knew hard work well, all day long, under a hot southern sun. That was her daily round, growing up in the rural south. Then she took to house-keeping, one of the few jobs a woman of her skin color could have in that era. So, if not by nature, her life experience had perfectly domesticated her. She was the undisputed queen of her home, and seemed to loved every minute of it.

I was happy with this new 'down-south' grandma. My mom's mom was raised on a farm in New Jersey, her family had come north from Virginia in the great migration. My maternal grandma grew up on a farm too, but under vastly different conditions. The north was free. Jim Crow did not live there.

My maternal grandma was decidedly northern. She married my grandfather and moved to Harlem, New York City before the Harlem Renaissance. She wore fancy dresses. She believed a woman was not dressed without hat, gloves and a purse. That was true in her day. No self-respecting woman would go out of doors, especially to anyplace important, without a hat, gloves and purse. She put doilies on furniture. She drank tea out of china. She had fancy things.

Contrast this with my new grandma, who drank out of jelly jars and seemed most comfortable in a housecoat. True, they were pretty, flowery housecoats, with snaps down the front; all the same, they were housecoats. I don't know if Mae owned gloves, and I don't think she cared. Maybe living with Jim Crow made things like gloves seem almost ridiculous.

I love going to Mae's. Before she moved to her home in Mount Vernon, New York, she lived with her family in an apartment in New York City. So we went often on Sunday's to see the family and have Sunday dinner. The visits to Mae's were fun, until they weren't anymore.

The shift happened after me and her youngest daughter engaged in sexual acts that disgusted me. It didn't happen all at once. It was gradual, like sliding into quicksand. No one drowns in quicksand in an instant. I'm not even sure why they call it quicksand. There's nothing quick about it. This was the same. A gradual descent into a dark place. We, me and my new 13 year old aunt, were often sent to her room to take naps. Back then, it wasn't uncommon for kids to take naps every day, or whenever the grown-ups got tired of us.

At first, we napped. Gradually, it morphed into something more, something disgusting. My young self felt and experienced it as disgusting. We descended into exploring sexuality in ways that introduced me for the first time to shame.

Before the acts, I didn't know about shame. If I did have any, I wasn't aware.

After feeling myself being sucked into the quicksand with her, I knew shame. Intimately.

I wasn't a willing participant, even though I confess I didn't know how to say 'no' either. Something in me was roped into doing things I didn't want to do. My heart was screaming NO. My spirit was feeling defiled. My mind was confused, dazed, shocked and horrified. My body was rigid. I hated the smells that came of what transpired in that tiny room in that New York City apartment.

Thankfully, it did not last for long. After a few incidents, I believe my mother, cunning, smart, connected, who watched us like hawks, caught on that something was going on that was untoward. She never said anything, she just made sure circumstances didn't lend themselves to anything shady going on anymore.

I was relieved and thankful.

Then Mae and her family moved to Mount Vernon, New York. I was relieved again. *She's further away, I'm safe.*

Decades later, I confess the day I heard Mae's daughter died in a car crash I had a momentary glee thought; *I'm glad she's dead.*

My own thought scared me. I was shocked at the contents of my own mind. I didn't know I harbored that level of hate, and for so long, until it jumped to the surface from deep inside. I had been toting, and maybe even nursing, that hate, heat, resentment and shame for over a decade by the time the accident that killed her had occurred.

By then, I was a grown woman, with children of my own. So was she. How could one mother be happy another mother is gone? Especially if she leaves behind little children?

It was relieving to hear that though her 3 kids were with her in the car, they all survived unharmed. When her car wrapped around the tree, her body shielded them from being hurt.

Ironic.

Someone who, I believed, was responsible for hurting a young person, namely me, is now memorialized as someone who protects young people.

Life is strange, bizarre even, with its twists and turns that challenge everything I think and held to be true.

The happy thought that jumped to the surface when I heard news of her passing informed me I had deep forgiveness work to do. I took on forgiveness as best I could then, not really having the tools to handle that kind of inner work at that point in my life. In my ever deepening walk with Spirit I eventually got the tools to re-frame the moments of horror I spent in that little bedroom, frozen on the inside, going against the grain of everything in me, and partially frozen on the outside too.

For years following, I would wake up in cold sweats, frozen in my bed. Sometimes I would lay there for God knows how long, unable to move and not knowing why. Maybe I was there an hour, maybe I was frozen all night. I could never tell. It was a frozen twilight of sorts. Night paralysis.

As a teen and young adult, I didn't connect the frozen moments in my bed with the frozen moments of panic in the room that indoctrinated me into shame.

Now I know. I no longer have them. I chose and choose to forgive deeply and allow divine amnesia to have its perfect way.

Dunked

I confess I've never laid eyes on my biological father. He flew the coop when he found out his 19-year-old unwed girlfriend was pregnant (so I was told). In 1961, the constructs of society made the idea of a child born out of wedlock a crushing load to bear. It came to me intuitively in my wiser years that he couldn't handle it, being young himself and more than likely terrified at the shocking news. We must also consider my mother was the only girl of 4 siblings and had 3 brothers who would not have had a problem protecting her honor. The intuitive knowing that came to me about the circumstances around my birth with regard to my biological father made me more forgiving, less questioning. Because I've never met him, and am not sure if he's still in this life, I've asked the universe to bring him to me.

My dad, who raised me, has always been quiet and firm, solid as a rock, never yelled (unlike my mom), and never put a hand on us growing up (quite an accomplishment in an age where "spare the rod, spoil the child" was taken literally, kids were dutifully taught and fully expected to be 'seen and not heard' and no practical child abuse rules, regulations or laws existed to prevent any grown-up from putting their hands on any kid for any reason).

Mom was the one who was quick to reach for a belt or a ruler to dole out corporal punishment, and when she didn't have those at her disposal, the back side of her hand across my face or a pinch on the underside of my upper arm administered enough pain to swiftly get me into compliance. She was a strict disciplinarian. The discipline serves me well to this day, even if the methods were untoward.

My Dad preferred delivering his discipline orally, from the Bible (another Bible Man. I can't seem to get away from them) for hours on end. Just as painful as a beating, if you ask me. But nobody asked me.

I must confess, some of the 3 hour talking-to's from dad, sitting on that little, round, 3-legged wooden stool in his room, with Bible scripture after Bible scripture being read and considered as both reasons and answers to changing whatever wayward, un-cultlike behavior I had been caught in, were not only the most boring thing I thought I would ever have to endure as a child, they also had the added effect of making me wonder if a swift beating from mom might not be the better option after all.

At least she was faster.

I confess I do not know which was worse, a swift and painful beating inflicted by mom, or a long, torturous talking-to from dad.

The double-pronged disciplinarian approach the divine arranged for me growing up was quite effective. If I forgot the whelps across my legs from mom I could not easily dismiss the Bible words in my head from dad.

After more than a decade of very thorough conditioning and rigid discipline from the Witnesses, through my faithful parents, in the form of 5 meetings a week — 2 one-hour meetings on Sunday morning (a public discourse and a study of the Witness seminal journal, the Watchtower) 2 one-hour meetings on Thursday night (the Ministry School and the Service Meeting, both designed to make me a better convert-maker) and a one-hour meeting on Tuesday night (the book study, more indoctrination) — in addition to Field Service (knocking on doors and walking the streets to make disciples) on Saturday morning, family study on Monday night, daily Bible reading and personal study, there was not much else to do other than follow the party line directive to dedicate my life to Jehovah and get baptized.

Which I obediently did at the age of 15.

I confess I didn't know what I was doing.

Witnesses have a different take on baptism than what I've noticed in other Christian denominations. They believe one should first dedicate their life to Jehovah God (which really means dedicating oneself to being in the Witness cult for life). They view it as one and the same. I do not. That dedication, according to the Witnesses, is then to be symbolized by water baptism. One's entire physical body must be submerged in water, the Witnesses teach, as they believe Christ did when he sought and underwent water baptism at the hands of John. Witnesses call the one who baptized Jesus 'John the Baptizer' versus 'John the Baptist' so as to make a clear distinction between the man in the Bible and the Baptist religion, which Witnesses believe is part of the World Empire of False Religion, also known as Babylon the Great, based on the harlot in the book of Revelation.

Before one can get baptized as a Witness, there has to be a thorough indoctrination into Witness dogma, creed and culture, which usually takes about 2 years. It can happen in as short a time as 6 months, from the time one starts a home Bible study to the time one is baptized, but that's not the norm. Baptisms are only done at large conventions or circuit assemblies, never at regular Kingdom Hall meetings, so there is a timing issue involved. If there's not an assembly or convention coming up, you'll have to wait for one to get baptized.

Please do bear in mind that I was affiliated with the Witnesses from 1964 until the 1990's, so this is my best recollection of how things were done when I was associated with the cult. Things have invariably changed. What you read on these pages in my experience.

With that said, let's discuss how a person actually becomes one of Jehovah's Witnesses.

The process goes like this: a Witness knocks on someone's door. The person accepts the magazines, or is receptive to the message the Witnesses are bringing. The person, once the Witnesses leave, is marked on the written records the Witnesses keep as an 'interested person.' A 'return visit' is made to the person. Return visits (formerly referred to as 'back calls') are made to specific addresses where someone has shown interest previously. They are usually made in the afternoons, after Witnesses have knocked on each door in a particular territory. When making return visits, there will have been a time lapse of a few days to one or two weeks from the first encounter.

Once the householder is receptive again on the return visit, they will be offered a home Bible study. If they say yes, a time and date is set up for the home Bible study to be conducted each week at a time that is mutually agreeable to the householder and the Witness. The Witnesses go in two's to return visits and home Bible studies.

The text for the home Bible study will be a book, produced by the Witnesses, that is used to augment the Bible and teach Witness doctrine. The book, along with the Witness Bible (the New World Translation of the Holy Scriptures) will be given to the householder for them to study in advance.

The person will also be invited to the Kingdom Hall, with Witnesses citing the scripture that instructs to not forsake the gathering of yourselves together.

If the person is faithful in having their home Bible study each week for a period of about 6 months, and is deemed to be progressing well, and is attending all 5 meetings regularly, they will be invited to prepare themselves to become a publisher.

When one becomes a publisher it means that their life has been found to be in alignment with Witness law and they are not committing any gross sins, such as fornication, adultery, lying, cheating, stealing. Being a publisher means that the person can go out in field service and begin recruiting more Witnesses. One does not have to be baptized as a Witness to be a publisher.

Once the person is a publisher, they will naturally be holding the goal, by this time, to dedicate their life to Jehovah and symbolize that dedication by water baptism. The water baptism must be witnessed by onlookers, the more onlookers, the better.

Before that can happen though, the person will receive another book — in addition to the many Witness publications they most likely have by now, required for the 5 meetings and deeper study — containing 80 questions that are to be prayerfully considered and satisfactorily answered before one can be baptized. The 80 questions are designed to cause a person to search themselves to know that they are truly ready to take this all-important step of joining the cult. I call it an 'all-important' step because once you're in, you can never get out (unless you're put out).

After studying the 80 questions on their own, the publisher will undergo several meetings with the elders of the congregation to go over each of the 80 questions together.

After that, the elders will make a determination as to the person's readiness to get baptized. Most oftentimes the answer is yes, considering all the hoops a person would have to jump through by the time they reach this juncture; no one just happens upon getting baptized as a Witness. By now, 6 months to 2 years, or more, may well have elapsed, and if you're in that deep, you're probably serious about what you're doing.

If the answer is yes, the person becomes a 'baptismal candidate' and will be baptized at the next assembly or convention.

Sometimes the answer is no. The elders find, for whatever reason, that the person is not yet ready to be baptized. Maybe they've dedicated themselves, which is a personal decision, and no one can really tell you if you're dedicated or not, but the decision to be baptized publicly as a Witness is in the hands of the Witnesses, not the person. It's the ultimate "yes, you're choosing us, but we've got to choose you too."

After completing the 80 questions, the answer from the elders for me is yes, so I am scheduled to be baptized in the summertime at the upcoming district convention.

I was baptized in a temporary swimming pool set up in Yankee Stadium with thousands of Witness and would-be Witness onlookers on a hot summer day in July 1977; a day, I might add, eerily not unlike the day we met the Bible man.

I wear a brand new swimsuit, me and my bestie Cynthia. We're both baptized at the same time; *makes it easier if you have a friend with you when you're doing something big*. My new swimsuit, bought for the occasion, as well as hers, is too showy, exposing more flesh than is comfortable or appropriate, so we're each handed an over-sized white t-shirt by the kindly sister who's monitoring swimsuits in the bathroom where all the baptismal candidates are changing, with the instruction to don it immediately. The modesty monitor having spoken, we quickly and quietly comply.

I pull the big t-shirt over my swimsuit and head out the women's dressing room, flip flops on, into the hot sun, with thousands of Witnesses watching, waving and applauding from the stands. My mother is as proud as can be. It's a celebration.

I am minutes away from being a full-blown card-carrying member of the cult of Jehovah's Witnesses.

When I descend into the pool, the water is cool, which feels good because standing on the line leading up to the pool (there are hundreds of people getting baptized that day) has sweat beads popping out all over me. The big t-shirt isn't helping.

I remind myself that this is not a fun day at Highbridge Pool, the pool I was used to cooling off at on hot summer days in Washington Heights in what we call Spanish Harlem. This is serious business, and I appropriately snap myself back to the gravity of the moment, away from fun thoughts of Highbridge pool, as much as I can, at 15 years young and not really knowing much about anything.

I am taken under the cool water, plunged backward, with my right hand over my nose, and my left hand holding the wrist of the right hand, over my heart, with the brother baptizing me holding me firmly at the middle of my back with one hand while the other grips the arm crossing my chest.

The Witnesses have managed to contrive the perfect manner for a man to baptize a woman without possibility of inappropriate touch. They practice it quite a bit. To be a brother who baptizes people is honorable among Witnesses. Yet one can never show any sign of getting a kick out of it. That's pride. You always have to hold whatever you do, no matter how good and honorable it is, in a *just another day at the office* fashion. Anything else is considered pride; a sure prerequisite to privileges being stripped.

Not being a swimmer, and being really nervous, my body movements cause a part of my anatomy to come up out of the water during the baptism the first time I go under. And the second. In the Witness world, I am still not baptized after being dunked twice, because a toe has surfaced the first time, and a foot has surfaced the second time while the brother has the rest of my body under.

Surely a sign.

You ain't baptized, Valerie. They have watchers to make sure. Under again you go.

Am I fighting this?

Before taking me under a 3rd time, the brother tells me to relax and keep my feet firmly planted on the floor (sound advice for life if you ask me). I do as he says. He dunks me a third and final time. Success. All of me went under, at the same time. It is done. I'm a full-fledged Witness.

Now what?

Well, aside from the teenage partying here and there and hanging out with friends, also Jehovah's Witnesses, all of life was basically the same: religion all the time, in an endless, dizzying, non-stop round of Bible study, field service and meetings.

Completely fanatical.

I confess there is a fanatical side to my personality that was fostered and fed in the whole setup. Doesn't it take a touch of fanaticism to be in a religion at all, especially a cult? I cannot say that side of me has been completely problematic. To the contrary, it's served me well in spaces and places along the way. Sometimes it pays to be fanatical, about the right things, but never about what somebody else thinks I should be fanatical about. That's what I've learned, don't take on other people's fanaticisms. Create your own.

I was in high school, and though the issue of college was on the horizon, it was considered by the Witnesses to be a den of iniquity, drugs and sex, so the mandate was to go to a vocational school or to take up a trade in high school, which trade one could use to earn a modest living, while spending the majority of time preaching the good news, the true Witness purpose, since the end of 'this system of things' was due to strike at any moment at the great war of Armageddon.

We were taught to always live a modest life. Never strive for a career. Why would one want a career in a dying old system of things anyway?

No time for college.

No time for careers.

You're dunked now Valerie, of your own accord, and even more than before, your life is about field service and more field service. The only exception to that is eating, sleeping, occasional play, and everything that prepares you for more field service.

That was the story of my life, and I did as I was told.

The choice for high school was the then all-girls' Washington Irving, which afforded two possible vocations that didn't require me to continue on to college: nursing and secretarial studies. Mom gave me the choice of one of the two. Either one, she reinforced in my mind, would earn me a modest living, while making sure to keep the main thing the main thing: preaching the good news as a Witness. That was to be my career, avocation and vocation for the rest of my life, until the end comes. That's your job here. We need more converts. We must spread the good news of Jesus Christ. And then the end will come. The end can't come until we spread the good news. So there's not a moment to lose.

I confess I was a reluctant convert.

I didn't 100% agree with the plan, but I can't say I had many ideas for alternatives either. My attitude was, I guess these people have it all figured out, and I've been with them now for over a decade of my life, and my mom is sold out that this is the best thing since sliced bread and is clear that there is no other acceptable way to live, so for now, I guess I'll go along with the parade.

The cult tide was strong, and I was uninspired to fight. Nor did I have real reason to.

Little did I know that high school was about to change everything.

The Beating Drum

N o one in High School knew I was a Witness, and even though I was dunked and sworn in to a life of field service, I confess I wasn't uttering a word about it.

I was secretly happy to keep my secret happily.

Up until the day I first set foot on the steps of Washington Irving High School, virtually my entire social, religious and friend world was ruled by and comprised of Jehovah's Witnesses.

Now that I've arrived on these very steps — of Washington Irving High School in New York's East Village — for the first time since we met the Bible Man on the street, I feel a new sense of freedom from the chains of home and religion, it is a visceral feeling, pumping through me.

It is aliveness. Freedom is aliveness. High school is when I make this connection.

We are meant to be free.

It felt good, really good. *Yes, this feels too good for something to be wrong with it.*

More than the freedom high school affords, it makes me curious, and for sure, curiosity sounds a death knell for religious cults.

In my new high school life, I take the train to school. The train carries my body downtown, where I am blithe to escape the Witness world for hours on end every day.

For the first time in my life, I am free to roam the city and explore, though I've lived here all my life. Having been tightly pinned in place under my mother's thumb for years, I almost didn't know what to do with myself and this new found freedom.

Besides that, for the first time in my academic life my mother did not make her annual September visit to my school to have a discussion with my teachers about why I would not be participating in anything that sniffed of anything the Witnesses didn't approve of,

Yes, every September I endured the humiliation of my mother coming to school on the first day of school, to meet with my teachers, with me in tow, to announce that we were in a cult (well, she didn't actually say cult, she said religion, but I think we all know what that means) and to lay out, in no uncertain terms, what was deemed acceptable and unacceptable to the religion as far as I was concerned, and any school activities under discussion. No birthday parties. No cake or ice cream. No coloring turkeys on Thanksgiving. No Christmas creations of any kind. No saluting the flag. Valerie won't even stand for the Pledge of Allegiance (the Witnesses view it as "the disgusting thing standing in a holy place" from a strange scripture in the book of Revelation, I believe, but don't quote me on that one).

"Valerie can sit in the hallway whenever any celebration is taking place in the classroom. She is to be dismissed before said celebration, and not allowed to re-enter the classroom until the celebration is complete." This was my mother's annual September declaration to the fresh round of teachers she was turning her child over to.

In hand she would always have the latest school magazine or journal the Witnesses made up for handing out to teachers with all the school rules laid out in writing (Witnesses never leave a stone unturned, gotta love a cult for being thorough). Said booklet was frequently updated and the new version released at a 'district convention' in the summer time to rousing applause from an audience of 10,000+ Witnesses in whatever stadium we were assigned to attend.

I always secretly scorned that particular publication, because I knew what it would mean for me come September.

Now that I've arrived in high school, mom not coming with me on the first day of school signaled two things. One, it was clear that it was up to me to stand on my dedication and baptism. Now it was up to me to tell teachers and students that I was a Witness, what that meant, and where I stood on celebrations of all kinds. Second, it meant that I was getting older, more mature, and with that, more trustworthy.

I was happy beyond words. Have you any idea how embarrassing it is for mom to show up at school every year to have that dreaded first day of school talk with my new teacher, while I squirmed in the chair, held my breath and begged for the whole thing to be over? Not the worst of it were — while mom explained, in detail, why Witness kids do not engage in any holidays or extracurricular activities — the furtive glances of a teacher whose thought is clearly 'you poor child.' Ugh. Top on my top ten list of things to hate.

Not so in high school. This September is different.

I'm free!

I have a whole new life, a life where people don't know I'm a Witness, and in fact, don't care.

In this new world, it doesn't matter a hill of beans what religion I belong to. No one's interested.

It's the 70's and life is about bell-bottoms, platform shoes and expressed creativity. It's "joy to the world and all the boys and girls" and nobody's assassinating anybody anymore, at least not publicly. It's students against Vietnam and peace for everybody. It's burning bras and women's lib. It's getting stoned on acid and LSD, none of which I had the courage, or bad sense, to do.

Students came from all over the world and hailed from almost every ethnicity on the planet, my school being a micro melting pot set against the backdrop of the macro melting pot that is New York City. For the first time, I have peers of every color and persuasion. My early years of school in Harlem kept me in circles with only black students.

Also a first for me in this new high school environment: religion doesn't matter.

Shocking as it may be for me, the reluctant religious convert, no one is the least bit concerned about what religion anyone is, or has been, associated with.

Refreshing.

Religion is a non-issue.

With that out of the way, it feels like we can get to the business at hand, living life!

Another first quickly happens. I forge a friendship with a black girl from France who speaks French. I had never experienced anything like that in my life. Strange as it may seem, at that point, I never knew there were black people who spoke French. I didn't know there were black people who came from France. I thought France was a 'white' country (remember, I grew up with 3 television stations and no internet).

For now, I'm in high school and loving it. I'm free of the Witnesses, to a degree.

The ironic thing about it was, up until my feet land on the steps of Washington Irving, I didn't know I wanted to be free.

I knew I harbored grudges and a complaining spirit about Witness life, with all the meetings, and even more so at having to get up early, especially in February to trudge through waist deep snow in New York City to knock on doors of people who, for the most part, are irritated at our arrival, when where I really wanted to be was home in my warm, cozy pj's sipping hot chocolate and watching Conjunction Junction like any self-respecting kid would be doing on a Saturday morning.

Even with all that, after having been in the Witness way for over a decade, I thought I had come to a place of acceptance about it, like a mole on my left hand; I may not like it, but I learn to live with it, especially if I think there's nothing that can be done about it. After a while I learned to live with discomfort, even accommodate it. I thought that's how life had to be. Discomfort now, for the life of bliss later. Live with the mole now, be beautiful later.

Going to high school, for me, was like waking up to find the mole had vanished. Imagine the elation.

I was definitely still a Witness, but there was now an opening for me not to be one.

The Witness plan for me forbade going to college, at the visible displeasure of my high school team of teachers and guidance counselors who were sure my writing would land me in newspapers, magazines and beyond as a journalist or author or both. The Witness stance then was that college was a veritable den of iniquity, full of unfettered sex, drugs and alcohol, and most definitely no place for an impressionable young person, especially without adult or Witness supervision.

Either way, without thinking ahead to what would happen, or not happen, after my freedom years in high school, while I was there, I was determined to enjoy myself.

I loved writing, and in high school, like never before, my writing blossomed and was celebrated. I took journalism, at the bequest of guidance counselors, who hoped my writing would garner me scholarships, which would hopefully make the case for college to my parents. I wrote for the school newspaper, for the school yearbook and took any and every opportunity I could to write. I also joined the high school drama club, under the close questioning and supervision of my mother, who was adamant that the main thing remain the main thing and that nothing creep in to deter meeting attendance or field service in our very Witness life.

My high school counselors pulled hard for me to go to college, to write, to be a journalist, to share my writing gift with the world. I could see they didn't understand the Witness perspective, and even disdained it. They thought it foolish to not get a good education, especially if you're a talented writer from the hood who could potentially have college paid for. So they kept encouraging me in what I was good at.

I felt the pull inside too. For the first time, my writing was morphing into something I never knew I had in me. Witnesses didn't have much room for creative writing, there was no need to write. We were charged to read, study and absorb the information we were given, on a head level.

When someone has your mind, they have you.

We were conditioned to believe what the religion wanted us to believe. There was no room, or tolerance, for having personal creative ideas, and especially not creative writing. What would you write about anyway? The Watchtower Bible and Tract Society (the distribution arm of the Witnesses) has already written everything you need to know, they having received it from the Faithful and Discreet Slave class (an elite group of elderly European men who, at any given time, are the be-all, end-all, say-so for Witness dogma, what the Witnesses believe and how they operate, purportedly based on the true revelation of scripture, which only they say they can receive, pope-style) with a Governing Body (also a small group of old European men who have charge of the entire global organization of Jehovah's Witnesses).

No, there was no room for creativity. Do what you're told. You're celebrated if you do, and if you don't, there are untoward consequences.

Hence my dilemma. I was never a do-as-you're-told kind of gal, although I didn't consciously know that about myself until I reached high school. I became a rebellious teen, wanting to assert my own will and way, but my mom was time enough for that with beatings, punishment and more religious conditioning, including the famed and effective trio of getting and keeping religious converts in line: shame, guilt and judgment.

Those are handy tools in the Witness toolbox; dare I say they're handy tools in every dogmatic system's toolbox.

It's clear to me now why my writing would have never been celebrated there. The only kudos I got was for having good grades in elementary and middle school, Witnesses do prize good grades, it means you're paying attention in school, which helps condition the mind to make you a better Witness. If one takes to the conditioning in school well, it makes the cult's job easier.

At no time can there be the risk of a free mind, following its own course, led by its own beating drum. No, that would be disastrous, and as such, is to be avoided at all costs. No creative writing. No creative ideas. No matter how loud the heart's drum beats.

Thus, religion kept us busy with much to do; taking extreme care that none of the prescribed activities were creative pursuits that would free the spirit and let the soul soar.

Soaring is not allowed in the Witness religion. They needed us to walk lock-step with all the other Witnesses around the globe so they could keep control. You can't control free-thinking, creative free spirits who are following the beat of their own heart's drum.

What are free-minded, free-spirited people good for? Changing the world? Yes! Helping people? Yes! Helping themselves? Yes! Perpetuating religious dogma? NO.

Therein you have religion's dilemma. They need you to be non-creative, cow-towed, and taking instructions from an outside party. Whatever it must do, it cannot let you get in touch, and stay in touch, with the beating drum within.

Well, in high school, my beating drum was too loud to ignore. There must have been a constipation in my spirit, because when I finally let loose with creative writing, I wrote so prolifically and furiously that it landed me in the office of the English Department, at the personal request of the department's Chair, Mrs. Freeman.

When I got the notice in my school mailbox that Mrs. Freeman wanted to see me, along with the time and date, I was petrified. Why would Mrs. Freeman want to see me? I quickly scanned in my mind the English assignments. They were all complete. As a matter of fact, I relished my English work so much that I did that homework first. I was most of the way through 9th grade, and couldn't imagine why I was being summoned to the office of the Chair of the English Department. In my conditioning, grown ups only called you into private meetings for scoldings. *What did I do wrong?* I'm nervous as all get out.

Nevertheless, right at the appointed time, I was sitting in Mrs. Freeman's office, bracing myself for a scolding. For what, I didn't know, I imagined it had to be that I was in some sort of trouble.

When I arrive, she isn't there yet. Oh goodie, my mind gets a few minutes more to persecute me with all the possibilities of bad things that could happen the second she walks through that door.

Much the opposite, Mrs. Freeman walked in with the biggest smile on her face, "Valerie, so glad you came."

Did I have a choice? If I'd thought I'd had a choice, I certainly wouldn't be sitting here, waiting for some kind of lashing, but I'm a good girl, my mother saw to that. Good girls don't have choices. They do as they're told.

"I've been looking at your writing..." she continued.

Uh-oh, here it comes, this is going to be bad... I brace myself, fingers gripping each other, sweat sticks my palms together.

"And it is absolutely remarkable. It's some of the best writing I've seen from someone your age."

What?!?!? That's why I'm here? Holy smokes, this isn't what I thought it was going to be...

The drum of my heart beats louder.

"I want to offer you a space in our English A program for next year..."

She's offering me an opportunity?!?!?

She describes the program to me, and shares that it's exclusively for exceptional English students, who write well, read widely and have 'above average' reading comprehension. It's a program that challenges students with college level work.

Then she says something I think I'll never forget.

"We read the great classics, written by some of the greatest authors of all time, Chaucer, Shakespeare, Wordsworth, Longfellow..."

Wait a minute Mrs. Freeman... are you telling me you want me?!?!? My mind is doing back flips. I was floored. I almost could not believe what I was hearing. If a fly was in the room, it would have found its way into my hung-open mouth with ease.

How often does it happen in life that you think you're about to get reamed out for God knows what and instead you wind up getting the offer of a lifetime to something so indescribably delicious that you can barely put words to it?

I'm in heaven; right here, and right now (and they told me that wasn't possible).

Mrs. Freeman was the first person to fan the inner flame of my creative spirit, she saw me. She saw through the facade. She could hear my beating drum. She was one of the rare ones who peered straight into my soul. And I let her, because she was one of the few who cared to.

She continued, "I teach the class myself, so it's very demanding. You're invited, yet I had to have this talk with you to let you know how challenging it will be, and to know for sure you're up to it. Though you qualify with your writing, grades and aptitude scores, you must be willing to take on the challenge. Are you?"

Before I tell you the rest of what transpired in Mrs. Freeman's office that day, and to understand how poetic and magical this moment truly was for me, from my then frame of reference, we'll have to revisit my childhood. Please indulge me for a brief moment.

One of my favorite things to do as a kid was immerse my head between the leaves of a book. I had books galore. My mom took us to the public library all the time. I bought home all the books from school that they would let me get my hands on in the school library, and as long as my mom had given them the once over, and approved them as Witness-friendly, and I had already done my Bible reading, and had read all the Witness literature, especially the Watchtower and Awake magazines, a new issue each week, then I was free to read the approved books.

And read I did.

I had a voracious reading appetite. I consumed books ad nauseum. I was rarely caught without a book. My tiny mind read so much that my teachers in 2nd and 3rd grade — based on my standardized test results that revealed I was reading and comprehending on an 8th grade reading level — wanted to skip me. Mom said no. Her reason: "she might miss something."

Now that you know that, for Mrs. Freeman to be telling me that we'll be reading all the greats of the literary world was probably the best news I had gotten from a teacher since I heard they wanted to skip me in 3rd grade.

I was beyond happy. I was ecstatic. I couldn't say yes fast enough.

I left Mrs. Freeman's office a different person.

And I never went back to who I was before that meeting.

Trajectory change. This time, a wholly pleasant one. I didn't know life could get this good. It had never been for me, as sweet as it was in that moment.

I glided down the hallways back to class, excited for this new world, and scarcely able to keep myself from daydreaming about Shakespeare and wondering what his writing life was like.

I'd caught a glimpse of life on purpose, and the light was blinding, not to the real me, to the me that had been carefully shielded, screened and guarded from 'outside' influences, when, in essence, I was being shielded from the real me.

Now, in high school, writing and setting my creative spirit free, I realize, on a soul level, that I am following the beat of the inner drum, doing what I love.

In a word, I color it glorious.

The glory was not to last.

Love, Sex & Witness Law

I met my first husband-to-be when I was 15 years young.

He was a tag-along with a guy who came to visit me, after a long talk at a Witness picnic that resulted in me giving him my address (we didn't have cell phones back then). Giving him my address was a no-brainer, since he was a Witness too, and we were all in a close-knit community where practically everybody knew each other.

I don't know why a guy would bring another guy with him to visit a girl he likes, especially if the tag-along is cute.

In this case the tag-along was really cute, and we instantly had a deep attraction. I call it love at first sight because it was an immediate knowing in my spirit that we would be together, in some form or fashion, though I cannot say that I knew then we were to be married 7 years later.

The first guy was out of the picture, just that fast, after I laid eyes on Benny (names have been changed), and he laid eyes on me.

He was a tad bit renegade. My mom didn't like him. She could sense his disregard and seeming disrespect, though I don't think he was being disrespectful as much as he was just being a 16-year-old.

Either way, mom thought I could do much better and voiced her opinion at every opportunity.

Benny was a deejay, had a rogue best friend (also a Witness), wore Adidas full attire (sweat suit and sneakers) and carried an enormous boombox on his shoulder through the streets of New York City. Not a pretty sight in retrospect, but pretty common back then.

My mom was disgusted that I was intrigued, and clearly smitten, by him.

100

I must confess, the 'bad boy' syndrome had taken a hold of me.

The 4 of us hung out a lot, me, my best friend Cindy, Benny and his best friend Danny (names have been changed).

Danny liked Cindy. He and she got married several years later. He was crazy, but we didn't find that out until she was already madly in love with him, and he with her. The news came to us when we got a frantic phone call from Benny saying that Danny was on the train platform about to jump in front of a train if Cindy didn't agree to be with him. She had recently broke up with him and his emotional state obviously couldn't bear it. She sensed the desperation in his threat and decided to stay with him.

Why I don't know. I tried my best to talk her out of it. He was clearly out of his mind. My argument was that any guy who would end his life — or threaten to — because he can't bear to be without her is not worth being with. But I think there was also a secret and silent longing for love in Cindy that made his antics okay, even welcome. When you don't know you're loved, anything that seems like 'love' will do, no matter how crazy it looks or is. And if someone is willing to jump onto train tracks if you won't agree to be with them, all the better.

She clearly had a different thought about it than I did, and it was her life to live, so I let it be. Years later, after Danny had been on pills to stabilize his mental mood swings, she told me he almost drove her and him to their death (during a period in which he didn't take his meds), swerving wildly down a winding road at breakneck speeds, threatening to end it all, on the heels of her proclaiming she was finally going to leave him, for real. I never understood their 'romance' but there was definitely a soul pact between him and her.

They went through that drama for about 10 or 15 years, until they finally parted ways for good.

I don't know where either of them is today.

Back to me and Benny. We didn't have a whole lot of regard for Witness law when it came to making out, and doing everything we could not to have sex but still have a really good time.

This is as good a time as any to talk about Witness laws on love and sex.

To begin, in the Witness paradigm, only male and female unions are allowed.

No gay unions.

If you are not in a relationship, there are still rules:

No masturbation.

No flirting.

No lusting after other people's mates.

Relationships between a man and a woman carry many rules:

No sex before marriage.

No tongue kissing before marriage.

No fondling before marriage.

No 'heavy petting' before marriage. 'Heavy petting' is considered any kissing and fondling that gets you worked up enough to want to have sex, even if you don't actually have it.

Once a heterosexual couple is married, the rules continue and expand:

No anal copulation.

No oral stimulation or copulation.

No menage a trois.

No kind of sex that is anything other than a penis entering a vagina.

They pretty much squeeze the fun right out of anything you want to do involving sex.

It's still a mystery to me how Witnesses manage to police married couples in their bedrooms, but they do. My husband was afraid to break the rules in the bedroom so much so that he never jerked himself off. If we didn't have sex, he would ask me to jerk him off, which I did, but hated. *What's the point*, I used to ask myself. Either have sex or jerk yourself off in the bathroom or shower or wherever you feel inclined to do so. No one's watching, and no one knows

Yet, the cult had convinced just about everyone that Jehovah God was watching all the time and would punish or reward according to behavior, so it was pretty easy to get compliance even from people's private bedrooms when threatened with 'God's watching.'

I always felt deep in my heart that what one does with one's own body to sexually please self wasn't anyone else's business if it presented no harm.

I sure as hell wasn't telling when I pleased myself. It felt too good for anything to be wrong with it.

One's sexuality belongs to oneself, not to a religion.

In the cult, we allowed our autonomy to be stolen. More accurately, we gave it away, maybe because we were afraid of it, or didn't want to assume responsibility, or thought somebody else could be trusted with it more than we could.

Back to the rules.

In the Witness world, there's no such thing as dating to get to know a potential mate. Dating is exclusively for marriage.

The only acceptable arena for getting to know anyone of the opposite sex is wholesome group activities, like bowling, going to see G-rated or PG-rated movies, attending Witness 'gatherings' (a get-together for Witnesses only at a home of a Witness) or apple-picking or ice skating or some other innocuous activity that will present little titillation and no opportunity for hanky-panky. Wholesome activities must take place in public and with a group of Witnesses present.

Because of the rules, we were accustomed to traveling in herds. You might see 10 or 20 Witnesses going to the movies, and maybe 30 or more of us going roller skating. We were taught it was safer to travel in packs. Maybe it is. Maybe it's not.

The most important thing to the Witnesses about this 'herd' mentality and behavior is that it discourages intimacy and provides public accountability.

Isolation is taboo. You must always be with a group, if you're unmarried. It's rare that you even see an unmarried Witness going out to dinner alone. Such a one would surely be questioned.

Once you've traveled in the pack for awhile, chances are you'll see someone who you think you may click with, or want to get to know better.

You can't date the person, or ask them out. Dating and courtship are strictly governed. The Witness mandate is clear: dating is only for marriage.

To get to know the person you're interested in, you must participate in group activities together. You're told that there's also opportunity for wholesome association at the Kingdom Hall and out in field service. You're encouraged to watch the person for several months. You ask them questions while out participating in a group activity, like 'what's your favorite color' while you're picking apples or horseback riding at a dude ranch with a bunch of other Witnesses. You continue building a relationship with the person in a group setting until you're reasonably sure this is the person you want to marry.

You and the other person have probably had a lot of interaction by then in the group setting, laughing, skating, going to movies and gatherings. Months or years of this kind of activity could go by; it's not uncommon for Witnesses to marry someone in the same congregation (group of Witness who go to a particular Kingdom Hall at the same time), or someone they grew up with.

Once you and the person have gotten to know each other in a group setting and are reasonably sure you want to get married, you 'ask' permission to date. It's not a formal rite, it's more of an unspoken ritual. If the girl's parents are Witnesses, it's appropriate for the young brother to approach her parents and let them know he'd like to date their daughter with the intention of getting married. If they approve, the brother's parents will also be approached, to get their consent as well. If both families agree, it's likely that the young couple will talk to the elders of the congregation, to let them know what's going on. This is not required, it's more of an unspoken rule in Witness culture.

If all is a go, and everyone 'approves', the couple starts officially dating, with the intention firmly in place to get married within 6 months to a year.

What that dating will look like could vary widely, yet it will be strongly enforced that the couple is not to be alone in closed quarters. My mom used to tell me "when attraction and opportunity meet, you have a problem." She's right. If you lust after someone, but never have the opportunity to fulfill the desire, nothing will happen. If you are thrown in close quarters with someone whom you hold no attraction for, it doesn't matter how long the two of you are locked up, nothing will happen.

But don't let two people who have the hots for each other get together in a private setting, especially if they're both virgins.

Witnesses strongly encourage marriage. If one cannot find someone whom they want to date, the Witnesses will then support the person in developing and embracing 'the gift of singleness.' They call singleness a gift, because it will mean a sexless existence, even sans masturbation (if you're following the rules) and to do that, one would have to be gifted by the divine for such a path.

More on dating.

If a brother gets a reputation for dating several sisters without following through with marrying any of them, he's heading for reprimand. You won't get the opportunity to date more than a couple of people before eyebrows raise in your direction.

Once a couple has dated for a few months, it's expected that they will become engaged and announce a wedding date. Witnesses discourage long engagements, for obvious reasons. It's presumed that we're talking about virgins here, and the virginity is supposed to be released on the wedding night at the honeymoon. The news from the dating couple of the impending nuptials will be met with extreme elation and celebration by both families and the congregation, if everyone is in 'good standing'.

Let's talk about people who are not in 'good standing.'

A Witness who's not in good standing is a Witness who has infringed upon the rules and has received discipline. Since we're talking about sexuality and Witness law, we'll address the ways this is handled, though there are other offenses that could warrant one not being in good standing, such as lying, thievery or not taking care of one's children or family.

In order to be punished, the Witness who has infringed upon the rules must come forward and confess their sexual misconduct to the elders (trust me, many of us never did).

For those who willingly confess, if the infraction is serious enough, there will be a 'judicial committee' formed to deal with it. A judicial committee is comprised of 3 elders from the congregation the person is a member of. One of the members of the committee is likely to be the Presiding Overseer (the person who is in charge of the congregation for a period of one year), the second in command and a secretary, who will be responsible for taking notes at all the meetings.

It's said that the elders get off on listening to people's sexual escapades. I don't know if that's true. I only know that the nature and extent of the questions does lend itself to a kind of 'audio porn.' The elders are trained to ask invasive questions that delve into the alleged 'sexual misconduct' in such a way that they get all the details. They find out who the parties are, whether both are Witnesses, or only one. They ask if the parties kissed, and if they did, if tongue was involved. They'll ask about genitals and if any were touched, by whom, how, and if the touching resulted in orgasm for either or both parties. They'll ask if and when any clothes came off, and where the incident happened (obviously the back seat of a car is very different from booking a hotel room). They'll dig into every aspect of the sexual escapade until they have all the information to make a ruling.

It's embarrassing to tell a committee of 3 men all the details of a sexual escapade (even if the escapade was really fun while you were having it). The person being investigated cannot have anyone in the room with them during the inquisition.

I've always found it strange that the elders would take a woman in the back room of the Kingdom Hall for questioning about personal sexual matters. The whole thing seems strange to me and always did. Not to mention highly invasive.

There may be several meetings with the judicial committee to get all the facts of the case. There may be meetings with both parties, if both parties are Witnesses, and there may be meetings with each of the parties individually to see if their stories jive.

After the elders determine they have gathered sufficient information (which could involve several meetings, each a couple of hours or more in duration), they will deliberate and study any and all scriptures that apply to the case in order to make a ruling (a decision about what is to be done). Sometimes they may ask the 'Society' what to do, in particularly hairy cases. The 'Society' Is a nickname for the Governing Body of Jehovah's Witnesses.

The ruling will fall into one of 3 categories.

The first category is 'private reproof', the second category is a stiffer punishment and is called 'public reproof' and the third category is the stiffest punishment, called disfellowshipping.

For the record, my status with the Witnesses is 'disfellowshipped.' One can never be disfellowshipped from God, so the term holds little, if any, weight in my consciousness, yet it can be a devastating event if one's friends and family are all Jehovah's Witnesses (which mine were at the time of disfellowshipping... see my YouTube channel for the video: "How I Got Disfellowshipped From Jehovah's Witnesses").

Let's look at each category to see what they mean, what the related punishment is, and how it is imposed.

Category 1 — private reproof — is for what the Witnesses call mild 'sexual misconduct.' Maybe a couple was tongue kissing, felt each other up a bit, but didn't carry it any further. Maybe they were in a private place, and no one knows about it except the two of them. They may be dating or not. They go to the elders of their own accord, and if this is their first offense, and they seem repentant (truly remorseful), and if they have no prior offenses, they may get off with the slightest discipline.

Private reproof means the elders will give them a stern talking-to from the scriptures, citing many Bible passages on why what they did is considered wrong, followed by a stiff warning against engaging in the forbidden acts again. They'll be watched, and may not be able to participate in field service for a period of time, generally 3-6 months.

Other privileges may be lost as well, like the freedom to raise one's hand and comment at the meetings or, in the case of a male, his being able to carry the microphone at the Kingdom Hall (which is considered a privilege of service) or any other position of service could be taken away.

During the probationary period, if all goes well and no relapses occur, the individuals will be back in good standing again, and may engage in field service, and have other privileges restored, after the elders have met with them again to be sure they're on the straight and narrow and have made the determination that they may again be in 'good standing.'

To the cult, it's a celebration when the elders meet with a person who's been on 'private reproof' for several months to let them know they are in the clear and have their full Witness 'privileges' restored.

Category 2 — public reproof — is the next level of discipline up from private reproof. This punishment is for sexual escapades where there is copulation of some kind or the circumstances of the case have become public knowledge. This punishment will also carry loss of privileges, at the elders' discretion.

In some cases, the forbidden act(s) may have resulted in a pregnancy. Since Witnesses are adamantly opposed to abortion (considered to be murder) the child will be born to the parents and the couple will be strongly encouraged to get married. Since the whole affair would be public in that scenario, Witness law dictates that the elders of the congregation address the matter publicly, in front of the entire congregation.

In the Witness world, it is completely unacceptable for a single woman to pop up pregnant with no explanation or disciplinary action.

Another scenario that could warrant this level of punishment is adultery, in which an 'innocent' mate is affected.

Because these acts have somehow become public information, or are considered grave in nature and/or scope (called 'gross wrongdoing'), the names of the perpetrators and the fact that they have been disciplined, and for what reasons, will be announced from the platform, in front of the entire congregation, on a night when the Ministry School and Service Meeting is conducted (a meeting that is generally Witnesses only with no visitors present, unlike a Sunday meeting).

At the point in the meeting where the announcements are made, an elder will slowly and somberly approach the platform, bearing a tiny piece of paper in his hands. He will carry a poker face and a sober attitude, adding to the drama.

We know what to expect. We've seen it before. Somebody's in trouble, and by this point, the grapevine has probably conveyed who the parties are and what they've done to almost everybody in the congregation who would want to be privy to that kind of information.

Nevertheless, for this announcement, everyone in the audience is still and quiet; you can hear the proverbial pin drop. The brother making the announcement is an elder, and would have been a member of the 3-man judicial committee that heard the matter and decided on the case. He will say something to the effect of: "in accordance with the scripture admonition at _____ (scripture quotation from the Bible like 1 Corinthians 6:9-10 or Hebrews 13:4 or Jude 1:7 or any of the plethora of writings Paul penned) on sexual misconduct, so-and-so has been reproved by a judicial committee."

Now the whole congregation knows you had a good time, and sparing the gory details, based on the scripture the brother quoted, we can pretty much guess what you did.

The punishment will likely carry the same scope of lost privileges, and maybe even broader, than being privately reproved.

Not to mention it's downright embarrassing; which is part of the whole system. In the Witness world, there is a heavy element of shaming people into doing the 'right' thing.

Category 3 — disfellowshipping — is the next level up in severity of punishment; the sternest punishment there is in the Witness world.

This level of punishment is reserved for what is considered 'gross wrongdoing', repeat infractions, or what is referred to as unrepentant or 'willful' sinners.

Not only are privileges taken away, but there is a strict rule not speak to, or associate with, in any way, a person who is disfellowshipped. It is an ousting. It is tantamount to a collective back-turning. Witnesses do not speak to disfellowshipped people, period, no matter where they may be encountered, or what they may be doing.

For family members of disfellowshipped people, any and all conversation is restricted to 3 topics: business, family and health. There can be no mention of the Kingdom Hall, or the Bible, or Witness literature or Witness activities.

The only people who can address religious topics with a disfellowshipped person are the elders.

The disfellowshipped person becomes as one who is dead to the rest of the Witnesses, hence why it is a powerful motivator to stay in line. The fear of banishment and loss of love this practice engenders is enough to make most Witness tow the line, even if haphazardly. Even the most reckless try to tow it enough not to be ousted, even if they have a challenge with remaining in 'good standing'.

No one in the Witness world wants to be disfellowshipped.

This punishment could last anywhere from 6 months to several years, depending upon the person.

I've been disfellowshipped for decades. It doesn't wear off. There's not a statute of limitations. If one no longer wants to be disfellowshipped, there's a process that addresses that. There are no exceptions.

If the disfellowshipped person comes to the Kingdom Hall on the night their name is announced from the platform (the night of the ousting), it is considered a sign of repentance, and may shorten the sentence. If the person continues coming to the Kingdom Hall for all the meetings (except the book study, which takes place in private homes of Witnesses and no Witness will allow a disfellowshipped person in their home for any reason, unless that person is a relative, and even then, there must be a good reason), that too is considered a sign of remorse and will also shorten the sentence. With regular meeting attendance, a disfellowshipped person could be 'reinstated' within 6 months. Reinstatement means the person is now allowed back into full fellowship with the cult again, though they may not have all their privileges fully restored yet.

Something in me always knew that withdrawal of fellowship from a person who's lost his or her way is not the best way to help people do the 'right' thing. Even when I was a devout Witness, and though I complied with the rules on disfellowshipped people, something in me always knew that withdrawing myself from someone was like withdrawing or withholding love.

It didn't feel good, like so many things I did as a Witness, but I confess I did them anyway, even at the protest of my soul.

Unbeknownst to me then, my spirit would not let that continue. My days of doing things against my spirit to stay true to a religion were barreling to an expiration.

I could feel it coming on.

Ultimately, I was disfellowshipped for adultery, being considered unrepentant and not willing to change my attitude to comply with the Witness way (more on that later).

To Witnesses, marriage is sacred. 'What God has yoked together, let no man put apart' and 'let the marital bed be without defilement' are the Witness die-hard creed and code. Married couples are expected to stay together for life, and to remain monogamous (with each other exclusively) for life. Though I don't know too many people who have successfully managed that, it's a worthy aspiration, if that kind of thing appeals to you. It's one of those things that looks good on paper, but try living it and you will quickly meet up with the side of your nature that doesn't at all agree with the rules and has no problem flouting them for personal gain and/or the thrill of the moment.

In the Witness paradigm, there are only two ways out of a marriage, no matter how bad the marriage may be: death or repeated adultery.

Even if a mate is abusive, a divorce is not warranted, though separation, for the safety of the abused spouse and any children in the household, may be well warranted and even encouraged. No one wants to think someone is being abused and nothing is being done about it.

Even if a mate who was being abused no longer lives with the abusive mate, they are considered still married, and that being the case, he or she cannot divorce, date or remarry. If the abusive mate is also a Witness, efforts will be made to 'reprove such a one from the scriptures,' so that they turn away from their abusive ways. When and if they do make a change, the mate who has been abused is expected to reunite with the formerly abusive spouse, when it's safe to do so.

If the abusive spouse is not a Witness, there's a chance that a divorce could be granted (only on grounds of adultery, yet that will have to be proven with 'evidence').

In order for either of the parties to be able to remarry, a divorce must be considered 'scriptural'. A 'scriptural divorce' means there are repeat adultery offenses in the marriage (each of which, once again, must be proven with evidence if there is not a confession from the adulterous mate).

Let's discuss evidence.

One cannot simply say their mate is cheating. They must bring evidence, which will serve as proof. Evidence can be anything from used condoms to stained sheets to pictures to the testimony of eyewitness of a mate in bed with someone else or any other such proof that a person has strayed or is 'creeping.'

It's a grave situation in the Witness world when someone is accused of repeated adultery.

Of course, the adulterous mate can always come forward and confess, sparing the innocent mate the unpalatable process of gathering good, hard evidence for the case, but that rarely happens. After all, the kind of person who would be out regularly getting their groove on with someone they're not married to, while married, is not likely to be the kind of person who would call a group of elders together to confess their deep dark secrets. Not that it couldn't happen, it has, but it's not likely.

What usually happens is that the adulterous mate is doing their own thing, and maybe even has left the marital home, and is off somewhere happily living their life, no longer according to Witness law and not even thinking about Witnesses (that was me). However, their mate may still be a Witness and cannot date or remarry because they do not have a 'scriptural' divorce. (This was right about when the elders came looking for me; my husband and I were separated, yet he couldn't date, have sex or remarry and remain in 'good standing' with the Witnesses, which he very much wanted to do.)

As far as divorce is concerned, it doesn't matter if you get a legal divorce. In the Witness world, if you do not have a 'scriptural' divorce, you are considered ineligible to ever get remarried. This is because they say that even if the law recognizes you as free, Jehovah God does not. 'What God has yoked together,' as is often quoted in these cases, 'let no man put apart.'

If it's unlikely that the perpetrating spouse will go to the elders (because they are no longer living the Witness lifestyle), the innocent party must get on with the task of racking up evidence, if they are ever to be free to date or remarry. It's not allowed to get a private detective or outside help with this. It's more of an unspoken thing that the evidence will somehow make its way to you, which it often does.

The reason the mate will rack up evidence (even though I imagine it to be one of the most unpalatable jobs on the planet, I mean, who wants to pick over their ex-lover's used condom) is because they want to be free. If the so-called adulterous mate/absent mate doesn't confess adultery, and the couple is not living in the marital home any longer, and their spouse is still a Witness, going to the Kingdom Hall and in good standing, that person cannot have sex, kiss, hug, date or remarry.

They are on total lock-down, until the evidence is produced. No one will touch them with a ten-foot pole when it comes to dating and romance, because they are still considered married.

Can you see why they would go about gathering evidence, even if they didn't like the job? They want to be free, and the thing that will set them free — other than a straight up confession from the wandering spouse — is evidence.

When adultery is the issue, and both parties are still living in the marital home, and both parties are still living the Witness code, Witness law only allows for divorce in cases where there has been repeated adultery (3 times or more). In this case, it's likely that the repeat offender has confessed, since they're present in the home and trying to live by Witness law. It's strongly suggested that the innocent mate should forgive the adulterous mate the first 2 times they stray.

On the first offense, the adulterous mate will be reprimanded from the scriptures and will be strongly admonished to 'drink water from their own cistern' (to quote an oft-repeated scripture written by Solomon on not straying from one's monogamous relationship). The elders will also encourage the 'innocent' mate to forgive the adulterous mate in a spirit of love, with no resentment. In addition, the elders will remind the innocent mate of their marital duty to serve up plenty of love-making in the bedroom so that the offending mate has plenty of sex to keep him or her happy at home. One should 'enjoy the wife of their youth' to quote another

Witness favorite of Solomon's wisdom sayings. On the second offense, the reprimand will be stronger, and the 'innocent' mate will still be encouraged to take back the straying mate into the marital bed, with full forgiveness and love. Though the innocent mate does not technically have to forgive and take back the straying mate, they are overtly or covertly encouraged to do so by the elders.

Once a 3rd adulterous offense occurs, it's pretty clear to all parties that this person is not going to stay at home, no matter how remorseful they may have made out to be the first two times they were in the elder's room. In that case, the innocent mate can choose whether or not to forgive and stay with the mate, or whether they will get a divorce. Only in that case is the divorce considered 'scriptural' and the innocent party free to date and remarry, after a reasonable passage of time. It's frowned upon for a newly divorced person to get married soon after their marriage has ended. There should be a passing of time that allows grieving of the old relationship before a person is clear to start a new relationship, which makes a lot of sense.

Here's a good time to add that elders are taught in all their dealings to use the Bible as a sword in order to decipher who's lying and who's telling the truth, so as to render just and true decisions. They're told to pray and to 'use the scriptures aright.' Jehovah God will reveal what's really going on, they are told, which is true. Deeds done in the darkness will one day come to the light, but not because we're talking about Witnesses, we're talking about how life actually works.

Like everybody, I believe elders are doing the best they can, in accord with what they believe is right. I don't fault them for doing their job; it's a job they sincerely believe is keeping them in Jehovah God's good graces.

Isn't that what we all are doing? What we think the divine wants of us? Or at least the best we can muster in any given moment, based on what we know and believe and feel to be right?

Only time and space will be the true arbiters of whether our actions were aligned with law or not.

Karma will do its beautiful work; of this we can be sure.

The Fanatical Years

I confess I became a fanatic. I don't know how else to describe how I conducted myself.

It's ironic that I was bred on the idea of moderation in all things in my Witness experience, except for when it came to practicing the Witness way. In that, we were encouraged to be fanatics. While the word 'fanatic' was never used, for me it was always implied.

I can't say for sure if anybody told me to become a fanatic, or if it's just a part of my nature, but I was most assuredly a fanatic. Somewhere in my pretty little head, I thought it was a requirement.

I was fanatical about the Bible.

I was fanatical about taking the Bible literally.

I was fanatical about going out in field service, knocking on doors, trying to convince people that they need to hurry up and come into 'the truth' lest they be destroyed at God's battle of Armageddon. No one knows the day or the hour! The end is coming!

Not very much different from Chicken Little, who ran around yelling, "The sky is falling! The sky is falling!"

It wasn't like he was completely off in his warning; there could have been some truth to it. But when you fanatically yell the same thing over and over, some of the sense of urgency gets sucked out of it. The words start sounding unbelievable, and after a while, people just don't listen anymore, *even if the sky really is falling.*

That's the problem with fanaticism. Even if there was some truth in the warning, the intensity with which the message is delivered, at near shove-down-your-throat levels, and the frequency of its delivery, daily, can have the opposite effect the deliverers of the message are going for; the message gets demoted, downplayed.

Just like that guy you see standing on the street corner, yelling to the top of his lungs, or into a megaphone, that the end is coming and you better hurry up and come to Jesus.

Does anybody pay him any attention?

Isn't that strange?

I mean, after all, if the sky really was falling, and someone actually knew in advance that it was going to happen, I'd want them to let me know.

The problem is when you get labeled a 'doomsday prophet', you just don't get listened to as much, not taken as seriously as if you didn't have the 'doomsday' part in front of the 'prophet' part.

Well that was me, a 'doomsday prophet.' It served me, for a time, until it didn't anymore. Then it got painful; painful to get out the bed in the morning to go preach the same worn-out message, to the same people, in the same neighborhood, a message I was having a hard time believing in anymore.

The worst part about it was, I didn't consciously know what was happening in me. I could feel the dissonance, the divide, the conflict deep inside, but I had the biggest challenge identifying the source of the issue.

Part of me was thinking, *all this doomsday prophesying and the end hasn't gotten here yet.* The Witnesses would have called it a lack of faith.

I was having a terrible time. Was I losing faith, or was I waking up?

I was waking up.

Not because what the Witnesses preach is not true. I don't know if it's true or not true, and for me, that's not the issue. The issue is: does it align with the Authentic Self, the Truth of who I AM? Is this the path of MY soul's calling? Is this me fulfilling my destiny, or is this me doing what I'm told?

Yes, I was waking up, waking up to the Authentic Self, to my soul's calling. My soul knew exactly what she was doing when she cast me in the role of Jehovah's Witness. She cast me in that role for a reason and a season, not a lifetime. She knew I'd have important breakthroughs there, that I'd learn discipline, like maybe nowhere else on the planet other than if I had joined the Navy Seals, and they probably wouldn't have taken a 4-year-old, so Jehovah's Witnesses, what I call the 'Army' of religions, was my soul's next favorite pick. I agree with her. I learned tons of discipline from going to 5 meetings every week, a ridiculous amount of 'personal study', daily Bible reading and field service 3-5 times a week for 26 years. If you lived in New York City when I was loose, I probably knocked on your door. Oh I was committed; maybe I should have *been* committed.

Like I said, I was fanatical.

I did what I was told, nearly all of it. It meant for me, being a true Witness, really living the principles, as best I could. There were a lot of us who were wearing the Witness name, and not living the principles.

Isn't that true of everything?

In every clan, you have 3 (maybe more) factions: the fanatical minority who comprise maybe 10% of the whole (the zealots and extremists, that would be me), the adherents in the middle, about 80% (who do pretty much what the group calls for and follow the lead of the zealots), and then you have the outliers, the remaining 10% (who do what they want while trying to hang on to the fringe).

I was never an outlier. It's not in my nature.

I was rarely an adherent, a middle walker.

I was always the zealot, the one out front, the Pioneer (as the Witnesses call it), running on the front lines with the pack that's willing to die for the beliefs, even if the beliefs weren't mine.

Fanatical.

Not because dying for your beliefs is fanatical. It's not.

Dying for someone else's beliefs is fanatical, and stupid.

When I'm a zealot in the wrong direction, I may get 2 points for being a zealot and completely committed, but I may lose 10 because I killed somebody in the name of something my soul wasn't on board with in the first place.

Christ asked a vital question: what benefit is there in gaining the whole world and losing one's soul?

None.

There's no way of knowing how many people I harmed, or how much havoc I wreaked, in the fanatical period of my life.

I pray to forgive me.

What is a fanatic? An extremist, a danger to self and others. That was me, armed with what little I knew, and a belief that what I knew had to be right, which made me dangerous to self and others. For me, that's the true meaning of 'armed and dangerous', not a person toting a weapon, but a person armed with fanatical ideas, intent on seeing those ideas through, regardless of what they have to do to make that happen. That's the stuff terrorists are made of, and while I confess that I have been fanatical, I also must confess that I am not now so.

I would rather meet up with a person toting a weapon than one who has been brainwashed with fanatical ideas that include death to people who don't hold the same idea.

There's no fanatic like a religious fanatic. A religious fanatic has a special brand of zeal that's deadly, in the name of God. They are amped up to the 10th degree.

I opt for its opposite.

The opposite of fanatical is live and let live.

Love.

Acceptance.

Non-judgment.

Let everyone be.

That's part of my overall life motto now, *let everyone be.*

God's got everybody.

I need to mind my business, I decided, and let everybody be, rather than running around the neighborhood hell-bent on trying to get people to see things my way, and if they refuse, to pronounce on them the 'judgment of God.'

What a farce. What human gets to pronounce judgment anyway? None of us. Even still it's a trap we fall into all too often, especially with ideas that are near and dear to our hearts, ideas that are on the verge of being fanatical or are fanatical. Ideas that may not even be ours, they may have been rammed down our throats, and now we're all too happy to ram them down someone else's.

Case in point: Jesus is Lord and Savior. I almost got bum-rushed one day when I stood up in a workshop — amongst Christians, would-be Christians and near Christians — urging each of us to examine EVERY belief to test its alignment with the Authentic Self.

I started with, "Jesus Christ is Lord and Savior." The women mutually nodded in agreement.

Then I asked a simple question that almost started a riot: "Is that true?"

Silence. Stares. Looks came at me like daggers, with the energy of *'you better hurry up with where you're going with this Valerie, because it looks like it could be blasphemy, and if it is, you are about to catch a beat-down.'*

What was my point?

Examine EVERY belief; especially the beliefs you hold most near and dear, *like Jesus Christ is Lord & Savior.*

If Jesus is Lord and Savior for you (only you know that by turning within to the Inner Presence and receiving your own inner guidance) then good. If you turn within and find something different, that Jesus is something/someone different for you, good. If Jesus is not in the picture at all, good. If he is, good.

Jesus will not be offended either way.

The important thing here is that we test every belief, I mean EVERY BELIEF, by going within, being still and asking. No belief is off limits, and no belief is too sacred to be examined. From what I now know, subjecting my most fanatical beliefs to rigorous Self examination — with an intent to know the Truth and align solely with It — is vital to my mental health and well-being, and the well-being of the people around me.

Ask. Ask. Ask.

Who are you asking? It doesn't matter the name you use for Who you're asking. If you pray, have pure intent, ask for wisdom and earnestly seek it, you'll receive answers. You'll receive the guiding light from your soul that points you in the perfect direction for you. You'll get what you need.

I did. I had to undo my belief house, brick by brick. And I had a HUGE belief house, built with the bricks I had been given, by mama, daddy, religion, school, society, the media and so on.

Don't go by what mama or daddy taught you. That may be all well and good for mama and daddy. However, you've got your own sea to sail, your own waters to chart. Nobody gets to do yours for you, and you can't do it for anyone else.

The amount of mail (emails and messages sent to me via social media) that contain cries for help from blessed beings of light on the planet who are trapped by what mama, daddy and religion think of them is staggering. It seems not to let up even when we're grown. We erroneously imagine that going against parental input and religious conditioning will surely incur social death, extreme discomfort, ousting, ostracizing or worse.

This is not how God wants us to live.

You are not created to live under duress or beholden to other people's ideas about you and how you are to connect with the Divine.

We're all in this together, yet we all get to come to our own Truth, each led by the Inner Light. For ultimate peace and fulfillment, we each have to find, get in touch with, and ultimately follow the INNER GUIDING LIGHT.

If I'd gone by what mama and daddy taught me, I'd still be holding on to ideas and beliefs that are radically misaligned with my Authentic Self. Those ideas and beliefs served me for a time and a reason, and when they had done their perfect work in my life, they were discarded, like a worn out pair of walking shoes. No one cries over old, worn out walking shoes. You buy more, and you let the old ones go. Unless there's some pressing reason, there's not a lot of emotion around it. The old shoes are not working for you anymore, so you let them go.

Do the same with any and all beliefs you have now that don't make your Spirit sing. Let them go. Don't hold on to them out of allegiance to mama, daddy, religion or anyone else.

Don't fight with them.

Don't try to get rid of them.

Don't try to prove or disprove them.

Just let them go.

Don't try to think of what your replacement beliefs will be. Just let them go. You don't need them anymore. They served their purpose, and now they're done.

See how easy that is?

Very easy. Except...

if you're attached.

If you're attached to your beliefs, like a toddler holding onto a blanket that's been toted around so long it stinks to high heaven and has holes in it, you're setting yourself up to have an unnecessarily hard time.

Get a mental picture of that toddler, you know the one, who falls asleep with that stinky security blanket under his head. You can't sneak it away to wash it, even in his sleep, because the moment you put your hands on it and try to pry it out of his tight little grip, he stirs and threatens to wake up. If he catches you with his blanket, he's going to scream bloody murder until he gets it back. You and he both know that blanket's not going anywhere.

That's what we look like when we hold on to outdated beliefs past their usefulness. Don't do that. It stinks. It's unbecoming of mature people. Paul said when we grow up, we put away childish things.

Ruthlessly and relentlessly examine your beliefs, all of them, especially your most cherished ones, the ones you'd die for, as they come up. No need to set up an interrogation of yourself on what you believe... you only need look at your life, honestly and openly, and your beliefs will quickly become apparent.

And why make this ruthless, relentless examination of ALL beliefs, especially the cherished ones? Why be so thorough, so vigilant, so determined to get to the bottom of things?

Because you're a Truth seeker, that's why.

You came here to get to the Truth, not to believe what people tell you. How do you know you're getting to the Truth? It has a ring to it. Truth rings. You'll hear it. You'll know it. It will ring in your Spirit. It will resonate for you. Follow it. Have the faith, trust and inner strength to follow your soul.

It knows the way.

In ancient Egypt it is taught that there are 7 aspects that comprise each of us. One of those 7 aspects is the 'Ba' or soul, the seat of divinity and nobility in the human, the highest aspect of self, the part of us that actually has the potential to become one with God.

Follow the Ba. It knows the way. Not only that, it's headed there in every moment.

Hitch a ride home to God.

Cold Toes

I confess I may have knocked on over a thousand doors.

If you add up all the time I spent as a devout Witness, from age 4 to age 30, and you consider that I went out in field service every week, and at periods in my life, every day, for at least 2 hours, and at times as much as 8 to 10 hours in a day, that is extreme door-knocking. (As of this writing, I don't think Witnesses knock on doors as they used to; I see them now mostly on the streets of huge metropolitan cities standing alongside displays of literature on racks or tables.)

I was a 'regular pioneer.'

In the cult of Jehovah's Witnesses, a regular pioneer makes a commitment to spend 90 hours per month in field service, spreading the good news. It's called 'full-time ministry.' Ninety hours per month averages out to about 3 hours per day, every day. So if I want a day off, I have to factor in those 3 hours into everything I do. That means 6 hours in field service the day before I want a day off. Or if I want a vacation, that means doubling up on hours for 3 weeks out of the month to have a week of vacation. It's called 'getting your time in' (which sounds frighteningly close to a jail sentence) and I had it down to a science. I did it oh so well, with conscience, until the day I discovered the cold toes.

I was in the darling period of my life, as I call it, because it seemed that everything was darling. I was living in a darling apartment in the Bronx, New York, with my darling husband and our darling new baby boy.

How did I get here? Well, let's go back in time a tad...

It's the 1980's and crack has landed in the hood.

I was in my early 20's and life was good. I was surrounded by all Witnesses all the time, I had an acceptable job that paid a modest wage, I was a secretary like I was told. Secretarial Science was one of two choices I was offered as a field of study by my very Witness mother when I was in high school (nursing was the other option).

Also like I was told, I didn't go to college.

I didn't know I was being smothered from the inside, but I would find that out soon enough.

I married at 22 and still a virgin.

Several years into the marriage, I was happy and very much in love, for a while.

We had our first child, our son Cory, in 1987, after 3 years of marriage. The second big life event Witnesses are big on, after getting married, is having children. The few celebrations they enjoy are mostly centered around married and family life: wedding showers, elaborate weddings, anniversary parties, and baby showers.

If you're tending to your family, as a wife or mother or husband or father, having kids, going to a modest job to support your family (but certainly not to get rich), going to the meetings, going in field service, studying at home and taking part in only the leisure, wholesome activities Witnesses advise, then life for you should be pretty good. No complaints, and no reason to complain. Keep yourself busy in Kingdom building, and you won't have time to get into any trouble.

Except I'm not vibing with that either. Never have.

In all appearances, life was perfect. What could be wrong with perfect? Nothing. Except the still small Voice deep inside that nips, nudges and nags at me, won't quit and won't go away; a nagging thing that questions what I'm doing and hints that there's more beyond the safe confines of the Witness walls I had built around myself, my family and my entire life.

Is there more?

No. There couldn't be more. Out there is the 'world'. This is the 'truth'. I'm in the 'truth'. And I'm not going to live in the 'world', that would be sure destruction. So stay here I must, whether I want to or not.... Right? I have to stay here. Right?

That's the kind of back and forth conversation I was engaged in with myself, all the while knowing, deep inside, there was another path for me, other than the one I was currently traversing, and that 'other' path beckoned relentlessly, at times with gentleness and at other times with a seemingly unfair boldness.

That nagging thing is the self-same thing that keeps you up at night, after you've made love to your lover, and the kids are asleep, and the crickets are quiet, there you lay, with the covers up around your ears, staring at the ceiling, wondering about the path that beckons you, and whispers grandiose wonders in your ear when no one else is around, the path that informs you, on a deeply visceral level, that you are so much more and that there is so much more.

This is the soul path that beckons, and it is insistent. Quiet, yet insistent. Not to be ignored. No, it will not long be ignored. And if you try, you will meet with certain death. The death will either be slow and painful, or swift and painful, your choice.

At that time, I confess I'd made an unconscious choice for a slow, painful death, living in-authentically, trying my best to make the best of it.

Until I decided to make another choice.

Let's talk about the unconscious choice first, and the cold toes.

I was out in field service, on a long pioneer day of about 8 to 10 hours. It was a Monday in the winter, somewhere around December or January. Cory, our firstborn son, was born in July, so he would have been about 5 or 6 months at the time. I took him in field service with me every day, since I was a stay-at-home mom, and since the 'inculcation' of young Witnesses begins like the biblical Timothy's: in infancy.

I loved toting him around all day because it meant I got to be with my baby. All the sisters in the congregation who were my pioneer partners loved seeing Cory. They had lit up every day when they saw me toting that huge belly up and down hills and sidewalk streets in New York 'preaching the good news,' and now they loved the born fruit of that womb. He was a good baby, and didn't ever complain about being out in field service knocking on doors for hours on end, up and down stairs, in his stroller, and in and out of people's houses for home Bible studies. He was a trooper. I was nursing him, so it was easier to get around without the concern for formula or where to make his bottles.

On the cold toes day, I remember coming home and doing what I did almost every day, rolling him off the elevator into our 2nd floor apartment in the Bronx. I took the big plastic windbreaker cover off Cory's stroller, undid his safety straps buckles and lifted him out. He was clad in a thick snowsuit, knit hat, warm socks and shoes and plenty clothes in layer upon layer for protection from the frigid New York City winter. In addition to that, I always had a blanket or two on top of him and tucked around him, keeping him well covered from head to toe.

Call me an over-the-top protective new mother.

As I took off his snowsuit and shoes, I felt his feet. His toes were cold. My heart sunk. I was so sad and crushed I nearly wept. He couldn't tell me his little toes were cold and I was devastated.

I must confess I do not know if I was overcome with these feelings because I had had him out in the cold so long that his little toes were freezing, or if I was sad because I didn't really want to be doing it in the first place, or if the two were really one big unwanted thing.

I was doing what I thought I had to do; a very deeply ingrained 'should.'

Should's are funny things. Interesting really, and so convincing. How do you not do something that you deeply believe you *should* do and still be able to sleep soundly at night? How do you look yourself in the mirror and be able to hold your head up when you know you're not doing what you *should* be doing? I hadn't figured that out yet back then.

Hence, I was sad.

Sad that I thought I had no choice in the life I was living; sad that it seemed the life I had chosen demanded so much of me and seemed to have a merciless lining, albeit unspoken; sad that my little baby's little toes were cold and I didn't even know it. How long was he cold? That question haunted me. He couldn't speak. He couldn't tell me he didn't want to go in field service, or that he preferred staying home in our quiet, comfy, warm apartment that day, or any day. He couldn't tell me if he really wasn't on board for the whole thing at all.

How long were his toes cold?

I still remember that day to the very day I write this, and it's been more than 30 earth years since those events unfolded. Yet it still plays out in my mind as crisp and clear as it did that day. Minus the fuzziness around the edges, the center of the picture remains crystal clear.

It was a watershed moment, another trajectory changing day, as if my short life of 27 years hadn't had enough of these monumental milestones already.

That day goes down in history as the day I decided I didn't want to be a pioneer anymore. I couldn't put my finger on it, and I didn't know why I was feeling what I was feeling, and I dare not share how I was really feeling with anyone in my Jehovah's Witness cult circle, but I knew I didn't want to do what I was doing anymore.

Something that had formerly been so zealous in me for what I was doing flew right out of me after the cold toes.

After that, I was not the same person. Not quite as zealous. Not quite as ready to stay in field service for 8 or 10 hours. I kept checking his toes after that. Was he cold?

Funny what little things in life can set us to thinking, and examining how we're doing what we're doing, and why we're even doing it in the first place, or if we even want to be doing what we're doing.

There was no damage to Cory, his toes warmed up quickly and he was fine.

His mother wasn't. I wasn't fine at all. There was damage to me. I was doing damage to me. That damage would eventually take years to undo. I was forcing myself to do something that went against my nature, my inner knowing, the core of who I am. That is the damage: going against my own grain.

Don't do that. Don't go against your own grain. Don't do things you don't feel within yourself you are to be doing, and don't not do things you feel deep within yourself that you are to be doing.

Don't go against your own grain.

I confess I went against my own grain for years, decades even. It was painful. That was my unconscious choice then: a slow, painful death.

Had I not gone into the deep depression 2 years after the cold toes, I may have exited this life long ago, an apparent victim of suicide. Had I not made a new choice in the middle of the depression, I may have exited this life then, faster, but no less painful.

The important thing is that I did make a new choice. I made the choice to be true to me, to go with my grain, to walk my authentic soul path.

When you walk the soul path, and you find your child has cold toes, you might look upon it differently, you might shrug it off, you might not be haunted by it at all. You might say, "tomorrow I'll put thicker socks on you" and take it all in stride.

But in the knowing that other people are being hurt, besides me — by me not only not being in harmony and alignment with my soul, but being fanatical as well — that was the unbearable part, especially to know that the one who was being affected by my lack of courage to walk my authentic path was my own firstborn child, the one person on the planet I loved like I loved no one else up until the magical moment of his appearance on the planet. I was hurting him. I learned the powerful lesson that my fanaticism hurt the people I loved most. That was unbearable.

That's where the haunting happens, when I am out of integrity with my soul, and my offspring, who rely on and look to me for care and protection, are somehow hurt by my actions.

I couldn't do it. I couldn't risk that kind of pain. I couldn't risk more cold toes.

Pain to myself? Oh I could do that all day long.

Pain to my baby? Absolutely not.

Something in me made a conscious choice to do things differently after the cold toes. I confess I started looking for an escape hatch from the Witness cult. It would not be easy. They studied my every move. Not to mention, I lived with an informant sleeping next to me in the bed. Witnesses are brainwashed to rat out husband and/or wife for the religion.

Yes, I **had** to find an escape route.

Gratefully, I found it. It's why I'm alive and well today, and why Cory's alive and well too.

The Man is the Head

In the Witness cult, the man is the head of the household and the congregation. Period. Not just the head of the household and the congregation, he's pretty much the head of everything that matters. For them, the man is head of the world.

I guess the woman is the neck. Some women say the neck turns the head.

In the Witness paradigm, the woman is subject, or is to be submissive, to the head, the man.

I confess I never fared well in that paradigm.

A woman who is a devout Witness would never set out to intentionally marry a man who is not a Witness. The concern is that if a man is not a Witness, and doesn't understand or agree with the Witness way, she may be putting herself under the subjection of an unbeliever, or a 'worldly' person, which is considered dangerous (if not for the person, for the religion). To an extent, she must do what he tells her, unless what he tells her is against the Witness creed. That's where the line is drawn.

As for the Witness women's personal wants and needs, these too are under the subjection of the husband's say-so. If he says yes, these will be granted. If he says no, they are not. This is what was taught (when I was in the cult), although on a practical level it didn't always play out quite that cut and dried.

Relationships are complex, as are the people who populate them.

There are many Witness women who do not work, as taking care of one's household is considered of prime and utmost importance, right after one's relationship with Jehovah God. If a couple can live on one income, the husband's, that's highly encouraged. Then the wife can stay home with the little ones, and inculcate the Witness way into them from babyhood. More soldiers for the front lines. If a family doesn't have to send their kids to daycare, better still. They like to keep the kids as close to home as possible until they absolutely have to go to school. It's not common among Witnesses to home school, though I'm sure it must exist, it's not taught or necessarily encouraged. What is encouraged is to send kids to school to be shining examples of Witness-dom so that more people can be drafted into the cult.

Maybe we could call them little bait. The kids.

Either way, one must take care of home first, and however that means is accomplished within Witness rules is encouraged and applauded.

In the time period that I was married, it unnerved me to have to ask a husband for money, though I confess I know many women who were not at all unnerved to ask their husbands for money, or to answer all questions about what the money is for, and to give an account of it when arriving back home from spending it.

I did it for years. Not the asking part, I'm far too independent for that; it's in the grain of the fabric I'm woven from to be my own woman.

Nevertheless there was an open accounting of where all our money went and was spent, under a complete merging together of all finances after we were married. I handled the finances, we both agreed on it, and it would have only happened if we both agreed on it. He knew I was better with money and budgeting, and would keep tabs on the money really well, and that I would actually do it and enjoy it. He, on the other had, hated doing bills or managing finances, so he abdicated it to me. It gave me a control of sorts, so I wasn't mad at the setup.

I also knew plenty of Witness women who were in no way submissive or subject to their husbands. They did as they pleased, when they pleased, with whom they pleased, whether the husband approved or not. These are considered unruly wives.

I think I was one of them.

Not blatantly. I would never have done that, nor would I have ever gotten away with it. The elders would have surely called me into the back room for a chastising with all manner of scriptures from 'the apostle' Paul, who loved to rant on how women couldn't do anything in the congregation or take the lead anywhere. I wasn't trying to hear that, so I did what a lot of sisters did: I was my own woman in a low-key fashion, kinda without letting anyone know I was doing my own thing. I just did it.

There is something in me that bristled whenever the words 'subjection' or 'submission' were pointed in my direction. I recognize that there is both a light and shadow side to this effect. On the light side, the divine in me knows I and everyone are equal, even if a religion tries its best to convince me that women are the lesser, subservient counterparts to men. On the shadow side of the effect, pride in me says I ain't listening to nobody, including God.

While I honor all that indwells me, both light and dark, I feed the light in me.

There was a light side gently telling me 'NO' when I heard, over and over, that I was less than men, and God put man in charge of me, and that my needs were secondary.

Let me state clearly that this is never the terminology Witnesses use. They do not pointedly tell the women that they are less than men. They tell us that we have a role assigned to us by God, an honorable role, and that role is to support the man. In that honorable role of letting the man lead us, we find God's favor.

I agree that there are aspects of this that are true and in divine order. In other arenas, there's a President and a Vice President, a Captain of the Ship and a Co-Captain. I understand that.

Where I take issue is that the man is the president all the time on everything. No one's that smart.

I agree leadership of a household is a must, otherwise the whole thing goes to hell in a hand basket and quick. This I know. I also know that order is the first law of heaven. There can be no order without effective leadership and without each player holding down their respective roles with commitment and excellence in any arena.

What we also have learned from thousands of years of human relationships is that co-dependence is born of inequality. In a committed relationship, if one is subservient to the other, there can never be an equal partnership, thus the relationship will always be co-dependent in some way, and thus, mutually restrictive.

This is not so with the parent/child relationship, as it is clear who is leading whom, or at least it should be. In my book, children and parents are equal souls, though they have different roles.

Witnesses do not adhere to the universal principle of equanimity. They espouse hierarchy, in almost everything. At the top of the hierarchy is God. Then Jesus Christ, then the 'Governing Body' (more on this later) then the 'Christian congregation' with its elders, then the man at the head of each household.

The woman gets to follow, follow, follow. Support, support, support.

She never gets to authorize, innovate, generate, invent, lead, take charge or make executive decisions, for self or anyone else. These are all considered the purview of the man.

I never asked to lead anyone else. God gave me that assignment, and trust me, on many occasions I have been reluctant to fulfill it. I haven't always been a willing leader. It wasn't like I wanted to take over the Witness organization women's lib style. I wasn't all the way on board for the women's lib movement in the 70's when burning bras was the new hip thing to do. I didn't want to take over the world. I didn't want to lead the men.

What I yearned for was autonomy. Self-expression. Authority of self. Responsibility for self. Ability and freedom to lead self. I yearned to feel, at the core of my being, fully supported in the truth that as a woman, I am the equal of any man, and that there is a divine unction, an inner urge to lead self, govern self, and make choices based on existence, not gender.

I never got that message while deeply entrenched in the cult, and would not have gotten it there. That's not what that system is about. If I don't like what that system is about, I am free to choose another path, as is everyone.

The starting point of the religious teaching that a woman is less than a man leads all too often to a point where the woman is neglected, ignored, abused, raped or even killed.

It is anything but a benign belief. It is one of the most violent beliefs we as humans harbor: that a woman is not equal to a man.

Before humans can do harm to another human, or take another's life, that human must be fully convinced, in its own mind, that the one he/she is about to perpetrate an act of violence on is in some way less than human, and certainly, less than self.

This is the beginning of the loss of the sanctity of life.

So while Witnesses never told me I was less than a man, it is the reading my soul picked up. It was the subconscious underpinning of my relationships, in the Witness world and elsewhere.

I could have never fulfilled my destiny as a teacher of Truth and Law had I been chained to the Witness way for the rest of my life. My destiny calls for me to speak to audiences all over the world, to stand up and share the inspiration of my heart, to write books, articles and blog posts on all things magickal, mystical and metaphysical, to explore the occult and teach it, to share my magickal experiences and to ultimately, I pray, be a way shower and guide.

In the Witness paradigm, the only way I would have ever been allowed to address an audience would have been by having a conversation with another sister in front of the congregation (without ever facing the audience) which is the 'setting' for a public talk on the 'ministry school' or a 'demonstration.' I would never have been allowed to face an audience, unless there was no baptized man present, which is likely to never happen. In the rare instances that there is not a baptized brother present, a baptized Witness woman must cover her head (with something, a hat, scarf, or in some cases, a napkin or doily) in order to address any assembly.

A woman is not allowed to lead.

A woman is not allowed to write books (for that matter, no one in the JW cult is allowed to write books; most of the books Witnesses read are written and manufactured by the Watchtower, Bible & Tract Society).

A woman is not allowed to have original ideas and execute these.

A woman is not allowed to teach (according to Paul's infamous one-liner at 1 Timothy 2:12: "I do not permit a woman to teach...").

I have often mused on the stark contrast between the life and teachings of Yeshua Ben Yosef and that of Paul. I believe many Christians give more credence, import and weight to Paul's writings than to what is afforded within by way of revelation from a deep, meaningful study of all the writings we have (including Gnostic texts and the Nag Hammadi library) that reflect the life and teachings of Yeshua Ben Yosef.

Yeshua's pre-eminent disciple was a woman, Mary Magdalene, who was also reportedly his consort and a master teacher in her own right. Even if Paul did not, Christ openly acknowledged and taught women and most certainly permitted women to teach, even when the rituals and customs of his day deemed otherwise. His was an open, gender neutral invitation to all as children of the Divine.

The Awakening

We moved out of New York in 1989, to Maryland, my husband, and our son Cory, who was two at the time. Shortly after the move, I discover I'm pregnant. I get depressed. I'm overwhelmed about being pregnant unexpectedly. My husband may be happy, I don't know for sure, but I almost cry my eyes out.

"I think you can Valerie" was his earnest and heartfelt reply to my tearful offering when I found out I was pregnant: "I can't have a baby without my mother!" My mother and father and entire Witness family were still in New York City.

At 29, I give birth to our second child. The baby came in June of 1990, and she was beautiful. A girl, just like I always wanted. We name her Sarai.

It is at this juncture in my life that the crap starts to hit the proverbial fan. I am in for yet another trajectory change.

After she was born, they say I may have had post-partum depression, but I say my soul was waking up, coming alive, and ready to end the charade. It had had enough of the Witness life/lie I was bearing through. I couldn't stop myself from not wanting to be a Witness anymore, even if I had wanted to, and I didn't want to. I was turning 30 and having my first major upheaval in consciousness. An awakening. A looking around at my life and asking, vigorously and rigorously, *'whose life is this anyway?'*

I came into the full awareness that I was not living my soul's authentic expression. What looked like postpartum depression — not being able to get out the bed, lazing around listless, with the idea of taking a shower dawning on me as an almost monumental undertaking — was, in truth, the

136

soul saying ENOUGH! *Get on your path of purpose or die.*

I confess I seriously considered the 'or die' part on the day I looked at the extra strength 800 milligram Motrin pills in the medicine cabinet I had received for pain management when I left the hospital after giving birth, and wondered silently *'how many would it take, to just go to sleep and not wake up...'*

My own thought frightened me.

What about my kids? Cory and the baby? How would they function without me? What am I thinking? I can't leave! But the pain of being here and not being me, not living my authentic soul's calling, and doing what I was told since I was 4 years old and met that Bible Man on the street, was too great to press on in. The pain of not being me is too heavy. Some part of me is choosing to numb out in depression, and is giving serious consideration to leaving the planet.

There has to be a better way!

My husband, still a Witness, was worried about me. I was acting 'strange' he said. He called my Mom to make his report, "there's something's wrong with her, I don't know what it is" and repeatedly tried to convince her to talk to me more about what I was going through, to snap me out of it, he honestly thinking that would be a sure solution, knowing how close me and Mom always were.

Mom didn't need much encouragement from hubby. She was on top of it with her own solutions. She talked to me over and over about Jehovah and keeping the faith. She wrote me letters, sent me cards, and still, nothing worked to cause a turnaround in the way they hoped it would.

The Witness life I had known for over 20 years was slipping away, and there was nothing anybody could do about it. Not even me.

Nothing can still or stay the soul once it decides to wake.

And no one can keep their own soul forever hinged in a coffin.

The Great Depression

I was ready. Ready to ditch the fanatical beliefs I'd been toting around, toddler style, for decades. And ditch them I did. I was forced to; I confess I didn't come to it of my own human accord. Had it been left to the human me, I probably would have opted to stay in the more comfortable position of being approved of by the people in my life who I wanted the approval of. I would not have opted, on a conscious level, to 'out' myself as a witch, or magickal, or anything other than what I thought the people around me could handle or be happy with.

That was my issue. I wanted approval. I wanted to be liked, accepted, even looked up to. I wanted love, and I wanted it from the people around me.

I didn't know then what I know now: I Am the Love I was seeking. I didn't know I'm approved of and accepted, just the way I am, by God. I didn't know I was designed by God.

Thank God the soul of Valerie didn't leave it up to the human Valerie to run the show. No, matters were solidly in the hands of my soul. My Divine Destiny on this planet, at this time, having been decided by forces more wise and ancient than the carnal me, kicked into full effect, no longer affording me the option of ignoring who I Am. My soul had taken over, and it was the new Law of my life.

Witch I was, and witch I am.

I didn't know it all the way then, but I was about to find out.

That's why I call it waking up.

After the depression, I made a deal with myself, or maybe it was part of

138

the deal to get out of the depression. The deal was that I was going to throw out every belief, save one, and start from scratch.

The one belief I held on to, the only one I knew for sure, beyond any shadows and any doubt: **God is love**. I knew that in my bones. I could die for that, but more importantly, I could live for it.

God is love.

Period.

At that point I told myself: *I don't know if God really sent his son here to die for me, or if I'm a sinner, deserving only of death (sounds more than a little harsh to me), or if I'm only here to live 4 score and 10 years and then return to dust, with the best I can hope for while I'm here is to have a little love, serve God, commit no sins, lead a good life, and maybe, just maybe, if I crossed all the t's and dotted all the i's, prayed enough, begged God in heaven enough, I might land in some wonderful place after physical death, or be resurrected to live eternal life in paradise on a cleansed and made new earth after all the 'bad' people were killed by God at the great war of Armageddon.*

I don't know if any of that's true.

They told me that narrow is the gate and cramped is the road leading to life, and few are on it, but broad and spacious is the path leading to destruction, and many are on it. That's what the 'Word' says.

I can tell you from experience, trying to walk that narrow road was a tall order, at least for me anyway. There could well be other people who are having a pure cakewalk on that narrow road, but I confess, I was struggling. It seemed daunting, near impossible. But daunting or not, if that's what it takes to please God and get the prize of eternal life in paradise on earth (that's what's drilled into the Witness psyche), isn't it worth whatever effort it takes? I thought so, and was willing to give it a good whirl, and did, til my questions about the whole affair got the better of me.

Can't I have paradise now? Why must I wait so long to feel good? Can joy be mine now?

And what about the seeming impossibility of actually being able to do what's required to get everlasting life and all the blessings of never ending joy and happiness and fruitfulness and fulfillment?

Why do I have to die or suffer before I get the goods?

What kind of cruel trick is that?

Did God invent that?

What kind of God invented that?

Has anyone talked to this God and asked Him about it?

Can I?

I was full of questions, the heretical kind.

No one seemed to like it when I asked questions like that.

After a while, I learned not to ask questions like that; not out loud anyway. But then I discovered a new problem: unanswered questions don't go away, only the methods by which we ask them. Suppressed, unanswered questions nip, bite and gnaw at me from the inside, I guess much like my mother's were nipping, biting and gnawing at her until she met the Bible Man on the street.

So I started by own independent search for Truth, or maybe I was driven to it.

You could say I was going rogue.

I started reading books that the Witnesses would never have approved of if they knew. So I made sure they didn't know. I confess, I snuck around. Who has to sneak around to read books when one has the true and earnest goal of seeking the Truth and gaining enlightenment?

One who lives in fear and needs approval like they need air.

Even still, I pushed on. I opened my mind to receive the answers I'd been searching for. I asked and asked and asked. I'm still asking. Seek and ye shall find is no mere notion. It's real. The more you seek, the more you find. Those who are content with eating what people give them will always have to get by on what people give them, and will have to settle for never having the true hunger of the soul satiated.

I was hungry, no, insatiable.

The meal portions I was getting in the form of the Watchtower and Awake magazines and the books and publications of the Watchtower Bible & Tract Society were not satiating my hunger. And the clear Witness warning to not read anything other than what came from the Watchtower Bible &

Tract Society no longer sounded like a protection. That fence took on a menacing air, stifling even.

Maybe they don't want me to know.

I needed more. I wanted more. And I knew, somewhere deep inside, that there was so much more than what I was being told and systematically given to eat.

They told me that what they were feeding me was the whole story.

It was not.

I feel the need to issue a word of warning here. Don't think that because it's the call of your soul to go on this journey that the journey is going to be joyful every moment. It's not. It's like any other road, part the way is rough, part the way is paved, there are ditches, and curves, gullies and dips, twists and turns, and there also are pristine views and beauty unimaginable.

When you consciously choose to embark on the soul's journey, because you read this book, or some other book, or you simply feel inspired to do it from the inside, don't think it will be an easy stroll through the roses.

There's some thorns in there too.

One of the biggest thorns for me, on this journey of the soul, this finding and receiving and accepting and rejoicing over and loving my Authentic Self, was the loss of relationships.

The whole 'man-is-the-head thing was getting real old, real quick.

I would soon feel the pain and devastation of the illusion of loss.

The Rebel

I confess my first marriage did not end well.

Nor did my second.

Which is why I am reluctant to do anything like that again. Maybe a better word to use here — rather than reluctant — is careful (full of care) about ever moving into marriage territory again; at least not under the conventional norms. Considering what I had to go through to get out of the agreements, I'd just as soon not do that again.

Maybe the marriage system, as I knew it, is broken. I confess I may have had a very skewed idea of what marriage is in the first place.

For me, God's way is love. That's all it ever is.

The cult espouses that God's way is rules and rigidity.

I have found that this is not the case. A Course in Miracles teaches that heaven makes no demands, while hell on the other hand, makes an impossible and endless list of demands, demands we could surely not fill. Why? Because the ego is insane.

God is not. God is love. God did not tell me to go to a courthouse to get papers to bind myself to someone for life. People told me to do that, and I did as I was told. There was a system in place that strongly encouraged me to walk that path, which should have been a tip off... why am I going to a courthouse to get married? The whole thing is rather strange to me now.

Hence why I would not do that again.

I am pretty confirmed in my thought that I will never go to courthouses again for matters of love. It does not seem natural.

When I went to the first courthouse to get wedding papers, the process was unsettling to say the least, and disturbing at points; unfortunately not disturbing enough for me to pick my tail up and head out of there as fast as my little legs could carry me. I was only 22, and there was so much invested.

There was 7 years invested in dating this person in an on-again, off-again turmoil ridden relationship that never seemed to steady into harmony.

There was the 18 years prior I had spent with the Witnesses, since age 4, being conditioned into what was supposed to be my life.

There was the engagement of several months he and I had carried friends and family through with us, including every bit of preparation for the big day, from shopping with my mom for fabric to make the elaborate wedding gown to visiting travel agents to get the best deal for the honeymoon in the Bahamas. (Might I add that there was no internet access for us in the early 1980's, so all of this was being done by foot, an odd and unbearable thought to the smartphone generation who does practically everything life calls for with thumbs.)

There was so much time, energy and money invested by the time I arrived at the courthouse steps that even if I thought the process of getting married was torturous and painful, I would have done it anyway.

Can't back out now. Nor did I want to.

I was a good girl. I did as I was told, for the most part.

There was the part of me that is a born rebel, and that is the part of me that would not be content with sitting on the sidelines while I made a train wreck of my life. The Rebel said "ENOUGH! We're not doing this anymore! I don't care what you were told Valerie, it's time to break free!!!"

Thank God for the Rebel.

It is she who, at about 30, decided she was going to end her marriage, an unheard of proposition in the Witness world.

It was she who decided to wear the mini-skirt.

Me and mini-skirt's have a thing going on. I love them. I love my legs. I bare them at a whim, and I love baring them. Part of it could be because I'm a Libra, and air signs love air to brush across their skin. It's exhilarating, electrifying. I feel alive in a mini-skirt, or anything that bares skin and feels free.

It was she who got me to buy my first mini-skirt. The Rebel. She knew I wanted it, in my heart of hearts, and she also knew it was forbidden.

Even better.

Forbidden fruit is undoubtedly the sweetest.

I do not know why this is so, only that it is.

It was a cute little black number that was sure to turn heads. I loved turning heads. Now, I turn them whether I want to or not. There's something in me or on me that whips people's heads around when I walk into a room. I don't think about it so much anymore, I just go with it. I think it's God they're seeing. I especially get it with babies. They catch sight of me and stare like nobody's business. I smile.

Because I could never wear the cute black dress anywhere that it was possible to be spotted by a card-carrying member of the cult (and expect to escape the attention and admonition of the elders) I tucked it neatly into my purse one night when I was preparing for a business meeting held at a Marriott hotel far from home. I was in a network marketing business, and had met a handsome and intriguing man there, who showed extra special interest in me.

We first met at the hotel one night when his network marketing company's meeting was occupying the room adjacent to where our network marketing meeting was being held. We were supposedly in two different camps, but our eyes locked, and the rest, they say, is proverbial history.

He and I had a little fling, I call it little because we never got a hotel room and never actually had sex. We did a whole lot of messing around though, and that was taboo for sure.

It was, like I said, forbidden fruit, and exhilarating. I was ALIVE.

He was married, and he said I gave him the best blow jobs he's ever had, and insisted that his wife wasn't doing it. You never know if that's true or not coming from a straying married man, he's liable to say anything to get head.

For me, my rebel was running the show. I was free! Out of the Witness rules! Doing whatever I wanted to do! Making myself happy! I don't know if I gave him blow jobs because I liked it or because I was determined to

144

see what it would feel like to do everything the Witnesses said not to.

I was over 30 and had never given blow jobs before. I must confess, there was something empowering about holding a potent member of another person's anatomy in my mouth, completely in control of their pleasure, and how quickly, or slowly, it would happen.

There's a psychological aspect to blow jobs that we didn't get to explore in any conversations in the cult. It's powerful. Maybe more women would love giving blow jobs if they connected with the potency and power in it, rather than thinking it's nasty. Just my thoughts.

Either way, we were having fun, me and him, hanging out after our network marketing meetings, going to the bar for drinks, smooching, feeling each other up and getting hot and horny.

It was thrilling, my first foray into the taboo world of blow jobs, seeing someone outside my marriage, and wearing mini-skirts.

I was breaking all the rules and never felt better! I felt like a teenager again!

Thank you Rebel!

She set me free.

Though one cannot live life by the mandates of the inner Rebel, I must confess it is a highly useful energy for setting one free from excessive rules, especially if the soul is stirring one in the freedom direction.

I acknowledge I could have been free by other, not so taboo means. I could have announced my truth, honestly and openly, to my husband, the religion and everyone else I had made any pacts with, and renegotiated the contracts. I know that now. Then, I was doing the best I could to keep my head above water. I love the me of yesterday, because she always did what she thought was best and is a good person at the core. She is love.

Of course, my husband of the time is getting suspicious. I go out every week to this 'meeting.' I come home late. I don't have sex with him (we've been sex-dead for a while now). I almost find sex with him repulsive. It's a duty, not a joy. That's because the relationship has disintegrated to a state that is not much more than 2 roommates taking care of 2 kids.

That would not last long.

Shocking Evidence on Me

Y ou would think I'd get caught and disfellowshipped for the first man I was tipping around with, to whom I was giving magnificent blow jobs, and who was the all too willing partner in my first foray into the taboo world of adultery and sexual acts beyond coitus.

Not so.

Nor was I disfellowshipped for the 2nd one I tipped around with during my first marriage; a neighbor whose kids attended the same elementary school as mine, and who, since he was a firefighter with a versatile work schedule, was routinely the only dad on school field trips. Since I went on every field trip with my first two kids from kindergarten to high school, and so did he, and since we both had more than one child in the same elementary school at the same time, he and I frequently found ourselves together on school buses.

He was REALLY cute and all the moms used to fuss over him because he was the only man with us all the time. I didn't fuss over him at all. He followed me around. I wondered why, even though there was an unmistakable attraction. I knew he was married, and so was I.

Though the Rebel had me firmly in her grip, I wasn't about to turn into a home wrecker with someone in our neighborhood. His wife was a nurse, I think, or in some helping profession, and it made me feel bad to think that while she was off saving lives and helping people her husband was lusting after me. I couldn't have part in that. So though I went to his house one day, supposedly under the guise of him looking at my network marketing products, it quickly became apparent that he and I were like moths to a flame and had best not be in a secluded place together. It got heated, so I ended the hanky-panky before anything serious could break out.

After his begging and pleading only got us so far until I had to clear my head, say no and mean it, he excused himself, went into the other room and jerked himself off, a totally strange thing for a man to do in the regions I come from. (As for the Witness men who were jerking themselves off, they would have never let on.) He came back to the room with a smile on his face, we bid each other farewell and I left.

And that was that.

No, I did not get disfellowshipped for that either.

I was disfellowshipped on the heels of a most fortuitous and strangely curious set of events...

My first husband and I physically separated in the spring of 1996, though we'd been emotionally and sexually separated for at least a year or two prior to that (more on this later),

One night, a few months after we were separated, one of my new lovers came home with me after a night of partying together. This particular lover was special from the beginning, there was an animal magnetism to him that I could not articulate, much less comprehend or explain. He and I met in the summer of 1996.

Little did I know I had met Twin Flame. Life is about to get a whole lot more interesting...

After he and I had had a good roll in the hay and fell asleep, at about 3 or 4 am, my son, about 9 at the time, on the heels of a nightmare, swung my bedroom door wide open and in one giant leap hurled himself into the middle of my bed, not a wholly uncommon thing for him to do (I thought my door was locked, but apparently it was not).

Except this night would prove to be one of the most uncommon ever.

Before I could do a thing to prevent it, my son came face-to-face with my lover.

I was mortified.

The only panicked thing I could think to do was grab my son and usher him back to his bedroom as fast as humanly possible, while trying to

147

convince myself that he didn't see a thing.

I would deny **everything** if asked **anything**. Or play dumb. Or ignore the questions. Or act like it was all a dream.

A very, very, very bad dream.

Yep, that's what I'll do.

And right then and there, my twisted plot was laid. The last thing I was prepared to do was have a conversation with my son about it and own up to what happened.

How could I tell him the truth? This bed, the same bed he had plopped into every time he had a nightmare, for years, had always contained his mother on one side, and his father on the other. Since the separation, only his mother was there. So when he plopped there in the middle of the night, there was me and plenty of space. I would console him and we'd fall back asleep. Those were the only 2 scenarios he was accustomed to when it came to my bed at night.

Now, a whole other thing had just happened that I was much too embarrassed to face.

The good news is that my son and I and the family had a good laugh about it years later, when I was able to own my stuff and talk about it with honesty and clarity, sans the guilt, shame and embarrassment.

It is what it is, and I love the Valerie of yesteryear.

Fortuitously for my soon-to-be-ex-husband — and as yet unbeknownst to him — shocking adulterous evidence on me had just been procured.

The Hedonism Period

I was home relaxing upstairs in our 3 bedroom townhouse when the elders came.

It's now the late 90's and my first husband and I had been separated for awhile. It was shocking, to say the very least, because Witnesses rarely separate or divorce. It's one of the biggest Witness taboos.

I had committed that taboo. I had put my husband out. Well, I didn't actually put him out. I went to the courts to file an order for him to be removed from our home. The cops came that night and carted him off amid tears and screams from the children.

With him gone, I felt relief.

For the past several years, from the great depression following the birth of my daughter (in 1990), I'd been slowly extricating myself from the Witness web.

It was an arduous task.

Every tentacle of cult living was deeply embedded in my flesh, and had to be removed one by one.

The tentacle of good friends. All our friends were Witnesses. All the young couples we knew for years and hung out with were Witnesses. We went on vacations together. We were raising our kids together.

Removing that tentacle hurt. It really hurt.

The tentacle of family was next. All my family members were Witnesses, of which my mom was the biggest.

How do you extricate that tentacle without ripping your own flesh to shreds?

No one tells us how to extricate ourselves from entanglements that include the whole clan.

Then there was the tentacle of my husband, who was still very much a Witness and intended to remain so.

That's how the separation happened. I didn't know whether we would ever get divorced, considering the Witness stance on that, I only knew that I was not going to be in that relationship configuration any longer. Yes, we were parents of the same children, and no, we were not going to live together as husband and wife.

On that I was clear.

The tentacles went deep. I didn't have a way to extricate them gently. So I did what many of us do when we have something painful to do, that we don't really know how to do... we do it anyway and see what happens. There's no training for some things in life, they have to be learned on the fly.

I was learning how to stand in my authentic self, without the clan, without the religion, without the benefit of familiarity.

I knew nothing about this terrain, had never seen it before. All I knew was, I had to embark on this path. I was compelled; driven by some inner force that could not sit comfortably where I was. It was like someone had put invisible, upright thumb tacks on my seat while I was in the bathroom. When I returned to the very same seat, I couldn't bear to sit on it anymore. What used to be comfortable now made me hop up.

I've been pulling away from the Witnesses for years, not going in field service, or to the Kingdom Hall, or to Witness events.

Then one day it all came to a head.

I'm at home relaxing upstairs, when I hear a knock at the door. It's the elders, doing a 'drive-by' as we call it (when elders show up at your front door unannounced). They usually do drive-by's on those who haven't been to the Kingdom Hall in awhile, also known as 'inactive' Witnesses, especially if they haven't been able to reach them by telephone.

In the months following our separation, my husband returned to his parents' home in New York. He wanted to be free to remarry, to settle down with a wife and have sex.

None of which could he do unless he was first granted a 'scriptural' divorce from me.

In my world, I didn't care what he was doing or not doing. I wasn't thinking about him any more than I was giving thought to the man in the moon if there be one.

Until the knock on the door came.

After the separation, my kids and I still lived in the same home our family had lived in for years (even while we were active Witnesses). That's how the elders knew where to find me.

My kids opened the door, invited the elders in and came upstairs to announce "Mom, the elders are here!" Damn it. They had already swung the door wide open and invited them in. Of course. They knew these men. They were not strangers to our family. Not only were they not strangers to our family, they were considered the guardians and helpers of families and believers. In these parts, we do not keep the door closed on a guardian (my words, not theirs, Witnesses do not use the word 'guardian' with regard to the elders, it's more my experience of them energetically.)

I reluctantly go downstairs to meet them.

The reason for their visit: my husband had informed the elders that I was sexually active with someone else. Which was true. I was having sex with my new man, and loving it. I hadn't been to the Kingdom Hall in years and had completely turned my back on the Witness lifestyle.

I was dropping it like it was hot in the clubs.

I was sleeping with whoever I felt like sleeping with.

I was doing everything I felt like doing; things I was never allowed to do, in good conscience, as a Witness.

That was over 26 years of pent up frustration. It burst out. I was on the loose, not thinking about God or a Bible.

As a matter of fact, years before that day, I purposely scavenge my entire house from top to bottom for every Bible and scrap of Witness literature I can find, deposit the whole pile in the storage room in the basement, and close the door on that chapter in my life with a silent oath that I will never pick up a Bible again.

I was done.

My hedonism period was in full glory... not a good time for me to meet up with the elders who were now sitting in my living room.

The Disfellowshipping

At this juncture I am clear, and have been happily living my truth for years now.

I am done with Witnesses. Forever.

There's not a thing these elders can say that will change my mind. Post-Witness life is too good to me and too fun for me to be anywhere near swayed to do anything different. I'm living unrestrained for the first time in my life.

I'm doing what I feel like doing, when I feel like doing it, with whomever I feel like doing it with.

That felt like freedom to me.

I must confess now I know it was rebellion.

The ones who are most tightly repressed are the very ones who spring into full-blown crazy when they're let loose. That was me. I was so deeply and reverently Witness, for so long, repressing so much of me and my natural desires, that when it came time to uncork the bottle, I was all over the place, completely unrestrained, and to exacerbate the matter, I didn't care.

It felt so good. I was liberated! Finally!

No religion!

No having to read the Bible every day!

No having to study the Watchtower for Sunday morning!

No waking up early on Saturday!

Hey, no more knocking on doors, EVER!

YES!!!

I could do cartwheels. I cannot even describe the feelings of freedom and relief I experience, that run deeper than the rebellion.

So for these elders standing in my living room, briefcases in hand, ready to whip out Bibles at any moment, who have before them the formidable task of bringing me to my senses and back into the 'fold,' it does not bode well.

They don't stand a chance in hell. But they don't know that yet.

They're about to find out.

I invite them to sit down at the dining room table. I excuse the children. We are privately talking. The elders ask if they can open with a prayer. I acquiesce, though I know what they're here for, and a prayer ain't going to help them. That's my thought.

Haven't you heard? I'm a full blown heathen now, and loving it.

They pray.

I respectfully bow my head and listen though I do not close my eyes nor do I express agreement with an 'amen' at the end.

They tell me why they're here. They've missed me at the Kingdom Hall. They've come by before, but haven't been able to talk to me.

Yeah, I know, I've been avoiding you.

They continue.

"We want to help you Valerie, but we need you to work with us. What have you been doing?"

They go in for their questioning. They question me about my lifestyle. They tell me that my husband has reported to them that I've had sex with someone else. They tell me that they know I know that this is a grave sin, and that the punishment for this is serious. Is there anything I want to say? Is it true or not true? Am I coming back to the Kingdom Hall?

Or have you completely lost your mind?

The last question wasn't a spoken one, more of a question that seems to be hanging around the edges of the others. Somehow I see and sniff that unasked question.

It stinks.

Something in me clicks. In a moment, I go from being respectful and patient to downright forthright.

I confess I don't know what possessed me to say to the elders what I hear come from my own mouth next.

"What I do is not your business. It's mine. I have nothing to say to you. You are free to leave my home."

What!??!? Did I just tell the elders to mind their business and get out?!?!?
Who is this new Valerie?

She has no tolerance or respect for the elders, the keepers of the Witness law, the very same set of brothers who the other Valerie had always revered, honored, and on not more than a few occasions, feared.

I don't know who this new Valerie is, but 2 things are clear:

One, she ain't the same Valerie that used to go in field service every day for hours on end and two, I like her.

Whoever she is, this new Valerie is a breath of fresh air. I really, really like her. She's fearless. She doesn't care. She's saying what she really wants to say, and taking no prisoners.

I never even knew this Valerie was in there until I heard her talking through my mouth. I thank those elders for introducing me to myself.

However, I don't think they are feeling the same wave of freedom and appreciation and don't-care-ness that has obviously swept over me.

They make a final pronouncement before leaving: "if you won't come clean, we'll have to disfellowship you. You leave us no choice but to assume that what we've heard about you is true."

Turns out, my estranged husband had told them about the incident when my son caught me and my new lover naked in bed in the middle of the night.

Yikes.

I was mortified.

I tried to brush it off, but kids are too smart. Under heavy questioning of my son about my lifestyle on a visit to his father's, the truth came out, and hubby had his 'evidence' on me: an eye witness report. No matter that the eyewitness was our 9-year-old son. When it's a matter of being free, and being able to have sex, and you can't have sex unless you get evidence to divorce and remarry, and you want to stay in Witness graces, a 9-year-old will have to do. You'll run straight to the nearest elders to tell them everything your investigation revealed.

There we have it, his evidence.

The elders were coming by to conduct their portion of the investigation. Was the evidence factual? It was only fair for them to bring the evidence to me, in order for me to confirm or deny.

I wasn't going to deny it. Why should I? I didn't care if they heard I was swinging from the chandeliers with 10 men.

I was past caring. After caring so much, for so many years, for so many souls, I was over it. I was done caring. About anything or anyone. Or at least that's what I told myself during the extrication. I had reached a point where it was too painful to keep caring.

Let me just have some fun became my new mantra.

My response to the pronouncement?

"Do whatever you have to do."

The air was thick and I was done.

Get out of my house had taken over me on the inside, so I could only imagine that it had by now written itself all over my face.

Before leaving, the elders make a request.

"Valerie, if you really want to show your repentance, it would behoove you to be present when we read your name off at the Kingdom Hall next Thursday night as being disfellowshipped."

Really?!? You have GOT to be freakin' kidding me!

I haven't been to the Kingdom Hall in years. I don't do that anymore. I'm not one of you anymore. What in Sam hill makes you think that I would set foot in a Kingdom Hall, to show people whom I care nothing about, and don't agree with, that I'm repentant for doing something I feel good doing and know damn well I'm going to keep doing? Have you completely lost your mind?

"Goodbye." And I mean it.

The elders leave. I never see them again.

My Biggest Thorn

My biggest thorn has been the seeming loss of familial relationships in my stand as a Christian Witch.

The death knell to me and mom's relationship was delivered tearfully in a conversation she and I had in her New York City apartment, ironically, in the very same room that was my bedroom when I lived at home.

She stated that, because I had been disfellowshipped, she could no longer have the same kind of relationship with me as we'd enjoyed for decades. According to Witness law, we could only communicate on 3 matters: family matters, business and health. The law is clear, and she was following it.

I confess it was no surprise. I know my mom well. She'd been a faithful Witness for almost 30 years by now. Nothing the Witnesses demanded of her seemed to be outside her capacity or willingness to do, including alienate or avoid family. She'd demonstrated that with her mother, what made me think it would be different with me?

The conversation and what ensued was emotionally devastating, for both of us. The intimate mother daughter bond we had engaged in since 1961, when I was born, was dealt a hard blow.

I know she believed she was doing the right thing. This kind of behavior, the Witnesses teach, is designed to bring an errant one back to the fold, by making them see the loss incurred by the error of their ways. So while it may sound like cruel and inhuman treatment, the Witnesses say there is a very loving underpinning to what they do, and that love should drive a person right back to being a faithful Witness, and when such does happen,

157

with the added benefit that the pain of being ousted will be so etched in the mind and fabric of the person that future wayward behavior would be out of the question.

A disfellowshipped person could turn around and become the most loyal Witness ever, even more so than the ones who've been there for years and never left, much like the prodigal son. He had to leave, see the wretchedness of his ways, then return home, only to be celebrated and elevated by his father. The one who had been there all along complained. Why not a feast for me? Why not a celebration of my faithfulness? I've been here with you all along Father. The father's response, in so many words: we rejoice greatly over someone who was lost and finds his way, even more than we rejoice over one who's been here all along.

As for mom and me. We sat and cried. We told each other how much we loved and cared for each other. What I could not have known then, that I know now, is that we were saying a goodbye of sorts.

The Bible Man's influence on our lives seems to be a long shadow.

That conversation happened when I was in the category of simply being disfellowshipped: the disciplined state for an unruly, unrepentant, wayward sinner who refuses to live according to the rules of the organization, rules that I had agreed to and that I had promised to live by forever, in my dedication to Jehovah God as symbolized by water baptism, and had since turned my back on.

That's the Witness take on it. I fully understand this, since I had committed to living this way myself, and had for 26 years.

Now, my understanding is: I made a dedication of my life to God, not to a religion. My dedication to God stands. Forever. In my mind, it was never a question, nor could it be.

After 'outing' myself as a witch, my brother, who still communicates with me (he's never been baptized so he can't be officially put out of something he never chose to join in the first place) informed me that the Witnesses have classified me as an apostate (I chuckle as I write this, not at the Witnesses, but at myself when I remember the feverishness with which I used to warn others against turning apostate). An apostate, according to Witness law and doctrine, is one who's committed the unforgivable sin: sinning against the Holy Spirit. Every sin is forgivable, except this one. I'm not sure what makes the Holy Spirit so special in this particular paradigm, but if you must affront any of heaven's hordes, make sure it is NOT the Holy Spirit, for, apparently, this one does not forgive.

Has anyone informed the Holy Spirit that there's an 'unforgivable sin'? Maybe not.

The Holy Spirit is my ever present guide to forgiveness, and ultimately, beyond forgiveness to the understanding and knowledge that there's nothing to forgive. There is no sin. Sin is a delusion of the ego (a human construct that thinks itself separate from God, and is, in all actuality, mad). The ego is insane. It made up sin. The part of us that believes in sin is actually mad.

Where there is belief in sin, you can be sure to find its bastard offspring: judgment, guilt, shame, punishment and ultimately, self-sabotage.

The Holy Spirit disintegrates all these, if we are deeply desirous and desperately willing, as I was, especially judgments (which get the whole party started anyway). I confess I call for this particular help from the Holy Spirit several times a day, considering my background of judging everything that moves.

The real question is: how does any one of us know the true condition of a person's heart and mind but God?

We do not.

Therefore, we cannot judge, if we be walkers in the Light, and I choose to walk in the Light. This is a judgment-free walk; free of judgments of me and everybody else.

Let everybody be.

If it had to take me forty-some odd years to learn it, it was well worth every moment, because the lesson of non-judgment is so profound, so life-fulfilling, so life-affirming, so welcoming, so expansive, so freeing, so empowering, and so loving that nothing can resist it.

Eventually, as my unerring faithfulness to my soul calling and heart path as a Christian Witch deepens and solidifies, my mother takes the position of not speaking to me at all.

While mom and I experience an outer shift in our relationship as mother and daughter, I confess the love is the deepest it has ever been. She had a habit of saying 'love you' when she ended every phone conversation. The inflection and tone in her voice and the warmth enveloping her words told me there was a smile on her face when she said it, accompanied by a soft spot in her heart. In this new post-disfellowshipping paradigm, whenever she ended a conversation with me, she no longer said 'love you', she said 'bye-bye'. If I were listening to the words only, something in me would have found reason to be upset. I did not listen to the words. I listened to the same inflection, tone and warmth she had always had as my mom. Nothing had changed. It still sounded to me as if she were ending every conversation with 'love you'. In essence, she was.

No amount of Witness law could steal mom's love. It peeked and leaked out all over the place.

For the oozing love of my mother that could not be contained — even in the midst of me not doing what she wanted me to, and indeed even in the midst of me doing what she despised — I am deeply grateful.

Soul Choice vs. Religion

I confess I was under a hypnotic spell... an errant belief that said I needed permission and approval from the people I loved before I could live and express my soul's knowing.

I was looking for the 'okay' stamp from my clan. I thought I would die without it.

That was then.

Now I know no one needs approval to make and live a soul choice.

Soul choices are not approval driven, they have nothing to do with who approves and who does not. They are not about that at all. The soul urges us to make a powerful choice: NOT to fit in, but rather to walk our unique God-appointed path, no matter how strange, no matter how bizarre, no matter what. It is the choice for AUTHENTICITY, another name for God showing up as a distinct creation while remembering It is One.

Soul choices are about saving that particular soul, in the ways and means agreed upon by that soul and the Creator.

Here's where soul choice and religion bump heads. Or, I could more accurately state that they go their separate ways, as the soul doesn't choose to bump heads. It only does what it's here to do. Evolve.

Religion wants all the souls in that construct (yes, religion is a construct of the human mind, no matter how convincing the people who propagate the religion are about the religion's divine origins) to act the same way, pray the same way, say the same words to the prayers, worship the same way, in the same place, at the same time, wearing the same clothes.

Sunday is the most segregated day in America. It's the day when most

161

people arise to go to their respective places of worship, their religious houses, and do what they do there, with people who look mostly like them, dress like them, say things like them, worship like them, and, by and large, live like them.

In my ministerial training and preparation to be ordained as a Minister of Spiritual Consciousness (which is what your soul cares about and is trying to evolve, your consciousness) I was charged with going to several houses of worship, including brands of Christianity unfamiliar to me. I was curiously enthused with the assignment, because for me it held the promise and potential of answering deep-seated questions I had about what people were doing in their respective houses of worship on Sunday mornings behind closed doors I had never ventured past.

There's only one way to get to the heart of the matter on that one, and that's to go to each one, talk to the people in that respective house of worship, and learn experientially.

Like I said, life's one big adventure.

Before I share with you the outcome of the assignment, and what I discovered about myself and my world in the process, I will say that the idea of visiting multiple houses of worship went completely counter to anything I experienced with the Witnesses in my 26 years of affiliation.

The Witnesses had books that told us about Buddhists, and Hindus, and Muslims, and other strains of Christianity, including Catholicism. We weren't allowed to explore any of those religions, their holy books, or their places of worship, on our own. We were taught the Witness version of what each of the world's religions is about, and the Witness view on why each of them is wrong.

So my experience of other religions was nil, save what the Witnesses told me, until such time that I made the conscious decision to find out for myself, from the people who could actually tell me how the religion worked: the ones who are in it.

My eagerness to take on the assignment of going to the holy houses of the major religions was a titillating one, because up until then, my study of the world's religions, in the years following my departure from the

Witnesses, was largely done through books in an attempt to assuage my burning, relentless curiosity.

Now, I'd get the opportunity to experience these religions for myself, for the first time in my life, at 48 years of age.

I went to the Jewish synagogue on a Saturday morning, the Sabbath, and heard ancient Hebrew words read aloud from a very long scroll, that had been carefully drawn from a big elaborate canister with tassels on it and unfurled by holy men. It was all so beautiful and poetic. I could actually channel Jesus and his reading of the scrolls and teaching from them in ancient synagogues as described in the Gospels. The Jewish congregation was most welcoming, above curious glances that must have reflected questions around what would bring a black woman they had never seen before into their synagogue on a Saturday morning, smiling from ear to ear like she was about to discover the secrets to the Universe.

Nonetheless, they were quite polite, shared the holy book, written in Hebrew, with me, and even helped me follow along with the service. They watched over me while I was there, making sure I got what I needed. I found that particularly exquisite.

When visiting the Hindu temple, I was tickled pink to see the word DEVOTEES at the station where we took off our shoes outside the room where worship takes place. To be called a DEVOTEE is fitting, I thought. *Yes, that's what I am, a DEVOTEE.* We entered the large worship space and sat on the floor on what looked like giant yoga mats, which causes a funny thought to scamper through my mind about what the big-hatted sisters at the Baptist Church would do if presented with this seating arrangement. I bring myself back from my silent reverie to the aroma of incense wafting through the air, devotees carrying fruit to the front, where a man collects the offerings in front of larger-than-life statues of Gods and Goddesses, all while devotees feel completely at home to move processional-style to each of several altars lining the walls, making prayers and offerings as they go.

Fascinating. I've never seen anything like this before.

After a period of singing and chanting, the prophet of the place comes in, almost floating on air, and delivers his message in another language.

Before beginning, he greets us, me and my sisters in ministry (who all have the same assignment). There are about 7 of us who have made this trip to the temple together.

I don't know what we must have looked like to our hosts, but we are warmly welcomed (and fed well afterward too). The prophet takes the time, care and attention to explain to us, right there in the worship service, before all the Devotees present, that his message will be delivered in another tongue, and that once he is complete, he will gladly translate his message into English for us. He then reassures us that he will make himself available to answer any of our questions at the end. My sisters and I then listen to the message, spoken entirely in another language.

Something in my soul knows the message is about love.

Sure enough, when he translated, among much more, he said, "the message today is about love, and that we must be connected to it, plugged in, like a lamp is plugged into the electric socket, then it shines…."

Beautiful.

It was prayer time on a Friday afternoon when I visited the Islamic Mosque. I covered myself from head to toe, as appropriate for a woman praying in that holy house. The women were on one side of the building and the men on the other. There were separate entrances for each sex. I didn't see the men worshiping or praying, they were on the other side of the wall, though I heard them. What I did see, looking around me, was one of the most beautiful sights I'd ever beheld, a roomful of women, on their knees, wrapped in colorful and bejeweled head wraps and scarfs, moving harmoniously as one, like a human tidal wave, in full-body prayer. There's not many moments I've had quite like that one. I do what they do. Though I do not understand the meaning of the words I am hearing or saying, I feel they are healing my spirit.

Breathtaking.

When my sisters in ministry and I went to the Native American Pow-wow, I was enthralled again, but this time in an altogether different way. Feathers, great and small, of all colors and sorts, adorned the people, from the chief, with his arranged in an elaborate head-dress that reached to the ground in back of him, to the tiniest one with a feather on their person somewhere, it was clear this clan esteems feathers. And drums. And community. And singing. And chanting. And prayer. And dancing. And beauty. And nature. And connectedness. I felt alive with the Natives. Raw and alive.

Divine.

Then I found a Buddhist circle and meditated and chanted with them. They said they could manifest anything with chanting, or solve any problem by chanting, or create any harmonious condition with chanting. I had never been exposed to the power of the word in such a way. Chanting works. The Buddhists taught me so. Experientially.

After having meditated and chanted with the Buddhists, devoted myself to God in song with the Hindus, engaged in full-body prayer with my Muslim sisters, found solace in the poetic cadence of ancient Hebrew words wafting from a scroll on the tongue of the Rabbi, danced at a Pow-wow, inhaled tobacco at a peace-pipe ceremony, caught the holy ghost at the Baptist and A.M.E. churches, and heard the melodious choirs of the Catholic church, there's one thing I can say with certainty, from my own experience: **God/Goddess is alive and well in them all**.

It was viscerally clear in every holy place and space I entered, that I was entering a house of God.

As I write this, in the years following my consecration and ordination, I still find myself irresistibly pulled to the holy houses and sacred spaces of the world in Africa, Bali, Indonesia and most recently India. I almost cried a river when walking through Notre Dame Cathedral in Paris for the first time.

Outside one of the temples in Bali where I cried like a baby, I was carefully outfitted with a sarong (the traditional and required attire for women entering the temple area; the signage outside also clearly states that menstruating women are not allowed entry, eerily similar to the Lakota sweat lodges I was not allowed to enter for the same reason) by a woman who looked to be about 100 years old and was as snappy as ever. The temple priests at the entryway who examined me for appropriateness to enter kindly asked me to remove my cap, which I did at once. Women must enter with an open crown and men must wear the traditional temple head wrap (which struck me as quite the opposite of our Islamic brothers and sisters).

This place, I think to myself, *has surely earned its nicknames*, 'Island of the Gods' and 'Land of a 1,000 Temples.'

The lotus pond outside the shrine in India arrested my body and fed my soul so deeply I could scarcely pull myself away from its edge. But the holy instant in India that I will always hold in my heart, soul, mind, body and spirit is the chanting sung in tandem by the men and women as incense wafts through the air, bells chime in the background and the holy men wearing only a white linen looking sarong religiously and scrupulously tend to the figure of the Gods with prayer and a rare devotion.

Who knew God had so many different kinds of houses?

Indeed, religion was constructed by us for one reason and one reason only: to consciously link us to Source. We, as humans, created religion after becoming acutely aware, very early on, of 2 facts about life on planet earth. First, that life here can be extremely perilous, and second, that hope is a very fragile, yet very necessary component to well-being, and that without it, the masses would quickly perish with nothing to believe in and nothing to hold on to.

We knew we needed help from somewhere.

Naturally, we inclined upward, since we're all born with the inner knowing that there is something greater than us, in each of us, that can successfully navigate us through, or around, or over, every one of life's perils.

However, to mass teach people to get in touch with this Thing within would be difficult, as the very nature of It is nebulous and nonspecific. We thought to ourselves that we had better devise systems for accomplishing this most important task of re-linking ourselves to the Creator. So that's exactly what we did. We made systems and formulas for worship, to get us started on the hope road. We surmised that somewhere along the road of 'say this prayer, in this way, using these words' something in our own spirit would kick in and connect us so deeply to Source that we'd never have to say another prayer again.

Instead, we'd become the prayer.

At that point, we'd transcend religion.

While 'say this prayer, at this time, in this way, using these words' sounds so helpful and supportive, and it is, it can quickly turn into rote or become burdensome if we're not mindful.

The system of reaching God is not the objective. It is meant to be a temporary fastener, to fasten you to God long enough, through chanting, or prayer, or singing, or meditating, that you'd never want to unlatch yourself again from the divine and you'd simply live in love, all the time. Then you would scarcely need religion. You may still participate in it, because you like it, or you enjoy it, but you're clear you no longer need it to fasten yourself to the Divine. You are forever fastened to the Divine, and could never not be. Once you know the Divine IN you, AS you, what would you need with a fastening device?

There's a great distinction between doing what you enjoy and needing to do something.

Religion is meant to re-link us to God, our divine indwelling nature, since it can be hard for us to sit still and get there on our own. We humans are brilliant, and figured if we built edifices to God, and invited people to band together to pray to God and sing to God and chant to God, that something really powerful would happen.

And it does.

Every time.

It can't not happen.

Religion is powerful, no question about it. It's meant to train us, not constrain us. It's meant to enlighten us, not condemn us. It's meant to inspire us, not load us with guilt.

It is not meant to be a substitute for God, nor is it meant to be a substitute for love, nor is it meant to be burdensome, nor is it meant to be exclusive, judgmental, condemning or dangerous.

Yet, somehow we've managed to make religion all these and worse, in spite of its inherent beauty and the purity of our intent in creating it.

It's like a super-strong Frankenstein monster we collectively create to do our humble bidding, when one day, all of a sudden, the monster gets out of control and wreaks havoc on the very townspeople that created it.

The very thing we created to help us and save us can become our destruction.

That's what religion has the capacity to do, when we let our own creation get out of control and run rip-shod over our humanness and our innate love of humanity and all creation.

Worst yet, when we let religion run rip-shod over our spirituality, we have created a definite plan for disaster. Frankenstein is loose, and can only leave destruction in his wake.

Let's not do that.

Let's not allow religion — our own construct, our own brain-child, created to solve a very real problem — turn into a Frankenstein monster and get in the way of how I lovingly relate to you and you to me.

Let's only love each other, shall we?

Fear Land

Y ou were born with magic. Everyone comes in with a unique brand of magic. The problems creep in when we're young and begin to forget our magic, usually because the people around us forgot theirs, so they pass the damage on to us, or they overtly shut us down, due to ignorance, or fear, or both.

For many of us, the people who influenced us most when we were being reared had parts of themselves that had taken up residence in fear-land.

It's important to state that not all of them lived in fear, and for the ones who did, not all the time. Our families of origin mustered demonstrations of courage, bravery and strength that we remember and from which we draw on for current courage, bravery and strength. They were able, many of them, to liberate themselves from fear often enough and long enough to perpetrate mighty and unforgettable acts of courage, of which we are both proud and grateful.

On the other hand, there were great swaths of their consciousness that were fear bound, even in the presence of the part of them that could act courageously on a moment's notice.

Because we were children, fresh arrivals from the purity and face of God/Goddess, we could clearly tell when the big people around us were in fear. If the fear they were in was associated with a particular display of our magickal powers, we learned, albeit subconsciously, to shut down that particular magickal power. The subliminal messaging we picked up: your power and gifts make people feel uncomfortable. Stop being so magickal.

Like my ability to 'see'. When I was a little girl, one of the things I heard most from my mother was "don't stare." I never thought I was staring. I only knew, as a child, that I could look at people and see things. I was only looking, or so I thought. The people on the receiving end squirmed, looked away, and looked back to check if I was still looking at them. If I was, they got even more uncomfortable. I still remember my mom's friends saying to her, "you better tell that child to stop staring at me."

From the unspoken and spoken messages I was receiving, it became clear to the child Valerie that my gift of 'seeing' wasn't a gift; it was an uncomfortability creator. I don't want to make people uncomfortable, so I'll stop looking. I'll stop seeing everything.

This is not a conscious choice, it's an unconscious deal we make with ourselves when we're little and we discover that our gifts or abilities aren't appreciated, or seem downright problematic.

If we'd all been raised by magickal folks, perhaps all our gifts would have been welcomed, encouraged and consequently enhances, honed and sculpted into magnificence. But alas, since this did not occur, at least for me anyway, we must work with what we've got.

We got fear. I got fear. So part of me also went to live in fear land, like the big people, though we could if called upon, at a moment's notice, do brave and courageous things.

In fear land, fear abounds.

Fear of ghosts.

Fear of spirits.

Fear of dead people.

Fear of the unknown.

Fear of things that don't have a safe, 'reasonable' or logical explanation.

Eventually, we learned to let some part of self live in fear, though we were born to live love.

Magick cannot happen in fear land.

Without memory of our magick, and the courage and encouragement to use it, we sank into feeling powerless. What we did not know is that these feelings are not the truth; we are never powerless. While it is true that we have thought ourselves powerless and have felt powerless, it is also true that we have never actually been powerless.

Because the feeling nature makes up our vibrational mix, and our vibration attracts to us more of what it is, by Law, we drew to ourselves experiences, conditions and people that made us feel even more powerless.

The downward cycle of feeling powerless continued until it got so painful that we sought desperately for solutions.

Maybe you've reached for solutions.

Maybe the solutions you reached for were in a bottle, or in a bed, or a crack pipe, or a line of coke, or pastries or any high that lets us temporarily escape reality.

Or maybe the solutions you reached for were in religion, getting or being 'saved', or singing in the choir. You hung out in religion for a while, but you still weren't able to escape that inner ache that came from knowing the people around you didn't really 'get' you.

You were strange.

Weird.

A little off.

You know what I'm talking about?

That was me, a little off, a little strange, never really fitting in, never really feeling like I belonged, and wondering why.

That's a debilitating way to live. It took me straight to the bed in deep depression after I had my daughter at about 30.

Today, I choose differently.

Will you join me? Trust that developing your gifts from the Creator will free you from powerlessness. The Creator never intended for you to be afraid of yourself.

Yet that's exactly what happens with beginning mages. We get afraid of ourselves, because the big people around us were afraid of us.

My daughter Varonika, who also has the gift of 'seeing' and is highly intuitive, and is a prophet, and has gifts of communication with spirits, particularly fairies, declared a prophecy once that set our neighbor's teeth on edge.

When she was about 5, she and I we were in our neighbor's van, about to take a short ride. She was sitting in the back, playing with a toy. I was sitting in the passenger seat, and our neighbor was in the driver's seat.

Varonika is pretty much an open vessel with little or no resistance to anything she receives from spirit, and has never had issue with saying whatever comes to her. She is the owner of a rare freedom.

All of a sudden, Varonika asks our neighbor, "Mr. Timmy (not his real name), how old are you?"

I'm a little alarmed, but not quite shocked, knowing Varonika. I think to reprimand her for being so forward with an adult, but before I could turn around and address it, he blurted out his age.

She looked at him and clear as day and certain as the sun said, "You have 5 years to live."

Then she went back to playing with whatever she was playing with. There was no judgment and no emotion. Just a simple statement of truth. It came out so pure, so clear, so calm and so unshakable that it startled me and scared the beJesus out of Mr. Timmy. His response: "I rebuke you in the name of Jesus! No! You are not speaking that over my life!"

She didn't respond. She didn't feel she had to. She had made her pronouncement, and that was that.

He could do with it as he pleased.

He was clearly rattled. Shocked. Uncomfortable for the rest of the short ride.

I never forgot that day. I did nothing but encourage Varonika in right use of her gifts. If she has a message, she says it, and I listen.

Because I was no longer afraid of myself and my gifts, I wasn't afraid of her and her gifts. Granted, it can be miraculous and shocking how the gifts show up, yet they shouldn't engender fear, only awe.

The Cross

I confess I almost recoiled in horror when I looked at the contents of the jewelry box he lovingly presented me on my birthday.

With child-like excitement I unwrapped the gift.

Inside was a cross.

I had never seen one up close and personal before, even though it was my 37th birthday.

It took everything in me not to shudder. That task added to the task of appearing happy at a beautiful gift, one that clearly held so much meaning for the giver, and came from a true heart space, was almost more than the mortal me could muster in that moment.

But muster I did, for I'm stalwart. Add to the affair that I'm a trained actress and there you have it. A perfect moment of "I'm shocked, but not for the reason you think."

It was a beauty; gold, encrusted with diamonds. Clearly a well-considered gift, chosen with care and love.

What could I say other than "THANK YOU!!!"

I didn't really mean "thank you," well, I meant it and I didn't mean it. I meant it because it was a beautiful gift, from a beautiful man, who later became my daughter's father and my husband, and it was a gift that meant so much to him, revealing his path as a Christian, and his agreement with me on my path as a Christian, and so was also a message, "I love you enough to buy you jewelry, and I love you more than a man loves a woman, I love you with the love of Christ."

Maybe he wasn't saying all that. Maybe I made it up. But what I made up made me feel real good.

Now for the reason I didn't mean the forced, shocked, trying to hide a shudder "thank you": I was trained that the cross is evil.

I hated the cross, and didn't know why. I knew why I used to hate it. I didn't know why I still hated it in the moment I was presented with the gift.

Until then, even though I had been away from the Witnesses for years, I never considered the cross as being anything other than what I was taught. I didn't think about it, really. It wasn't a conscious knowing that I despised the cross. It was just one of those things I had heard so many times that it had embedded itself in the fabric of my consciousness, much like a bedbug, or a tick. As with most embedded mental constructs, we do not question them.

Neither can we do anything about them, for we have long forgotten that they are there.

This is why the Uni-Verse, in all Its love, will call forward, at the perfect time, the very situations and circumstances that render it near impossible for us to remain ignorant or unaware, and that demand (lovingly and gently or brick over the head style) a piercing examination of the beliefs we have unconsciously chosen not to question, yet are firmly holding to, whether they serve us, or anyone else, or not.

I cannot imagine how much unexamined, unquestioned mental material I'd still be carrying around had it not been for these timely expose's.

I make it a spiritual practice not to be ignorant.

The deal was sealed with a declaration to the Powers that be: *I desire to see and know all of me, with the intention of ascension and release of any and everything that no longer serves me. And so it is.*

KNOW THYSELF — the two word charge displayed over the entryway to the Temple where the Oracle of Delphi sat — we find is of great necessity in our work of magick. How can one change if one is not aware? We cannot. Alchemy does not take place in the dark. We must become aware. We must wake up. We must know.

I didn't know, up until the Uni-Verse bought it lovingly to my attention in the form of a gift from my lover, how much I hated the cross.

And why did I despise the cross? Because I was taught to. The Witnesses made a valid 2-pronged point about it that made it above question in my younger mind.

First, they taught, Jesus didn't die on a cross. They say he died on a tree, a straight up and down wooden beam. They say the word used in the original Greek (in the New Testament, which Witnesses refer to as the Greek Scriptures; according to them, referring to parts of the Bible as 'new' or 'old' is inappropriate for it is always immediately applicable) to describe what Jesus was impaled to is 'stauros' meaning 'tree.'

From this, they surmise that Jesus was impaled to a tree without the branches or a cross bar, called, in Witness jargon, a 'torture stake.'

The torture stake is the symbol you will see in Witness literature when pictures of the impaled Christ appear, between two 'evil-doers' who are also impaled to torture stakes, one on his right and one on his left. In these renderings, his arms are stretched over his head, with his hands impaled by means of a nail driven through both, one over top the other, rather than stretched out to his sides. The 'evil-doers' are impaled in likewise fashion. They cite much data, scientific, historical and otherwise, to prove their point.

Whether you believe Christ died on a cross or on a tree is up to you. I'm not here to convince you either way.

I believe the deeper reason Witnesses do not abide the cross is to further the divide between them and any and all other Christian religions. They are ruthlessly committed to the differences between them and all other religions. There is no partaking with, as they say, Babylon the Great, the World Empire of False Religion. In the Witness world, every Christian denomination is wrong, and, as part of Babylon the Great, will be destroyed.

Except them.

Let me reiterate here why I share this information with you. It is for the purpose of awareness, and prayerfully, to promote understanding. Though you may not believe what Witnesses or any other religion espouses, if we understand why they believe the way they do, though we may not agree, we are that much closer to peaceful co-habitation on this planet.

What we are not aware of cannot be changed and what we do not understand, we fear.

There are Christian denominations that handle poisonous and deadly serpents, based on Jesus' words at Mark 16:17-18 and Luke 10:19. Also cited is Paul's experience of being bitten by a venomous serpent with no ill effects whatsoever. (Acts 28:1-6) Whether you agree with serpent handling or not, if you spoke with a dyed-in-the-wool serpent handler, they would speak to you with conviction and sincerity about why their beliefs are true and right for them.

We cannot argue with that. It is not a matter of who is right or wrong. These are judgments. It is a matter of what is right for each soul.

A pastor in West Virginia died at the age of 44 from the venom of a snake he was handling in a religious service. He sat the snake on the ground and sat next to it. The snake bit him on the thigh. He died 10½ hours later. His father, the former pastor, died at age 39, also of snakebite from a poisonous serpent he was handling during a church service.

If you stepped over into the afterlife and asked this pastor and his father if they would have done anything different, I'll bet you a quarter the answer will be "of course not!" How could they have done anything different? Both got to die for what they believed in, whether you or I or anybody else likes it, agrees with it or gets it.

Let us have open dialogue amongst religions about our beliefs, no matter how bizarre these may seem to the next group, without judgment, and perhaps we shall get somewhere. The somewhere I pray we get to is peace.

Understanding and non-judgment are especially called for when encountering beliefs among our brethren that could be considered borderline and/or just plain crazy. For the most part, it's not considered strange to get dressed up and go to church on Sunday morning to praise the Lord, no matter what church that might be. It may, however, be considered strange to get dressed up and go to a church on Sunday morning where they pass around a poisonous serpent.

But even serpent handlers need love, and we're not here to judge anybody. Let everyone be. That's love's true call.

Christ said to love your enemies and pray for those persecuting you. He also said that if you love those who love you, what are you really doing? There's no stretch in that, it's easy to love people who love you.

But how are you doing with loving people who are strange to you? Or loving people who are weird to you? Or loving people who handle serpents like you love your own children? Or loving people who hate crosses when you love yours?

The true test is in how much you're willing to stretch your understanding and love to encompass everybody, snake handlers, Jehovah's Witnesses, Buddhists, witches, everybody.

Now that I am more familiar with Roman torture and death sentences than I was as a Witness, having studied more extensively than they would have ever allowed, I know the Romans used crucifixion widely as a means to carry out the death sentence. Peter too was crucified. Many were crucified. The nature of the Crucifixion (with a capital c) is an extreme teaching lesson, as taught by *A Course In Miracles*. It was an integral part of Yeshua ben Yosef's destiny as a soul: to suffer an ignominious, painful, humiliating, public torture and death, only to raise from the dead completely unscathed 3½ days later. It was his calling to live and 'die' as he did. Because of what it stands for, his Crucifixion is different from all the others who were killed this way (though we acknowledge all these lives). It is a symbol, and like all symbols, the beholder is the ultimate arbiter of what it means. The Crucifixion means only what it means to you.

The 2nd reason Witnesses give to abhor the cross is to avoid idol worship. Witnesses view the cross as an idol, an object believed by many to be the mode of our beloved's murder. If a loved one was killed by a gun, Witnesses say, we would not idolize a gun by wearing it around our necks to commemorate that one's life. Even if Christ did die on a cross (which the Witnesses hold he did not) why commemorate his life by shaping the instrument of his death into an idol?

Well, I guess the answer to that question can be anything you want it to be. Why do we commemorate people's lives by lighting candles? Why do we remember the World Trade Center as two smoking towers? Why do we put markers on graves?

We do it because we are human, making lives into history in every moment. We are the only sentient beings on the planet who can thus commemorate life, though it's been observed that elephants in the wild never pass elephant bones without mourning and acknowledging the life of the deceased elephant in a complex ritual involving examining the bones with trunks, picking them up and caressing them, and touching them with their feet. It is quite a spectacle to behold, one that is almost guaranteed to bring tears to your eyes.

We wear crosses for the same reason that elephants wave their foot over elephant bones. Yes, it looks strange, but deep within ourselves, there is meaning, and that meaning is precious to us, and we shall keep doing it, whether others understand us or not.

Now, I love the cross. I have several of them all over the place, including 3 hanging from the rear view mirror of my car.

No devout Witness would enter a home or car where they see a cross prominently displayed, for fear of opening themselves to demon attack.

I have long since discovered this is simply not true for me.

I have never had an attack of the demons, and have never experienced any ill effects or untoward outcomes from having crosses around. I found it to be quite the opposite. My relationship with the cross as a symbol of love and freedom from mortality has enhanced my walk with God and deepened my desire to attain Christ-hood.

Where was the turn-around?

It started in the very moment I saw the now somewhat legendary golden cross encrusted with diamonds staring back at me from inside its cozy spot on white fluffy padding inside a gold colored jewelry box. How I kept the gasp from leaping out of my throat is anybody's guess, but I'm glad I did.

What I learned from the experience is that a belief shattering event could show up at any minute, and most times make their appearance when we least expect them, like on birthdays.

Be ever ready for shift. Yep, that's what I've learned.

My shift started right then with a glorious opportunity to examine my beliefs for old, outdated constructs that no longer fit me, mental monuments that I could now safely, gently and swiftly dismantle and release. In the fresh vacuum created, I could choose anew, redefining what my relationship with the cross would be, if any, from a place of full awareness. The void could be filled with love, light and understanding.

In my moment of almost recoil, I remember a thought shooting through my mind *I'll take it, but I'll never wear it.* That was the unquestioned belief speaking, the dying Witness dogma trying to get in its last word.

It didn't win.

Thank God.

A new awareness was dawning. *The cross is not evil, Valerie, no matter what you were told... it may even be a gift.*

I accepted the gift. And yes, I wore it. I actually let him put it around my neck in spite of the visceral feeling that there was a possibility I could combust into flames right there. I didn't. The heavens didn't part and lightning didn't strike. I was just fine. What a relief!

I had been having another of those post-Witness moments: petrified to look under the bed, but when I summoned the courage to get down on my knees and take a peek, much to my relief, there was no monster.

I almost laughed at myself. *How can you combust into flames from wearing a cross Valerie?*

The cross is a deeply meaningful symbol of freedom from mortality and unconditional love for a billion or more souls on the planet, and is a nod to our ancient Egyptian roots as a child of the Ankh, which is tattooed on my right arm.

With the Ankh tattooed to my right arm and the cross hanging from my neck, I'm about as ready as I'll ever be to examine all I believe as I gallop on in this lovely, luscious life as a Christian Witch.

Forbidden Zodiac

I confess I did not know my sun sign for the first 2 plus decades of this incarnation.

I was somewhere in my 20's when I found out I was a Libra. Even then, part of me didn't care. To that part of me it didn't matter.

I was trained that way.

Witnesses do not believe in the Zodiac, or in any form of astrology, Eastern or Western. All astrology is taught to be a tool of Satan the devil, and, as with all tools of the devil, it is crafted for one purpose and one purpose only: to draw one away from Jehovah God. For those who are away from Jehovah God, there is only one place they could be: squarely in the devil camp, aka the eternal annihilation camp. With that warning, it's no wonder astrology is avoided like the plague.

There was so much heat on it from the Witness perspective that we didn't talk about birthday's, or sun signs, or astrology at all. Your date of birth made no difference. It was a completely random event, not to be remembered, or celebrated, or memorialized while you're here or after you're gone.

We made no mention of it at all. My birthday came and went, with not so much as a word uttered about it. The same was true for my mother's and my father's, and all my sibling's birthdays as well. It is also true for every devout Witness.

It was simply the day you were born, with no more significance than the day before or the day after.

That's it.

To talk about any of it is taboo.

My view of it now is that we are missing vital information about self and the soul's destiny when we choose to ignore or omit important birth information, especially the sun sign and astrological chart, Eastern astrological sign, Tarot birth cards and the Mayan Galactic Signature.

It's all vital information; clues to the greater mystery that is life. With life being this ginormous jigsaw puzzle to solve, I can use all the help I can get. If my date of birth — and the position and activity of the celestial bodies at the precise moment of my arrival on planet earth — holds valuable information for me, I want it.

From years of studying all things magickal, mystical and metaphysical, I discovered that my birth date, the very date and time my soul chose to enter this physical plane, has the potential to unlock a veritable vault of information about me, why I came here, what my inclinations and proclivities are, my strengths, and where my weaknesses could trip me up, what people are helpful to me and which are not, what helpers I have on the other side, how I operate within and how I show up in the world and a whole lot more than I could put into words in this tome.

Our birth information is too vital, too detailed, too accurate, too soul specific to cast off and dismiss as unnecessary, or to choose to ignore.

If you are a conscious, aware being, it would be irresponsible not to know the cosmic weather and all manner of influences, that you can know, which occurred at or around your arrival on this planet.

I was so in the dark.

I was blind.

Now, I see.

I also confess that I could not have seen when I didn't. The light, at that point, would have had an adverse effect on me. At that juncture, I wasn't much different than the dwellers in Plato's cave, scrounging around in the dark, knowing there's more, yet not ready for the light.

What a place to be.

The only thing that can save one from such a state is time, and an intense yearning for the truth.

I had that longing, and still do. It's voracious; I want to know, I yearn for truth. The more I walk with God, the more truth is revealed. It is this phenomena that keeps us walking forward, though the road be rough and rocky in spaces and places along the path. I can't not walk this road, even when it gets rough and rocky.

I heard it said that the truth sets you free, but first it pisses you off.

That's true.

The sad irony of where I was in my Witness walk was that I thought I had the truth, which meant I wasn't searching for it at all. You don't search for what you think you already have.

That's where I was. So how could truth seep in? Truth needs a space to fill, a void, a vacuum. When there's none, truth waits silently at the door until we open to it. It never presses, coerces or convinces. It simply is, and will become clear in due time.

That's what happened for me. The 'truth' I thought I was living and teaching was not. It's not that it wasn't the truth, it's that it wasn't *my* truth.

I remember the other part of me that experienced a silent elation, a quickening, upon learning I was a Libra. *What does that mean? Tell me more!* That part of me wanted to know everything about Libras. I wanted to know what it meant for me, for my life, and for the future. My then belief system didn't allow for talking to anyone about the future, that was a downright sin too, sure to carry one straight to the devil, but at that moment, I silently got real curious about what a Tarot card reader, or astrologist, or, like the Bible called them, a Magi or one who could read the stars would have to say about me and this Libra discovery.

What mysteries did the stars hold about me?

I couldn't silence those questions. They wouldn't go away. I tried. I gave it my best Witness shot. It was no use. The soul was already breaking free and there was nothing my little human mind could do to contain it. My soul was choosing to wake up, to explore everything. First on the list of things to explore: the forbidden... specifically, the things I was told **never** to explore. That's where I wanted to head first, like a curious child who gets determinedly fixed on the very thing you tell her not to do.

I was determinedly fixed on the forbidden: the Zodiac and my birthday. What do you do with that?

Especially when you're in a community of people who are around you all the time, listening to what you say, watching what you do, taking tiny mental notes of your every move, even when they don't want to be doing it. We can't help it. We were bred to constantly monitor each other, not in an I'm-looking-so-I-can-catch-you-doing-something-you're-not-supposed-to-be-doing kind of way, more in a conditioning of the religion sort of way. If you are taught, for instance, that lima beans will kill you, and someone shows up with a lima bean, you jump on on high alert real fast, and are definitely not chowing down. Not only that, you will do your best to prevent the other people from enjoying their lima beans too. You're going to make sure no one around you eats lima beans. Not because there's anything wrong with lima beans, only because you're under the mistaken belief that there is.

That's how it was. We were conditioned to believe so many things, that when something other than one of those beliefs shows up, it causes alarm. Some things were considered extra deadly: like anything supernatural. They carried the warning of having the possibility of causing one's home or possessions to become demonized, which for Witnesses, is a harrowing and terrifying experience. We were fed stories of people whose homes or possessions became demonized after that person came into contact with some item of the occult, like an Ouija board, or an item from another person who was already demonized. The demons needed a bridge, we were told, and will take any item or opportunity as a path straight to you.

To Witnesses, the thought of one's home or possessions becoming demonized is tantamount to strychnine in your food; to be avoided at all costs, highly detrimental and potentially deadly.

If we want no parts of the devil or his demons, anything we're told that could take us in his direction will become suspect, disdained, feared, avoided or a target for expulsion.

Including people.

That's what happened for me. My ideas and free way of living became

183

too heretical for the Witnesses. I was cast out. Disfellowshipped.

Ironically, at the time I was disfellowshipped, it was not for occult practices. It was for immorality. The charges: adultery. They were right. I was having sex with someone else while still married to my husband, even though we were separated.

Even still, to the Witnesses, if anything, or anyone, in any way, could possibly connect us with the devil or the demons, that thing, or person, must go.

I confess I used to be 80% on board with that belief.

I'm not now.

It is a belief that is not grounded in universal law. Universal Law rules that another person cannot take me to the devil. I am the creator of my reality and the master of my destiny. If it looks like someone is taking me to the devil, that's only a facade. If I'm going in the devil direction, it's because I want to go in that direction. The story of how I get there is almost inconsequential.

Universal law teaches me that no one has more influence in my life than me.

No one can lead me to the devil if I don't want to go.

And no one can prevent me from heading in a direction in which I want to go.

I agree that people around us influence us for the positive or negative, and in some relationships, it's a bit of both, or more one than the other, and I get to decide what I'm going to do in those relationships.

The bottom line of it is: no one can create my life other than me, and no one can create your life other than you.

The idea of expelling people because they may be contaminants flies in the face of love. Love is embracing, accepting and draws us in, even when we are errant, or not being lovable, or being absolutely ornery.

Love never pushes away.

It only draws us in deeper, deeper into itself, deeper into the lap and heart and arms of God/Goddess. This is where our healing is: in the unconditional love of the Almighty.

Love makes us different, better, more refined. It draws us in, and never casts us out, though it is adept at casting out the energies that have attached to us that are not love.

I am deeply grateful for the love of the Goddess.

When I was ignorant enough to not know my own sun sign, as an adult woman, and afraid to learn it because I thought simply having that knowledge would connect me with evil, I can only say that God's love saved me from ignorance. Having emerged from it, I can state with utter confidence: ignorance is not bliss. While I am deeply in love with the ignorant woman I once was, the younger me, I am also aware that she did what she was trained and taught to do, and she did it all for the right reasons, to be pleasing to God and to serve and save her fellow man. This was always her motive. I cannot be mad at that.

I confess part of me felt duped, mad and hoodwinked. I choose to forgive. People can only give you what they think they have.

The questions that used to flash across the screen of my mind, even after years of forgiveness work: *why did they so thoroughly convince me of things that weren't true? Why were they seeming to withhold valuable information from me? I trusted them... why did they instill in me completely erroneous information about what God wanted from me? Greater still, why did they say God was going to punish me, or kill me, if I didn't get myself together enough to live, eat, sleep, talk and walk as the religion told me to?*

Why? Why? Why?

After years of asking *why*, I stumbled upon a significant discovery: why is not a helpful question.

What came to me from the Inner Being is that the answer to a why question is always the same: *because.*

Why did they so thoroughly convince me of things that weren't true? Because.

Why were they seeming to withhold valuable information from me? Because.

I trusted them... why did they instill in me completely erroneous information about what God wanted from me?

Because.

Greater still, why did they say God was going to punish me, or kill me, if I didn't get myself together enough to live, eat, sleep, talk and walk as the religion told me to? They made God look like a villain. Why?

Because.

Why? Why? Why?

Because.

When I heard that simple one word answer to all the 'why' questions I will ever, and have ever, asked, I was stunned. Then perplexed. Then mad.

What it means to me now is 3 things:

1. I may never know the answer to some of the questions I'm asking. I get to be at peace anyway, even if I never get answers. You may not always get answers. You can still be at peace. Peace is a choice.

2. Does it really matter anyway? What would I do with the answers? Get madder? Be more resentful? Hold an even bigger grievance? What does it matter 'why' something happened? It happened *because*. Learn from it and move on Valerie.

3. Is it making my life better now? If I knew 'why' everything happened the way it did, would having that information really be all that helpful? Maybe. Maybe not. Even when we finally obtain the much sought after answers to the 'why' questions we're asking, it seems that life does not automatically drastically improve like we thought it would. It doesn't follow that you say 'oh, I get it, now that I know 'why' that happened, I'm good.' No. Improvement is not automatic. Sometimes knowing 'why' has the potential to make us feel worse.

Trust that the universe is always only revealing to you the information you need to have. If you don't have it, you don't need to have it.

Yes, I learned a lot from being taught that knowing my Zodiac sign was a sin and celebrating my birthday was displeasing to God.

I learned that people believe what they want to believe. I can either agree, or move on. I chose to move on.

I learned that they taught me their interpretation of the cosmos, and that from love. They can only teach me what they know.

I learned that they sincerely believe they are doing the right thing, with love for Jehovah God as the prime motivation at all times. I can't be mad at that either.

I learned that the space I was in was necessary for me to occupy then, in order to be the woman I am today. For that I'm grateful.

I learned that the more time I spend pointing my finger at anyone outside myself, asking 'why', I live in victim land and out of power country. I choose to live in power.

Yes, there's much I learned from not knowing I was a Libra. And there too was much joy in throwing myself the birthday party of a lifetime, my first, at 40. The party lasted 2 days.

In it all, I confess I would not change a thing.

Keys

My son, at one station in his life, was running a large and successful business with lots of people on his teams, and was in possession of a lot of keys. In his business, keys to a new building for a new manager represent growth, opportunity, financial advancement, promotion, respect, success and a whole lot more.

Keys are important. They're a symbol of power, and power equals responsibility.

I've gotten a lot of keys, and you probably have too. Some were wanted and welcomed, like keys to new cars or new homes we'd worked for, and some were not so welcome, like keys to a new office that came with a promotion at a job you were about to quit.

Either way, if you have a lot of keys, each one of those keys probably represents and commands some kind of responsibility. Each one of those keys was entrusted to you, for some purpose. Each of the keys I was entrusted with were given to me by people, entities or groups who thought I would do a good job with those keys, i.e. pay the car note and take care of the car, pay the rent/mortgage and take care of the home, or take care of the matters in the office/business that pertained to those keys.

Sometimes I successfully fulfilled my role and responsibility with the keys that were entrusted to me, and sometimes I did not. When I wasn't responsible, the keys got taken away.

Magick has keys too, many of them. The distinction is that in magick, the keys are granted to you as you prove trustworthy of receiving them, not the other way around.

188

While humans will give you keys to try you out, the Universe does not. When humans grant you keys, they never really know if you're going to do everything they expect you to do with those keys, as they expect, when they expect. In many cases, they're taking a very well calculated risk, after having you fill out paperwork, or checking your credit or other credentials and referrals.

In all cases, what will happen after they turn the keys over to you can never be known for sure.

In magick, it's been my experience that you must first prove your trustworthiness, your devotion, your stewardship ability, your purity of intention, and any other requisite tests of those particular keys, and only after having been proven, oftentimes by fire, do you receive the keys.

The Universe knows when and where to grant you access, and to what.

Let's start with Tarot. I first started studying Tarot in this lifetime, as a conscious choice, in May of 2005 when I went to my first Tarot workshop with Geraldine Amaral, an amazing Tarot teacher.

I didn't have the keys to Tarot that I have now, and I am also convinced that there are many more that I do not currently have access to or even know about.

This is the nature of ascension of the Magician's consciousness. You are given keys along the way, at the appropriate times for you. Each key unlocks a mystery that deepens your wisdom, understanding, and therefore, mastery of the Magickal Arts & Sciences you are studying and practicing.

I don't know how many keys to Tarot there are, and I guess I won't ever know if I've gotten them all. I don't even think getting them all is the goal. The goal, for me, is advancement to enlightenment, ascension to the Christ nature, such that I realize oneness with God. The Enlightenment of the Buddha, or the Ascension of the Christ. This is what my soul is seeking and working for in every magickal operation, some consciousness ascending, expanding, transforming or evolving experience that leads to growth, mastery, maturity, purity, wisdom or some other divine virtue or spiritual ideal.

Yes, there's a point to magick, a final destination of sorts: Enlightenment.

Then it's on to the next task: Enlightenment for all beings everywhere. Alas, the Magician's work is never done until all have achieved this Enlightened state of being.

Nobody's free until we're all free.

Subtle Superiority

Witnesses have their own Bible. It's called the New World Translation of the Holy Scriptures.

I was taught it was a purer translation of the Bible. They say it has the name of God (which they believe to be 'Jehovah' from their interpretation of the Tetragrammaton) restored in all its rightful places (over 6,000 instances). The line of reasoning is that the 'other' Bibles use the word 'LORD' (in all caps) when the Witnesses purport there should be the usage of God's name.

It's also taught by the Witnesses that the New World Translation is a translation of the original Hebrew, Greek and Aramaic languages into modern English, whereas they believe many Bibles are versions (i.e. King James Version). I was taught that the New World Translation is a labor of love that had been painstakingly undertaken by people who love Jehovah. The Witnesses do not use any other Bible except their own creation. They do not allow any members to use any other Bibles. They expect that if you become a Witness, you will get rid of any other Bibles you have (by throwing them in the trash to prevent anyone else from getting their hands on 'rogue' copies of the Bible) and that you will adopt full and exclusive usage of the New World Translation of the Holy Scriptures.

Bullshit.

Pardon my french, but from where I speak to you now, after having defied the Witness code to venture into an undertaking of reading all the different Bibles I could get my hands on, including the Apocrypha, and enjoying the flavors of them all I might add (though some more than others) I can

191

categorically state for myself: there are no right or wrong Bibles. There are the Bibles that speak deeply to me, and those that don't. I go toward the ones that speak to me, without bemoaning the existence of the ones that don't.

It's your choice what Bible you use, if the holy book of your choice is a Bible.

The reason I'm bringing this up for discussion is the very subtle sense of superiority I believe this whole Bible issue fosters among Witnesses.

I was under its hypnotic spell, until I wasn't anymore.

You're only under a spell weaved by someone else if you don't, or can't, see it. Once the spell is revealed, it begins to lose power over you.

Maybe I was the only one under the spell of subtle superiority and better-than-ness, done in by my own pride and arrogance, and this I'm more than willing to confess. I've had my goodly share of run-in's with pride and arrogance, and their unruly offspring, destructive demon seeds seeking to wreak nothing but havoc.

So I'll speak for myself here, and for no one else. I cannot speak for anyone else anyway, and, having become aware of my ineptitude at speaking for myself in very human moments of frailty or forgetfulness, won't even try.

What I will do is share with you my story, my feelings, and my take on the experience, and leave it all before you, like a sort of buffet, to choose what suits you and pass over the rest, without disdain for the presence of any of it. We don't disdain the food we don't eat on the buffet, nor do we mourn or bemoan its presence just because we're not eating it. We just pass it over. Do the same here. Take what feeds your spirit, and pass over the rest. There's a lot here, and by my own confession, will be very hard to swallow for some who are partaking in this particular buffet.

Back to subtle superiority. When I went out knocking on doors in field service with my Witness Bible, which I was strongly encouraged (okay, maybe a little more than strongly encouraged, let's say I was wrestled) to read each day, I carried with it a very subtle, almost imperceptible, or maybe very perceptible, sense of superiority; that *I've got the goods and you don't,* that *I know something that you don't,* that *I've got the right Bible, and you don't* air. I came within a hair's breath of saying, *that thing you read every day, that King James Version or some other 'version' of the Bible, is not an accurate translation, and what's more, it doesn't have Jehovah's name in it all 6,000 times that it's supposed to, and it doesn't have plain English that we can all understand, and it doesn't have the whole and true message that Jehovah God really wants you to hear, in the way Jehovah God wants you to hear it. It's clear you need one of our Bibles.*

Like I said, bullshit.

It was, nonetheless, my story. Thank God it's not my story anymore. I get to turn it over and examine it as I write this, and trust me, what I find in the turning over and examining can be horrific. No matter, it was my experience, horrific and all, and I wouldn't change a thing. My soul called it forth because I needed it.

For there is no home so sweet as humility to flee to for one engulfed in pride and arrogance and sees clearly their folly, and no castle so lovely as truth to find shelter in for one pounded by monsoons of religious doctrine.

That was me, engulfed in religious superiority, Biblical pride (if there be such a thing) and unholy doctrinal arrogance; all in the name of saving lives (whether you needed/wanted saving or not).

Either way, I was coming for you, fist poised in midair, ready to knock on your door, to blatantly and unapologetically interrupt you in the middle of watching TV, or feeding the baby, or sitting on the throne, just to let you know, in no uncertain terms, that how you were living your life was wrong, and to persuade you, by any scriptures necessary, to quit your wicked ways (they being proof positive that you have been caught in the snare of Satan the Devil), and come to Jehovah God, through Jesus Christ, to save your life from everlasting judgment and destruction at Armageddon, and live with the rest of us in the 'Jehovah's Witness only' paradise here on earth for an eternity, just like God meant for it to be from the very beginning, when He created Adam and Eve.

Side with us and live, or don't and die.

Those were your choices.

What's it going to be? That's me, at your door, looking you straight in the eye, tapping my foot, pointing at the watch, *time's a ticking, Armageddon's coming and we ain't got all day, I got other doors to knock on and more souls to save, are you in?*

And I presented it all with no apology, and with fervor even. Why should I apologize? This is what the Bible says, you can read it for yourself, right here in this very carefully selected series of scriptures I'm going to read to you, one by one, all of which have been carefully crafted to prove my point. Give me a JW Bible and an hour and you were in for an earful.

That was then. This is now.

I still have my New World Translation of the Holy Scriptures. When we were little, we were trained to never let our Bibles touch the floor or be unkempt or not presentable, so we went through a lot of Bibles, with all the daily use. This 'Witness Bible' I've had for years hasn't worn out yet. I look at it sometimes, when I want to see how a particular scripture reads. Frankly, the memory of that Bible isn't the happiest for me (issues I'm still working through, call it religious conditioning recovery), so I don't read it as often as I read some of my other Bibles.

My heart and soul are absolutely and irrevocably in love with the Amplified Bible, it's on my night table and stays open to passages that feed me. I read her every day. She's a blessing to my soul, and has only good mojo for me. I have 7 Bibles as I write this. I made a count of Bibles in my home the other day, and was shocked to find that I had less than 10. *I need more Bibles*, I heard myself say. I love collecting them, they are strange and weird and wonderful things, Bibles. You never know how one is going to hit you. You just open it up, land on and read a passage that breaks your heart wide open right there and then and has you weeping for the rest of the day. Or you could pick it up, land on and read some strange tale of a king who tortured and killed a woman and her 7 sons (like I did today in my New English Bible with Apocrypha in the book of Maccabees, definitely a no-no for Witnesses) and be mortified beyond belief. Even if they're not real, there are passages in the Bible that took the route of being shockingly horrifying to get the point across.

Yes, the Bible is a bizarre book; there is no question in my mind about that. And it's my knowing that, for me, it is holy and inspired and perfect and beautiful, in all its weirdness. And if a person were to find themselves suddenly marooned on a deserted isle, with nothing else for miles around, I would pray that that being would have a Bible. It's a magickal book to me, maybe even one of the biggest and best magick books of all time. It gives pure insight into the Mind of God, and this I eagerly search out with hunger and abandon. I want to know the Mind of God. I want to understand. I want wisdom. I'm a seeker of truth who asks a lot of questions.

In my Witness days, if the answer didn't come from the New World Translation of the Holy Scriptures, or the people who were behind it, it wasn't the right answer.

That's not true for me anymore. No one gets to tell me what's true for me. I can read the same passage of scripture in 10 different Bibles, and get touched in 10 different ways, maybe more. The New World Translation may be the touch I need in a given moment, or maybe it's the Amplified or the New English or the New International or the New Authorized King James that reaches out from thin, crispy leaves, eager to touch me in the way my soul is longing to be touched in that space in time.

I confess I have long since let go of attachments to where and how I get my God fixes, as long as I get them.

Each of us has to discover truth on our own. Each of us has to undertake a very private, and at times very frustrating, search for wisdom, the elixir of life, the Holy Grail, as legend calls it. We must each go on a quest for truth, justice and wisdom. No one can give these to you. And if anyone tries, ask a lot of questions before you follow. No, I'm certain of it, you must find these on your own, led by the unfailing, unwavering inner light that knows not how to flicker, but only how to lead the way.

Since Witnesses couldn't have other Bibles, I didn't pick up another kind of Bible until I was well over 40 years old, and even then, I felt somewhere deep inside like I was committing some of kind of sin, a sin of infidelity to what I was taught, a sin of disloyalty, or at its worse, betrayal. Was that true? No. How do I know it wasn't true? By how it felt. It didn't feel like love. It felt like guilt. And guilt is not love.

What I was experiencing was the effects, the insipid results, of religious conditioning in the form of old beliefs and worn out judgments trying to surface again, in a futile attempt to stay lodged in my consciousness. A good way the ego gets you to hold on to something, even if it's killing you (which are the only things the ego presses us to hold onto anyway), is by making you think, feel or believe that you can't possibly dispense with the thing that's killing you. No, it argues and defends, you must hold on to those old beliefs and worn out judgments, no matter what they're costing you. It wouldn't be right to let go of those 'sacred' religious beliefs, no, you can't do that, whether they're serving you or not, they should be kept and prized, like an old, beat-up pair of shoes with holes in the soles that hurt your feet that you can't bear to throw away, even though you have newer and better and more beautiful shoes now that fit you perfectly. Those old ones just have so much darn sentimental value.

What is sentimental value but an attachment to the past? And if the attachment hurts, why keep it? Worse still, if the attachment causes guilt, what's the motivation for holding on?

That was me and the New World Translation. It was the be-all, end-all of inspired Biblical truth for me in my Witness life. I remember I used to get mad when I heard people say about us that we had our own Bible, and that we invented it. It's funny, because in a way that's true. Maybe I got so mad because I knew in my heart of hearts that there was truth to what I was hearing. The inner feeling of subtle superiority and better-than-ness was emitting an attracting signal. What it was attracting to me were people who said, in essence, "You think you're better than us and you think your Bible is better than ours, but it's not, because you made it up anyway."

They were only mirroring what was going on inside me. What else could I be faced with other than what was going on inside me? By Law, it's impossible to be faced with anything in life other than what's going on, or what has been going on, inside us.

Under all superiority and better-than-ness, there is sure to be found unworthiness and less-than-ness, seeking cover, hiding just beneath the surface, not wanting to be seen for what they really are, trying hard to blend themselves into some other background, like a chameleon, and not succeeding at that either.

People can always sniff when something's amiss, even if they don't know exactly what they're sniffing.

Yes, I suffered from religious superiority and participated in prideful gloating, just like a little 3-year-old, *nananeenana, my Bible is better than yours.*

God saved me from myself.

I sit here happy now, smiling about the me of yesteryear, and the me of today that accepts all of me, even the prideful parts and the arrogant parts, and the better-than parts who are trying to hide the less-than parts, it's all in the mix, and it's all me and mine. I'm grateful. Really and truly grateful to look at and accept and honor and smile at the whole beautiful tapestry of my life and know it's all perfect, down to the very last stitch.

The Devil

This tome would not be complete, to my mind, without a fleshing out of this 'devil' business, as fully as I can manage without inciting boredom.

Some say Witches are of the devil. This is an all too common misconception.

It is mostly those who believe in a devil who say this, I've noticed. As for Witches, of the ones I know, do not believe in nor do they subscribe to the Judeo-Christian idea of a devil.

Including me.

Yes, I was bred and raised on the devil. I was taught he is evil incarnate, the very opposite of God, and that he is a roaring lion seeking to devour someone, and that he has hordes of demons who will overtake me at the slightest misstep: from bringing an item into my home that a 'demonized' person had owned, to not reading my Bible. According to the religious philosophy I was reared in, the devil is the ruler of 'this world'. He is bent on destroying humanity, mostly by the doorway of our vices. He has been described as beautiful and appallingly ugly, taking shape and form for whatever his particular mission may be at the time, which also makes him a shapeshifter. He was given quite a bit of attention and focus, with the reason being that we ought to be hyper-aware and on guard as to how he operates. He was a larger-than-life character for me, especially growing up, when one has no way of putting into some cohesive and intelligent context what the big people are talking about. Kids have no point of reference for the devil, they haven't seen enough 'evil' yet, so it's pretty hard to get them on board with the whole devil idea.

No, most kids I know do not believe in a devil. They're smarter than that.

Back to what I was taught. The devil will meet his ending, as the story goes, in a great battle, the battle called in the Bible Armageddon, bringing to an epic end the eons old war between him and God for the souls of humanity.

And yes, as I write this, I am becoming aware that this story is even more fantastic than it was the first few times I heard it. Yet, like the other beliefs I was being force-fed, there wasn't a lot of room for push-back or even negotiation.

There was, however, room for questions, a beautiful merit I award to my mother, her being an excellent teacher, certainly the best teacher I have had in this life, and teachers love good questions from good students.

Questions shape learning.

Good teachers know this well.

Questions reflect that the student is at least interested enough to know more, a good teacher's paradise.

Questions also let the teacher know what has been heard, learned and/or assimilated and what has not. The teacher, any good teacher worth her salt, then gets to reinforce the weak or missing links.

This was my mother to a tee.

She did not shut down my questions. I guess I could now say, on looking back at it all fondly, that my mom and I were in an ongoing game of question and answer while I was a kid. I was curious. Really curious. And she had all the answers, the answers that worked for her anyway. And if nothing else, she stated and taught them with a certainty that made them more of an 'of course' in my little mind.

Including this 'devil' business.

So for the first 33 years or so of my life, I lived with the devil idea in an uneasy, fearful, ever so slightly confused way. That, however, did not stop me from teaching the devil idea to as many people as my door-knocking could get me an audience with.

Yes, Satan the Devil was the most despicable character ever. His legions of demons (fallen angels) would think nothing of roasting me to shreds, only after torturing me with paranormal behavior, like hurling dishes around the kitchen, as was the case in some of the Witness tall tales of people whose homes had become 'demonized'. If a person's home is demonized, lifting one item from that home would form the necessary bridge for the demons to enter your life and home.

And once the demons were in, there was scarcely ways and means to rid oneself of them, better to move, and leave all your possessions behind. The Witnesses were not the exorcising type, being much more content to leave the whole business alone and move on, not even with so much as the shirt on one's back.

I pray to describe to you, in some capacity of fullness, the all encompassing idea of the devil, and how much psychic space he and his demons took up in my Witness psyche.

It never felt quite right, to my soul, that so much attention should be given to the one who is the self-proclaimed enemy of God, and our tormentor, accuser and adversary, yet, again, it was the party line, and the party line I learned was best to tow with no resistance.

I did that until I couldn't anymore.

I no longer subscribe to the belief in a devil.

It took me years to come to this place of peace in me. I will try my best to share my journey to this truth here with you now, with the prerequisite that you remember I am not trying to proselytize, or tell you how to think, or what to think, or what to believe. I have no interest in any of these.

I am sharing with an intention to cause you to ask questions, seek truth and have the questions answered in your spirit from a space of communing with the Master Self I AM, resident in your very being, without undue pressure or influence of religion.

You must break free of what you've been taught to learn anew. I did, and am still doing it. It is not a one time affair. It is the call of the soul that you seek and live your truth, your AUTHENTIC TRUTH.

My authentic truth and religion butted heads on not more than one occasion. When that happens, usually the conditioning we've had in the religion is so complete and so thorough that we push down our own natural inclinations, questions, stirrings of Spirit in us and soul calls.

Calls to magick, let's say, as I've always had.

Back to the devil story.

This devil business is where my authentic Self and religion took complete opposite paths.

First, I have no basis or evidence for belief in a devil.

I know that sounds strange, what with all the wars and crimes and atrocities we heap on each other on this earth plane, yet there is something in me that tells me all this is not the work of a red, evil, pitch-forked, lying, invisible persona running amok outside of ourselves.

No. That is not the answer. Of this I'm sure.

I do have evidence for men's minds made made by fear, and heaping atrocities on others.

I do have evidence for mental dis-ease and the killings and horrors some strands of it have caused.

I do have evidence for an egoic mind that tells us, not infrequently throughout the day, that we are either better than others, or worse than them, and that we must scratch and claw and fight our way through life to get what we really want, as all that we want is currently in the hands of someone else, which means we'll either have to manipulate them into giving it to us, or take it by outright force. None of these options have seemed unacceptable to the vast masses of humans. We've all used these methods, whether they create lasting peace or not, and even whether they're lastingly effective, or not.

Yes, I have evidence for fearful humans, for crazed humans, for egoic humans who have completely edged out God.

Yet, I have no evidence for a being outside of ourselves who is the origin of evil, a power almost equal to God such that there would be any significant battle between the two.

All this symbolism, does, however, *mean something*, and we are pressed, on the journey of the soul, to discover what it *means*.

There is a battle between one side and the other. We have dramatized this battle and placed it outside ourselves, it's so much easier to have a scapegoat to pin everything. The 'devil' is a great scapegoat.

Rest assured, you will never be let off the hook because you chose a scapegoat. The idea of scapegoats came from the Bible, when a goat was sent into the wilderness every year, carrying all the sins of the people. It was a symbol, a metaphor. One goat can't carry away the sins of a million people. Yet it was a beautiful ritual that reminds us of the eternal truth.

That's what rituals such as this do, remind us of eternal truth. When you get caught in the ritual, and miss the meaning, you are stuck in religiosity. That is a point of ignorance.

Don't do that.

The scapegoat was not to give us an out. God devised this beautiful ritual for the people of Israel to relieve them of the burden of whatever sins they thought they had committed during the year. It was to show that heaven holds nothing against anyone. See this goat walk away into the wilderness, with all your 'sins' attached to it, watch it walk away and know you are free and clear.

It is a beautiful symbol of freedom. Yet, we have, as is not unusual, taken something beautiful that God has created, and turned it into something sick and twisted, that has one purpose only, to do us in.

Back to the devil. He is not a scapegoat. He is not real. He is a figment of men's imaginations, and yes, he has captured our imaginations almost as much as God.

This is a good time to tell you about my missions trip to Kenya with 18 Christians. I was not a member of their church, however I traveled with them because of a synchronistic turn of events ordered by my soul. While on the trip, I heard, almost non-stop, "the devil is a liar!" or, "that's nothing but an evil spirit!" or "I rebuke that in the name of Jesus!" or "the devil is busy!"

These oft repeated phrases bought way more attention to the supposed enemy of God than I think the people mouthing the decrees realized or desired. Energy flows where attention goes. Speaking of a devil repeatedly will make everything look like the devil. Almost like the boy's mother in the movie The Water Boy. Everything she saw was "nothing but the devil!"

How is one to live a centered, peaceful life in God with so much energy poured into the polar opposite? It cannot happen, that is the Law, spiritual Law.

Spiritual Law says that what we focus on expands. Some people take this law to mean they are right. They have boundless evidence in their lives that seemingly prove their beliefs true.

However, that is a trap. It is the trap of belief. Your beliefs, my beliefs, and everyone's beliefs, are all manifesting, all the time. This is because beliefs manifest, and not because the beliefs are necessarily true.

Example. Our life in New York City was, by belief, fraught with danger. We were told continually, be careful, watch behind yourself, don't walk down dark streets alone, stay where a lot of people are, and on and on.

I am not saying these are not helpful statements. I am saying that the statements were heaped on a daily, the result of a consciousness that was steeped in fear. If the belief is fear-based, what will it produce? After its kind. Fear-based life experiences. It's not because living in New York City is an inherently dangerous place to be, there are people who have lived there all their lives and have not had a dangerous experience, and there are people living in the middle of supposedly one of the safest places in the world and have dangerous experiences. The place you are in does not determine your experience. There is one thing and one thing alone that determines and creates your life experience: your consciousness. That's it. It's stunningly simple. As all truth is.

Your consciousness of the 'devil' is creating all your 'devil' experiences.

Once I made that not insignificant discovery, I decided to shape and mold my consciousness around God, and God alone.

It's worked for me.

Me dropping belief in the devil — though quite strongly ill-advised — never did anything but help me.

I can think of at least 7 ways I have been helped by dropping my belief in a devil. I offer these here for your prayerful consideration (once again, don't believe me, I am not religious and therefore do not need converts, I want you to wake up).

I relaxed. This is the biggest benefit, for me, of releasing belief in a devil. The devil idea has people on edge, untold billions around the world are walking on edge of an untoward enemy who could do us in at any time. This is not a comforting belief. Drop it.

I found out God wasn't mad at me. God wasn't mad that I dropped the devil idea. God smiled at me for doing so, as if I had graduated into a secret circle of knowers. I assure you, God will not be mad at you if you drop your devil belief. But you'll have to find that out for yourself.

I found out that the real enemy is inside my mind. I was clear that the thing I needed to be on the lookout for was inside my mind. There was nothing sneaking up from behind me that was doing me in. Every time I had a wayward or unkind or unloving or harsh or dangerous or seemingly 'evil' moment, it had originated in my mind. I started watching my mind more closely, rather than watching my back. God's got my back. I need to watch my mind.

I tested and disproved the belief that if I didn't believe in the devil, I would be especially susceptible and easy prey. Not true. I tested it. I went there. I did not become any more susceptible to anything because I woke up and dropped the devil belief, except that I became more susceptible to wisdom.

I grew up and took ownership and responsibility. Without a devil to blame things on, I could no longer rightly or sanely continue to avert, duck or dodge my responsibility for all of my life experience. I could not, in truth and in good conscience, continue to blame an outside entity for tempting me. My scapegoat had walked away into the wilderness.

I enthroned God in God's rightful place in my mind, life and world: on the throne of omnipresence. God is omnipresent, omniscient, omnipotent, the All in all. Where is there room for a devil in that? There is none. God has nothing to prove. God is God. God did not create anything that could raise up and offend or challenge Itself. God did not create anything that is — or could potentially become — against Itself. A house divided against itself cannot stand. There is no division in God. A devil who came about as a challenge to God would mean that God was not smart enough to have seen that one of God's creations would go rogue, and subsequently induce lots of other of God's creations to go rogue along with it. It postulates an impossibility: that God could create something that could go rogue. This, to me, is nothing short of pure lunacy. There must be more to the story, some deeper metaphysical meaning, that, if not presently perceived in its entirety, is more than worthy of our intentional, soulful exploration. The very nature of your relationship with the divine is rooted in this intentional, soulful exploration.

I set myself free. I proved to myself that I am the Master of myself, and I am free to choose what I believe, and what to drop that no longer serves the highest and best of me. It is incredibly liberating, though I am clear liberty and freedom are not one and the same. I prefer freedom, it being the inner being-ness that creates a life of liberty. Yummy.

So there you have it, my not entirely complete list of reasons I simply dropped the 'devil' idea, as it was handed to me.

Now that that's said and done, let's go farther, deeper.

We can now delve into alternate ways to look at the 'devil'.

In Kabbalah, the ancient technology for the soul, we learn there is a force — not opposite to God — that actually helps you in your soul's journey to God.

This force is called Satan (pronounced su' tahn).

This force is not inherently evil. This force is not out to kill you. This force is not your enemy.

This force, we are taught in Kabbalah, which wholly aligns and agrees with my soul, is our worthy adversary, our opponent.

Any good adversary, or worthy opponent, as in a game, lifts us to our highest self. It is our strengthener.

Christians, hold on to your hats (and wigs). I promise you I am not being heretical, nor am I making a bold and audacious claim that the 'devil' as taught in the Judeo-Christian way is helping you. It is not.

This is something differently entirely, and if you are willing, we will now embark upon a deeper metaphysical exploration, that you are free to take, or not take. It is up to you. I say, that since this information and invitation is being presented to you now, and God never presents us with anything we are unprepared to handle or cannot handle, then, my exhortation to you would be to dive in.

Here we go.

Breathe.

Think of it this way: you love, as we all do, watching a basketball game, or a football game, where the two teams are evenly matched. We seldom enjoy watching unmatched teams play in games where the outcome is all too sure. We want the hard-won victory. We want to see two sides battling it out to the end, bloody noses, grimy faces, to the unknown win, which could go to either team. Yes, we want to see evenly matched teams play. We want games where it is risky to go to the bathroom lest we miss some major shocking event that turns the tide. We love this! And why do we love this? Because a deeper spiritual significance to the game, it is the inner game we are all playing, all the time. In the universe, it's always game time, not just when the bell rings.

We have an inner game going on. It's the game of fear versus love. They are worthy opponents, both being so completely and totally absorbing and engulfing. Being engulfed by either fear or love is beyond what most of us want to experience, consciously or unconsciously. This inner game is a game in which we are *always matched*.

The more you evolve, the more the opponent in you evolves too. The more sophisticated you become, the more sophisticated it becomes. The more you work out, the stronger it gets. Not for the purposes of doing you in — quite the opposite — for the purposes of making you into a stronger, faster, better, wiser being.

This is what any worthy opponent does for us. This is what the energy known as the adversary does for us.

If we look at it in the simplest terms possible, Satan is helping you.

Wow.

Did I just say that?

Yes.

And I meant it.

Let's go further, shall we.

Satan, as a force that is a worthy opponent, your adversary, causes you to stay in the gym longer, the spiritual gym, in prayer, meditation and study of sacred writings. Knowledge of a worthy opponent in a game, that you'll face on Saturday, means you'll stay in the gym longer on Friday night, eat well, go to bed early to get all the sleep you need, wake up and get yourself pumped and ready for the showdown of the century.

Without that energy in your life, you'd quickly disintegrate into a lump of mush. We need a good workout. The gym, or exercise of your choice, does good for your body. The spiritual gym does good for your mind, body, spirit and soul.

The correct response to a worthy opponent is not fear, it is respect. You respect that you'll play a big game on Saturday against the team who currently holds the championship.

Wow! What a rush! Nothing to fear, everything to look forward to!

It completely changes your whole perspective on your life and world when you look at the energy known as Satan as an opponent designed to challenge you into your greatness rather than an evil originator bent on destroying you.

The former incites you to be better, for being better's sake. The latter incites you to fear.

Which would you rather live in? The potential of being your best, or at least striving for it, consistently and enthusiastically, or the fear of being overtaken by evil? You get to choose.

Choose wisely.

I made my choice on how I am going to live.

A word here about God and what God wants you to believe. What does God want you to believe? Nothing.

We're stuck in thinking God wants us to do something, or to believe something, for God's sake. We think if we don't believe the way our good Christian religion has taught us, God will be mad, or pissed off.

For the record, God doesn't need anything. *God is everything.* God is All.

God doesn't need you to believe in God. God doesn't need your allegiance. God doesn't need your worship. God doesn't need your prayers.

You need all these, to get to God, at the center of your being, where God has been quietly waiting for your attention all along.

When you really get that God is All, needs nothing and wants nothing, you'll decide to stop trying to jump through hoops for God. It's simply not required. Maybe a full 99% of the stuff I was taught God required of me is not so.

I had to make this discovery on my own, and though it wasn't easy coming to this deep understanding, doing so has freed me on more levels than I can write about in a thousand books and most importantly, put me solidly in an ecstatic love relationship with God, more than I could have ever could hoped for or have had access to in the religion of my upbringing.

I just could not fall deeply and richly in love with the God I was taught about. So I had to nix those ideas and go on a soul journey for myself, to discover the God within my own soul whom I was always madly in love with, and I use the term madly purposely here, for a love relationship with God, a true love relationship with God, is born from a bit of madness in the human mind, the willingness to strike out and do something seemingly radical, to give up so much, to risk the love and approval of family, friends and religious acquaintances one has had for decades, to go on some nondescript, unconventional, non-prescribed, don't-know-where-it-will-all-end, journey of the soul. Yes, that is mad. It makes no sense. In this respect, I love being mad.

It's All Cerebral

Witnesses keep their people cerebral.

That's how the plan works best, when it's all in the head. That worked for me while I was there. Being an air sign (Libra) it's my natural instinct to go to the head in my dealings rather than drop to the heart. It's a soul signature I chose to come in under in this lifetime, so that I could learn, among other things, to challenge my natural proclivities to think my way through and instead claim and exercise the right to live from the heart.

Because the Witness way is more about structure, dogma, doctrine, discipline and compliance than it is about finding and following one's true heart's calling, they have to keep everyone in the head space. They must find, and/or devise, ways to capture the attention of the 'disciples' and hold it, in order to successfully mind program them.

Yes, it is mind programming.

This is why it is a cerebral religion and not so much an experiential one.

A few examples for clarification.

The Witnesses are convinced that they are the only true religion, and that all other religions, including all other Christian religions, will be destroyed by God at the battle of Armageddon.

Though this teaching never 'felt' right in my spirit, because it was oft repeated, with supposedly incontrovertible evidence from the Bible, what was a girl to do but believe?

The basis for this teaching is supposedly a Biblical one.

They call all other religions, including all denominations and strands of Christianity, 'Babylon the Great'. The Witnesses draw this term from the 17th chapter of Revelation, wherein is described a whore riding a red, 7-headed, 10-horned beast. The beast is covered with names that are an insult to God, as Revelation reads. The woman is drunk with the blood of the holy ones.

Witnesses believe the meaning of 'Babylon the Great' to be: 'the world empire of false religion'.

They claim that this woman symbolizes the world empire of false religion, to include all the earth's religions outside of Witnesses.

There is also a clear delineation, a line of demarcation, that the Witnesses necessarily make between themselves and all other denominations of Christianity (yes, Witnesses do consider themselves Christian). They brand it all as false.

This blanket stamp on all religions as false does not end at Christianity, however. The Witnesses have a book (at least they did when I was there) that examines each of the world's major religions, pointing out their tenets, and concludes each segment with a this-is-why-that-religion-is-false-and-thus-not-pleasing-to-Jehovah section.

They have their reasons, very specific reasons, for why every religion on the planet, other than Witnesses, is false, and therefore not pleasing to Jehovah God (the Witnesses say 'Jehovah' is the closest in pronunciation and spelling to the true name of God).

To get you to believe any of this is a cerebral exercise. You won't believe it if allowed, or encouraged, to think for yourself.

You won't believe it if you drop to your heart.

You won't believe it if you are simply still long enough to engage the deeper wisdom.

Hence, all these self-reflective, meditative, contemplative rituals are banned.

What I know about religion, by and large, is that it does not encourage one to think for self; it encourages, and in many cases, demands compliance.

In an experiential space where spirituality is freely explored and one is encouraged to turn within and have their own experience of the divine, and supported in being led in that direction, and that direction only, we blossom.

When we're being told what to do, along with being on the receiving end of heaping doses of judgment, guilt and shame (favorite religious tools for keeping 'disciples' in line) we don't get to explore Self, the only exercise that will ultimately lead to freedom.

Everything else is an exercise in futility.

Yes, listen to your pastor, as long as it aligns with your spirit. Yes, listen to your teachers, as long as what you're receiving aligns with your inner knowing. Yes, listen to spiritual leaders you resonate with, as long as they are supporting you in being your true, Authentic Self.

Witnesses do not, under any circumstances, want you — nor can afford for you — to discover and live from your true, Authentic Self.

Your Self is the enemy of organized religion. Not because your Self does not like religion. Much to the contrary. Your Self does not even see religion.

Religion is a man-made construct; it is our attempt to understand the world around us and our place in it and somehow, in it all, reach the Source for which we all long.

The Self is not human. The Self, Who you really are, the I AM THAT I AM, that exists as you, does not comply with, nor does it support religion.

Religion is bottom up. It's us trying to reach up to God.

Revelation is top down. It's God reaching down to us.

When you let religion, our own man-made attempt to reach God, take precedence over revelation, your own experience of God, you are completely out of order.

It's like treasuring the map rather than the treasure. The map is only supposed to get you to the treasure. Once you have the treasure, you don't need a map. Who cherishes a map rather than the treasure? We would call that one insane.

Yet, we do it every Sunday in churches across the world. We subject the God in us to the religion around us. We let the religion tell us what to do, when to do it, how to do it, and even let it dictate to us what we can and cannot do when it comes to our relationship with God/Goddess/I AM. It sets itself up as such a prominent place in our mind space that we believe it over what God is whispering within our own hearts.

How can we expect to live this way and be happy?

We cannot.

Something must give.

Back to the cerebral nature of the Witness approach.

For 26 years, my mind was conditioned as a Witness. The conditioning is so complete, so pervasive and so all-encompassing that it does not allow room for doubt or questioning. If you talk to a devout Jehovah's Witnesses, it is likely they have been so mind-trained that they will not budge from their beliefs, even if they are not aligned with what they feel on the inside.

Cerebral.

In order for the conditioning to work, Witnesses convince their 'disciples' that there's an authority, set by God, of a group of men on earth who have the sole ability and responsibility to interpret God's word for you, and what it means. This group is called the Faithful and Discreet Slave (a class of men, all white and elderly) who live in Brooklyn, New York, at the world headquarters of the Watchtower, Bible & Tract Society, the arm of the Witnesses that make and distribute their literature.

The Faithful and Discreet Slave is the be-all, end-all for Witnesses when it comes to doctrine. What they say goes. There's no questioning it, no doubting it, no watering it down. The Faithful and Discreet Slave have meetings behind closed doors, in which they decide and come to agreement on what the Bible means and what the doctrine of the Witnesses will be, or how it will change or shift. An example is having to change their stance that the world would end in 1975, a well-known Witness prophecy that they said was based on the Bible (complex calculations from the book of Daniel and Ezekiel). Well, 1975 came and went, and no doomsday. Here we are (as of this writing in 2013) almost 40 years later and no end of the world yet.

You can imagine that the Faithful and Discreet Slave had to amend their calculations about 1975 and come up with another story, one they also said was based on the Bible.

Once again, you'd only believe it if you didn't ask your own inner Wisdom and guidance.

The Faithful and Discreet Slave has what's called a Governing Body. They are like the executive arm of the Witnesses, making sure the dictates and mandates of the Faithful and Discreet Slave are carried out. The Governing Body are responsible for the Witness workings around the world. The Governing Body is made up of 13 or so men (also elderly and all white, I make this point for a reason soon to be revealed, hang with me for a minute) who are all going to heaven, an afterlife reward for only 144,000 according to Witness belief. The rest of the good souls will live here on a paradise earth.

These 13 or so men (no women can be members of the Faithful and Discreet Slave or the Governing Body) are very similar in appearance and ethnicity. I've always wondered about that. I've always wondered why there were no black members, or Asian members or Hispanic or Native American members of either the Faithful and Discreet Slave or the Governing Body. I've been around Witnesses, as one or in association with one or more, for close to 50 years and this has never changed, as far as I know.

There's something strange about that in my spirit. Yet, in the cerebral head space, you can be convinced of damn near anything if the people who are convincing you are really good at mind conditioning. I believe the Witnesses are some of the best mind conditioning agents on the planet.

I also believe that Witnesses are the army of religions. They wake up early, knock on doors in all weather, including weekends, when the mailman is taking a rest, attend 5 meetings a week, 2 circuit assemblies (a gathering of several Witness congregations – a congregation is about 125-150 Witnesses) per year and a district convention (a gathering of several circuits) per year. Some, like I did, may even travel to distant territories to help save the souls who live in outlying areas that don't get knocks on their doors very often.

Then there's the Circuit Overseer and the District Overseer. Overseers (strangely similar in name to slave drivers) are tasked with keeping the flock in line and ensuring compliance.

The much needed compliance for the whole thing not to blow up and fall apart is carried out by the ones who've proven stalwart in the 'faith' for several years.

The hierarchy goes something like this:

There is a local Kingdom Hall of Jehovah's Witnesses, in which 2-3 congregations may meet. Each congregation is comprised of about 125-150 'publishers', on average. Publishers are the ones who have proven 'clean' enough to go out, for at least 10 hours per month, and proselytize (though Witnesses will never call what they do proselytizing, they call it spreading the good news, not the gospel, that's too much like churches, it's the good news). Being 'clean' enough means you are married to a person whom you are faithful to, with no freaky sex (yes, Witnesses moderate sex, even among married couples, to make sure they are not engaging in oral or anal copulation, only vaginal copulation being approved) or, if you are single, you are not having sex at all (fornication is sex outside of marriage and is an offense serious enough to get one booted out of the 'faith'). Sex is a big issue, they're hard on compliance in that arena. The next issue is that a publisher must understand that his/her behavior and comportment are being seen at all times — at work, at school, at play — and that they must always be exemplary for 'worldly people' so that they will not bring reproach on Jehovah's name. This is a big deal, 'reproach'. Witnesses are urged, guilted into and pressured to comply so that they do not fall into the reproach category.

It's an effective compliance tool as reproach leads to disciplinary action, which could include simple behind closed doors reproof (stern talking-to by the elders, with a warning not to do your dirty deed again) all the way up to disfellowshipping, the Witness total removal of one who is not in compliance.

I am disfellowshipped. And in a way, happy to be, because it means Witnesses will have little or no contact with me. The average Witness is sternly charged not to speak to disfellowshipped people at all. They quote Matthew 18:15-17 and 1 Corinthians 5:11-12 as their basis for disfellowshipping.

Since no one wants to be put out of anything, least of all the brotherhood they have been bred on, sometimes for years, it's easier to gain compliance if the threat of being ousted is seriously held over your head, with examples right in your own congregation to prove that the Witnesses mean business.

They systematically and thoroughly search for, address and, if need be, remove those who are in any way suspected of inappropriate Witness behavior.

The biggest offenses in the Witness world are adultery (probably number 1 given their views on the sanctity of marriage), fornication, homosexuality, lying, stealing, and the mother of all crimes, the sin against the Holy Spirit: blasphemy (from which Witnesses say there is no return nor forgiveness for). One who falls into this category is considered 'apostate', the worst form of falling away from the 'faith' that can be committed in the Witness paradigm.

I have heard, from my brother, that the Witnesses now consider me an apostate.

I laugh.

It makes no sense, other than if you're not thinking, opting instead for letting the religion do all the thinking for you, which it is more than happy to do. If that's the case, then it makes perfect sense.

An apostate is considered especially dangerous, as they can bleed to other believers and sway them away from the 'faith'.

Translation: people who have waken up and are now thinking for themselves, and can see the holes in the religion, and are no longer willing to be under its vice-like grip, and who have made the decision and soul choice to be free, are considered dangerous to the 'flock', the ones who are still under hypnotic mind control.

If your very existence depended on the energy supplied by people who live in the matrix, a person like Neo (who's free and, not only that, is now on a mission to free more minds... the very minds that are housed in the bodies that serve as your energy source) will seem very dangerous.

If religion is the matrix, I'm firmly on Neo's side. Having been trapped deep inside the matrix for years, my soul was crying out: FREE ME!

I remember a powerful conversation with my teacher about the Witnesses and being disfellowshipped. She asked me if I really wanted to be there. I said "no". Then she shed a bright light on the whole experience when she said 'so, you didn't want to be there anyway, but you were too afraid to be authentic, so you let them throw you out.'

Wow.

That was it exactly. I was too afraid to stand up, be my true authentic self and say, 'hey guys, it's been real, and I'm out!' Instead, I did what I wanted to do, including rebelliously breaking the rules, knowing I'd be kicked out sooner or later. Hindsight *is* 20/20.

Next up from publishers on the hierarchy are pioneers. Pioneers make a commitment to proselytize for 90+ hours per month. They are the generals in the Witness army. They lead the charge in placing literature (the Witness term for giving their magazines, the Watchtower and Awake, and other books and Bibles away to 'interested' people), conducting home bible studies (the Witness method for beginning the indoctrination into the Witness way), and bringing people into 'the truth' (what the Witnesses call their religion, 'the truth').

Publishers and Pioneers can be both men and women, with the large majority of pioneers being women.

Next are Ministerial Servants, men only, who serve in the congregation to keep order and who are on the tract to become elders. Ministerial servants are to follow the code set out in 1 Timothy 3:8-13 and may parallel the position of deacon in a traditional Christian church. There may be 5-7 or more ministerial servants in a congregation and are mostly comprised of young men who are mature enough to help with the compliance issue and are eager enough to want to become elders one day. Women are not allowed to become ministerial servants.

Next up on the totem pole are the elders, of which there may be 5-6 in a congregation. The elders, like ministerial servants, are all men. Women are not allowed leadership or teaching roles in the Witness world (other than to conduct home Bible studies, or a small gathering of Witnesses for a 'book study', only if her head is covered and only if no qualified, baptized brothers are present). A woman cannot teach in the presence of a baptized man.

The elders are responsible for the order and compliance in the congregation, and to make sure everything is unfolding exactly as the Faithful and Discreet Slave says it's supposed to. They are like quality control agents. Having this role means they are sold out Witnesses, and have proven that fact over many years.

Among the elders, there is a hierarchy as well. There is one brother who serves as the Presiding Overseer for a year. He is in a sort of rotation, as brothers only serve as Presiding Overseer for a term. There is also a secretary, who takes down vital information at the elder's meetings, of which there are many. The elders generally meet after each meeting at the Kingdom Hall, on issues pertaining to the congregation. There's also an accounts servant, who is responsible for counting the money deposited into the collection box and making sure it is documented and sent off rapidly to Brooklyn, New York, the headquarters of Jehovah's Witnesses. There are some funds that are used for expenses at the Kingdom Hall as well. Each publisher, pioneer, ministerial servant and elder works and makes their own living. No one is paid a salary; it is all volunteer work.

Groups of congregations, maybe 10 or so, form a 'circuit'. There is a 'circuit overseer' who ensures compliance on the circuit level, and who goes around, on a schedule, to visit all the congregations in his circuit. He is assigned a circuit by the powers that be in Brooklyn, New York. When I was there, a circuit overseer would serve for a period of 2-4 years, visiting each congregation in his circuit every 6 months. Each congregation thus gets a week-long visit from the circuit overseer and his wife (circuit overseers must be faithfully married for many years to get the position in the first place) twice a year. During that week, the circuit overseer works out in 'field service' with the congregation, meets with the pioneers to encourage them, and meets with the elders to, once again, ensure compliance and deal with any issues of non-compliance in the Witness way, sternly and swiftly. A circuit overseer has generally been an elder for many years.

Next up is the district overseer. A district is several circuits put together and could comprise thousands of Witnesses. While a congregation may not often receive visits from the district overseer (it's deemed a privilege to have the circuit overseer and the district overseer visit the congregation and the red carpet is surely rolled out) Witnesses do see the district overseer every 6 months at the circuit assembly (when the entire circuit comes together for an all day Saturday and Sunday meeting). There is also a once per year district convention, that generally lasts for 3 days (they were 4 days long when I was a wee tot, lasting from Thursday to Sunday), Friday to Sunday. These are all day affairs, usually from about 9 am to 4 or 5 pm, and include skits enacted from the bible (called 'dramas', a highlight of the assemblies) and talks and demonstrations and are saturated with Witness 'success stories', stories of faithful Witnesses who stood up to doctors who were trying to convince them they needed a blood transfusion to stay alive, yet they refused, or a Witness wife who stood up to an 'opposing' husband who didn't want her to go to the Kingdom Hall, but she decided to go anyway, or a 'youth' who didn't go along with the pressure from peers to take drugs in school and is standing before the assembly to share the story. There are also stories weaved in from Witnesses who have seemingly impossible conditions to live through, and are yet being 'faithful' in meeting attendance and field ministry.

More mind conditioning.

The bigger assemblies are designed to clearly display that the Witness world is oh so much larger than the local Kingdom Hall, and that solidarity is firmly in place. The Witnesses' strong clan mentality makes fear of ousting that much more effective.

Up from the district overseer is somewhat of a mystery, rank and file Witnesses aren't told what goes on behind closed doors, or high up the food chain. The bulk of the information that flows down is rules mixed with doctrine.

Between the Faithful and Discreet Slave, the Governing Body, the district overseer, the circuit overseer and the congregational elders, close tabs and a tight rein are kept on Witnesses all over the globe in a system of control and doctrine that is purportedly gleaned from the Bible.

This is a cerebral exercise in mind control. I call it thus because this is my experience of it, having been there for 26 years and now having been free for almost 23 years. This gives one a lot of time to reflect, meditate and contemplate. As I contemplate my life's journey, I can say the with certainty that the Witness walk was a necessary one for me. I could not have not had it. It has gone into the wonderful mix of who I am today, and to be sure, I love who I am today. I have the Witnesses to thank for a large part of my journey.

Yet, also residing next to my gratitude for what I learned and grew through while I was there, is a clearer understanding of what was really happening.

Gratitude does not imply agreement, nor does it condone. It simply says 'thank you for all I received' from deeper than a thinking place. Gratitude lives in the heart space. I am grateful, from the heart space, for the Witnesses and all I experienced in the portion of my life journey that I walked with them. I am also clear that the whole affair was a complex exercise in mind control.

It's all cerebral.

And when people outside yourself have control of your mind, you are in a sad predicament indeed, with little hope of escape the longer you stay in the clutches. The longer we are subjected to mind control, the weaker one's will becomes to find anything else. The Witnesses are masters of eroding one's will for something other than what the religion states it should be, by using the favorite tools of fear of abandonment or loss of love, guilt and shame.

All in the name of Jesus.

The only thing that got me free was that my soul had made a choice to be free, and it was going to live out that choice, or die. That was the mandate from my soul, be free or die.

Since the death option didn't appeal to me, I chose the former, to be free. Freedom has its price.

For the most part, as far as I can tell, and I am open to learning something new and different today or tomorrow, but what I know from where I sit right now is: freedom is VERY expensive.

It cost me my most cherished beliefs. I had to turn them all over.

It cost me my relationship with my mother. It forever shifted after I stood in my soul choice.

It cost me my relationship with all the Witnesses I knew. Most of them live in the space somewhere between loving me very much, not speaking to me at all, being surprised when they see me, wondering what I'm doing behind closed doors, and some may be secretly wondering if I'm the anti-Christ. I'm making these statements based on observations of Witnesses when I've come in contact with them, not on what they've actually told me. So I can say that my observations may be completely off and not factual. I can only go by what I experience, and since they've pretty much made a decision not to speak to me, it's unlikely I'll be able to poll the. Nor would I want to.

I'm surprisingly happy with how it turned out. Just as much as they don't want to speak to me is equally how much I would not have them in my circle. Not so much because I don't want them around as it is because they don't fit into my current paradigm of freedom.

People still living in the matrix cannot comprehend people who are free.

And so while we are not together, and I do not wish for us to be together, I'm grateful for what I learned, and happy to share it here.

Most of all, the Witnesses taught me, by the opposite means, to live in the heart, from the heart, fully, all the way.

And they taught me in the most strange and contrary way that it could have happened, by trying to control my mind.

Had I not had the experience of mind control, I know not if I would now so deeply value a free mind and an open heart.

Thank you Witnesses.

If They Have Your Head They Have You

I do not want to convey the idea that the mind does not need controlling. If you got that connotation from the previous chapter, let me expound. The mind absolutely does require control and conditioning for the best possible life on planet earth.

There is no question about whether the mind needs controlling and/or conditioning. I absolutely want my mind controlled and conditioned.

The question here is who or what is doing the controlling and the conditioning?

In a tiny nutshell, if any entity outside of yourself is conditioning your mind, be sure the conditioning is faulty at best and deadly at worst.

There is no entity — including religion, politics, school, parents, clan, tribe, culture, country — that should have control of your mind.

Your mind is created to be under the subjection of the spirit of God within. This is the only influence we are to turn our minds completely over to.

Anything short of that is, in my opinion, deadly. It could be a slow death or a fast death, either way, if your mind is controlled by any entity outside yourself, you are slowly dying.

And how many of us allow our minds to be controlled by entities outside self?

Note the word 'allow' is used here, to indicate and remind that any mind control is voluntary, at some point, even if it started out when you were a young tyke, like mine did. At some point, the mind control became voluntary, and I could opt out. This is true for all of us. All of us, to be sure, received mind control while growing up. We were conditioned to believe certain things, probably the same things the ones who conditioned us believed. We were taught that these beliefs were 'how life is.' Somewhere along the way, we got the idea that what we received was the truth.

It's not.

The best we received was a pile of opinions.

Maybe we got some truth swirled in there, encoded in scripture, parables, old folks sayings or idioms. Yes, there was some underlying truth to some of what we got. Yet I must confess that the bulk of what I got was opinion mixed with religious fervor.

A nasty and particularly compelling combination.

Which brings me to the other scary issue with mind control and conditioning. It can be used for any cause, very effectively, whether that cause be for good or for evil. When you turn over the control of your mind to an entity outside yourself, you are now an ally with them. They are using your energy to forward their purposes. In essence, this is the matrix of machines using humans as an energy source. How were they able to do it? Mind control. They kept the humans mind's fixated on and in and illusory world, while using their bodies for their own purposes.

This is the danger of mind control. When someone has your mind, they also have your body and your vital life force energy.

Think pimp and prostitute. The prostitute could up and leave the pimp at any time. She has multiple opportunities to get away, if she really wanted to. However, because the pimp has her mind, in most cases, her body stays put. It's less strenuous physically to control someone's mind than it is to control their body. Without mind control, no sane person will let you hold their body captive for any length of time. They will eventually revolt and free themselves, freedom being the highest aspiration of the human spirit.

But if you have a person's mind, their body ain't going nowhere. Such is the case with Jehovah's Witnesses, and perhaps many more of the world's religions, or perhaps even religion at large.

My biggest pet peeve, or maybe I should call it a concern, about religion is that it does not, in its current form, seem to be fulfilling the purpose for which we created it: to lead one to one's Self.

The religions we have today seem to be leading converts to the religion. When your intention is to control and navigate a person where you want them to go, you will have to control and/or condition the mind in order for your aim to be successful. You will need to crush something in that person's spirit as well, as no human is willing to let themselves be controlled on a soul level. We may submit to it temporarily, all the while seeking an out. Or we may tell ourselves whatever we need to tell ourselves to make bearable our pain, the pain of being controlled or contained, against our inner will.

To control or contain a person against their natural inclination to be free, you will need to employ effective methods of mind control, including:

Fear of retribution and/or punishment if one does not comply – the Witnesses have this feature of mind control mastered, as was earlier mentioned, with the fear of being ousted as the ultimate retribution. I cannot stress enough how devastating this fear can be to the Witness psyche, especially if one has been a Witness for many years. After making sure that I only made friends with Witnesses, as association with worldly people is not allowed, other the necessity of work or school, after which all association is to be cut off, and even association with family members (who are not Witnesses) is frowned upon and cautioned against, lest they contaminate the Witness (they quote 1 Corinthians 15:33 as the basis for this, "bad associations spoil useful habits" is an oft-repeated phrase/affirmation for Witness mind control). Once association with all other people, save Witnesses, has been adequately achieved, and ones' entire support system and network is comprised almost entirely of Witnesses, the fear of being kicked out is artificially heightened. This was my case. I was afraid for years to leave the Witnesses, with the thought: *where would I go?* It was for me to discover that fear could not rule my life. I had to make a different choice. That choice was, and is, for love.

Seclusion – a key part of Witness mind control is secluding their members. Cults often do this by physically living in a closed community or compound (think Jim Jones). Witnesses have a clever way of attacking this aspect of mind control by making everyone who is not a Witness an undesirable. This makes it easier to create a cult-like allegiance without the hassle of setting up a compound and secluding all the Witnesses in it (the Witnesses do have a version of a compound in Brooklyn, New York, though all Witnesses are not required to live there, more on that later). There is incessant and insistent urging to avoid association with anyone who is not one of Jehovah's Witnesses. After all, if they don't come to Jehovah God, they're going to die at Armageddon anyway, with no hope of return, so why would you want to associate with them? They're practically the walking dead. The only exception to this rule that is somewhat tolerated is a 'sister' (a female Jehovah's Witness) who is married to an 'unbeliever' (a person who is not one of Jehovah's Witnesses). This is a sticky situation for sure, and usually happens when a woman who's married decides to become one of Jehovah's Witnesses. Her husband, not being a Witness, is under constant pressure to become one, if the wife is doing her job. She is strongly encouraged to bring him to the Kingdom Hall, suggest that he have a home bible study with one of the brothers, invited to all the events, and exposes him to the brothers at the Kingdom Hall each chance

Praise if one complies – there's huge upside potential in the Witness organization for complying. They award their members with 'parts on the program', meaning that you could be showcased on stage, at a major event, like a circuit assembly or district convention, if you are particularly faithful in doing what you're told. The religion calls it being faithful to Jehovah and views obedience to Jehovah God and the religion as one and the same. This is one of the biggest reasons I left.

These are the major, most compelling and effective tools Witnesses use for mind control.

To make the whole affair easier, mind controllers must make the individual think they are doing what they are doing voluntarily, that it is one's own idea to be in subjection to another. This is, for me, the most insidious and destructive form of mind control. I was convinced, over many years of mind conditioning, that being a Witness was the best possible thing I could do with myself and my life, when that was not the truth of my soul at all. Yet, on a mental level, I was totally convinced of this idea. I was so convinced of it that I was on the front lines, out trying my best to convince other people of this self-same flawed belief.

What almost makes me chuckle is the indignation one religion will muster at another religion who is doing the same thing, in a different way. I noticed that other Christian religions seem to have a disdain for Witnesses, the very same disdain Witnesses seem to have for all other branches of Christianity. Christians of other denominations love to say that Witnesses aren't Christians, when if you ask a Witness, they will tell you they are Jehovah's Christian Witnesses. They will tell you they preach the good news (not the gospel, as that sounds too close to churches) and they will also inform you that Jesus is the way to God, the truth and the light. They will tell you that you cannot get to God without going through Jesus Christ, and you will be hard pressed to find a Witness that doesn't end his or her prayer "in Jesus name, Amen". They are sold out for Jesus Christ, just not in a churchy way.

Because they're exhibiting their sold-out-for-Jesus-Christ-ness in a way that's quite different from most other Christian denominations, they're thought of as not Christian. I think one of the biggest reasons they are thought of as non-Christian is because they do not celebrate Christmas.

Jehovah's Witnesses are clear on the origin of many holidays, this I appreciate, they've done their research. They, to me, are not like most Christian denominations, who openly celebrate and practice holidays that are pagan or non-christian in origin. It is part of Witness core curriculum to know and understand fully, with 'biblical' proof, that all the religious holidays are pagan in origin, or not substantiated by the Bible. They say there is one sacred day on the calendar, and that is the Lord's Supper (also called the Lord's Evening Meal), which Witnesses commemorate each year with a depth of reverence that is rare in some holy day celebrations. This once a year celebration is said to be the only day Christians are charged to commemorate each year. They do not so much view it as a celebration as they view it as a commemoration. It is a sacred time of remembering, remembering why Christ came, and a time of reflection on his life and work. This annual commemoration, they say, was instituted by Jesus Christ himself, at the Last Supper, when he reclined with his 11 apostles (Witnesses say that the true ceremony did not begin until after Christ dismissed Judas Iscariot), broke bread, thanked God in prayer and gave it to his disciples, with the instruction that this represents his body. Then he blessed wine, passed it and instructed that this represents his blood, that would soon be shed for mankind. Witnesses re-enact this meal all over the world on the day on the Jewish calendar that equates to Passover, as this was a Passover meal. Therefore, the actual date changes each year. It is usually around the spring time, not far off from Easter. They are adamant that it has nothing to do with Easter, and Witnesses do not at all celebrate the resurrection of Christ. They say there is one day, and one day only, that the Bible specifically says to commemorate each year, and their interpretation of Christ's words to 'keep doing this in remembrance of me' means to do it annually, on the same day Christ did it.

Most other Christian denominations take a different tack — although they are commemorating the same Biblical event — by having holy communion once on a month, many times on the first Sunday of the month. The beauty of the Catholic church is that one can receive communion daily. How divine.

Either way, it seems all Christians, from all denominations, are clear that the last evening meal, on Passover, that Christ spent with his disciples was an important one to commemorate. His charge to keep doing this has stuck with us for thousands of years. This is poignant and profound when considered with reverence. Though religions vary greatly about how and when they do communion, or what they call it, there is a beautiful unity in it. All are united in their allegiance and loyalty to carrying out this most sacred ceremony.

For Witnesses, the only ones who can eat the bread (unleavened bread that Witnesses get from a Kosher store so as to have exactly what Jesus Christ used) and drink the wine (the very same kind of red wine they think Jesus Christ used) are the ones who are members of the 144,000 who will be living and reigning with Christ in heaven.

Witnesses believe that only 144,000 people will have the honor and privilege of going to heaven to live with God and rule with Christ. This belief is based on Revelation chapters 7 and 14. Witnesses take the number 144,000 quite literally, and say this is the exact number of people who will go to heaven.

All other righteous ones are part of what Witnesses call the 'great crowd' spoken of in Revelation 7:9-17, who have washed their robes in the blood of the Lamb, making them white (to indicate purity and cleanliness). They did not defile themselves, and they worshiped God in his temple day and night, and so they receive the blessing of the Lord. This 'great crowd' will live on a paradise earth, according to Witness interpretation of scripture.

To me, this teaching of only 144,000 going to heaven was always somewhat incredulous, and I must confess, I never quite understood it. The doctrine left so many unanswered questions in my mind. Though Witnesses try their best to keep their doctrine tight with fancy footwork they say is from the Bible, and complex time calculations involving the books of Revelation and the prophets, there are holes that cannot be ignored. A few of my unsatisfactorily answered questions:

How come only 144,000 people get to go to heaven when there have been billions of people on earth. Something about that doesn't seem fair. The Witness response: because that's what the Bible says in Revelation. Period. End of story.

When did these people get chosen? People have been living on the earth for eons, yet, according to the Witnesses, there are still members of the 144,000 living on earth now (a few thousand, according to their count). The Witness answer: God didn't start choosing the 144,000 until 1914. Only people who were around on earth then and since then can be chosen.

Which begged the next question, *what was God doing up until 1914, just watching people on earth? Why did He start picking people then?* The Witness answer: because that's how the Faithful and Discreet Slave says it is, therefore, that's how it is. It would be best for you to use your time and energy remembering the scriptures we're using to support our doctrine and teach it to other people rather than asking questions. (And no, the Witnesses did not actually say that to me, it was what I received as an undertone of the message.)

How does God choose them? They all seem to be old, white men, with very few women, and hardly no minorities. Doesn't God want people of different colors in heaven? What about women? Are any women going to heaven? This question was big in my mind growing up as a Witness, considering that all the people with power and authority in the Witness world seemed to me to be old, white men, most of whom were Jewish. I was confused and wanted to know. The Witness answer: that's God's business how God chooses them. We can't help it if they're all old, white men. If that's what God wants, that's what God gets. My response? Hmmmmmmmmm...

How does a person know if they are chosen? Witness answer: God's spirit speaks to their spirit (based on their interpretation of Romans 8:15-17) and they know they are adopted as sons of God.

Which then begs the question, doesn't everybody get the same opportunity to have God's spirit in them let them know they are adopted by God? Who gets adopted and who are 'orphans'? I don't get it... The Witness answer: you're not supposed to get it. Just believe what we say. (Once again, they did not actually say this to me. It was implied.)

Another question, what happens if one of the 'sons' of God changes their mind and doesn't want to go to heaven? Witness answer: if one falls away, God will replace that one. Though it is rare, the Witnesses say it does happen. This is the only way a younger person (under the age of 50 or so at this point) could get chosen, since the number was already sealed and God had done all the choosing already. Now, we would only have a few replacements here and there.

Mind you, Witnesses watch like a hawk at the Lord's Evening Meal to make sure no one partakes of the 'emblems' (the bread and the wine) unless they have been completely vetted and accepted as a member of the 144,000 after rigorous questioning by the elders of the congregation. One cannot just up and decide that they are members of the 144,000. They will be questioned, and if not able to pass the test, they will be dealt with as one who is either completely disrespectful of Witness lore and doctrine, or they will be considered mentally incapacitated on some level. Witnesses do not take lightly their commemoration of the Lord's Evening Meal and anyone who would even touch the 'emblems'. This is considered a high holy offense. The brothers who pass the emblems at the Lord's Supper consider it an honor and privilege.

I would encourage you to go to a Witness commemoration of the Lord's Supper one year to take in what the event is all about, then draw your own conclusions.

I'm not here to call Witnesses right or wrong. Like all of us, they're free to believe anything they want to believe.

My concern is, and has been, the mind control used to gain compliance. Witnesses are not seeking to get you to turn within for your own answers and a direct revelation of God within your spirit. They are clearly indoctrinating members into a belief system that is at points completely incredulous and at other points a stretch if you want to say it's all based on the Bible. They are Fundamentalists, and Fundamentalists concern me. I recall an unforgettable truth I heard from a Kabbalah teacher, learned in Hebrew, the Torah (Jewish scriptures) and the Zohar (Kabbalah holy book) who stated quite definitively: "anyone who takes the Bible literally is a fool". Wow. I agree; could not have said it better.

I guess it was more the way he said it than the actual words he said. His words were infused with an of-course-ness that made his words common-sensical. *Of course*, I thought when I heard it, *that's exactly right, this book is not meant to be taken literally.*

I came to that conclusion and I am far from a scholar of Hebrew, the Torah or the Zohar. Though I am an avid student of the Bible, I am far from a scholar of that as well.

Yet I don't think you have to be a scholar of any kind to start getting — even if it's the first time you've ever picked up a Bible — that this book is loaded with meaning, and it may not mean what it seems to be saying.

One has only as far as Genesis to traverse in the Bible to come to the conclusion that this is a book of allegory and prophecy and symbology and mystery and mystical meaning and metaphysics and, and, and.

I cannot sum up in words what the Bible is. I don't think anyone can. It, like all holy books, defies description or categorization.

All I know is: it ain't meant to be taken literally.

The Witnesses take much of the Bible literally — at pure face value — a practice that inevitably leads one to flawed interpretation. I do not say this to say Witnesses are wrong in their interpretation of the Bible. I am not the judge of that. I do not purport to know who is wrong or who is right, nor do I desire or aspire to. That is not the point here, which I feel I must stress, lest these words be misconstrued. This is not a treatise condemning Witnesses. I have no reason nor right to condemn nor to approve.

What I am saying here is that there may be more to the story than the Witnesses teach, or more layers of meaning inherent in the Holy Bible, or that there is more room for what the Bible is saying to each one of us personally, without requiring the Faithful and Discreet Slave to tell us in every moment what every inch and word of the Bible means for each and every person.

It's like reading the Bible and having someone look over your shoulder telling you what every word means.

I would respectfully offer to that person whispering over my shoulder, 'perhaps that is what it means to you, and I'm not knocking that, more power to you, and at the same time, may I be free to receive what it means for me? Thank you very much.'

I don't think that's too much to ask. Let me read the Bible for myself, and find out what it means for myself. Let God speak to me through the pages of the Bible, if that's where I happen to be looking for a Word from God in that moment. I can find the very same word of God on a tree bark, or a rose petal or a butterfly's wing or a sunset. No one has to tell me what they mean. The meaning of all these — indeed of everything in the universe — is already encoded in the soul. It's for you to unwrap these mysteries for yourself. Isn't that part of the delicious-ness of life on planet earth on this journey of the soul? That you get to unfold timeless mysteries for yourself? That you get to ask any questions you want, and receive the answers in any way you and the universe agree to communicate? And that you get to receive the ancient, timeless wisdom for yourself, in your own spirit, in your own way, in your own perfect time? Isn't it beautiful that you get to choose? Without being force-fed someone else's beliefs or knowing or revelations?

YES! This is the great reason we are here, to evolve the soul, to grow, to ascend, to understand, and ultimately, to *know.* Not to be told.

To *know* for ourselves.

Dinosaurs

I confess I did not believe in dinosaurs for most of my early life and well into my 20's. Witnesses don't believe in dinosaurs.

I'm not sure how anyone on the planet can, at this point, not believe in — or deny the existence of — dinosaurs, when just about every museum on the planet has one.

Which brings me to the point of conceding.

Witnesses, as far as I know, do not concede.

When it has become overwhelmingly clear, as proven beyond doubt by hard scientific data, that they have been mistaken in doctrine or 'prophecy', they will not concede (an example of this is the doctrine that the earth is only 6,000-7,000 years old; Witnesses take much of the Bible literally, including the 6 creation days of Genesis, with each day, they say, representing 1,000 years, based on 2 Peter 3:8). This failure to concede, I believe, is one reason many in the scientific community may be at odds with religion; because of the religious zealots who will not, even in the face of proven scientific facts (like dinosaurs) concede their religious views. In the face of whole skeletons, they will still say dinosaurs don't exist (as if dinosaurs needed anyone's belief). They walked the planet, and flew above it. They don't anymore. Period. What's to believe, or not to believe, about dinosaurs, as whole skeletons lay, perfectly preserved, in layers of rock and ice, moments of our storied past kept safe by the Earth Mother herself? Are we not past 'belief' in dinosaurs? Are they not by now a fact?

Even still, Witnesses will not concede.

They will make doctrinal adjustment, only if advantageous, claiming that said adjustment is the result of the 'light getting brighter' (based on Proverbs 4:18). The light getting brighter is the Witness way of saying 'we need to change something... what we told you before didn't happen, and we have no clear reason, or excuse, so give us a minute while we come up with something else.'

It's a clever blanket statement — supposedly supported by the Bible — that serves the more covert purpose of neatly cleaning up Witness missteps in doctrine or failed 'prophetic' announcements. It is also handily used as a general scapegoat anytime the Witnesses want to change anything.

The light keeps getting brighter is the party line when a 'prophecy' does not materialize (such as the infamous failed Witness prophecy the the world would come to a cataclysmic end in 1975... based on this prediction alone, I personally know Witnesses who did not get dental work done because they were convinced Armageddon was coming; 30 plus years after the fact, what those teeth look like now is anybody's guess).

While it is true that our walk with God does cause the light to get brighter, as the Proverb teaches, we understand that dogmatic positions are not the light in the first place. They are man-made. Like all man-made constructs, they are temporary, by their very nature. Nothing we can make in this world will last. Nothing here is eternal. Doctrine is a man-made construct. It is man's attempt to tell another man what a holy book means. While none of us have any business telling another what any holy book means, we may have been fed doctrine, nevertheless.

This is unfortunate. For me, it took years of taking off the Witness glasses when reading the Bible. The dogma and doctrine was so thick and mucky that it took years of extricating myself from it to be clear. Even now, I still, if I'm not careful, will read a scripture and the Witness version/translation/meaning of it will come to my mind. Not that the meaning from the Witnesses wasn't helpful. In that moment in time, when I was receiving it, it was very helpful. It was exactly what I needed. Yet I recognize it as a rest stop along the train ride that is my life. It's a place I visited in consciousness, not somewhere I was supposed to set up camp and live in.

Some of us are stuck at rest stops when God has long ago whistled for us to get back on the train.

There's somewhere good and wonderful and divine God is taking all of us. We're to grow there, not go there. You won't get to your personal Nirvana by express train ride. Evolution is a process, an unfolding, a lovely train ride through the country. There are stops along the way. Some rest stops are 15 minutes. Some are 5 hour layovers. Some are bathroom or smoke breaks. All of it is part of the ride.

So I cannot bemoan the Witnesses because they were at one of my God ordained rest stops. The divine's in charge of all the rest stops and who there to meet and greet you at each one. There are no accidents, mages know this well. Everything is by design, even when it looks like total chaos.

So please never get from this tome that I am not thankful for the very necessary walk I had with the Witnesses. To the contrary, I thank God for all the gifts I received while there.

When you graduate to high school, as Rev. Michael Bernard Beckwith teaches, you don't burn down your middle school.

When we graduate spiritually, we cannot, in good faith and deep gratitude, curse the mechanism of our growth. For me, the Witnesses and all they brought me was well warranted and serves me well to this day. The more I reflect on my journey, the more I'm deeply grateful for all of it. I see the magick of the universe at work in the gentle, guiding, ever-present, invisible hand leading us ever onward and upward to a higher plane.

With that said about dogma and doctrine, what I learned from it is this: never be dogmatic. About anything. It may seem right and true today, but it could be proven an absolute lie by tomorrow. Maybe I think I know something today, I may totally abandon it tomorrow. Anything I can think is not real. I cannot think of eternal things. The eternal is not a thing one can perceive with the regular thinking mind. Thus, because my mind cannot think of the eternal, anything I think must be temporary.

Including all my beliefs. They must all be temporary, by their very nature. A belief cannot be permanent. One the eternal lasts forever, and the eternal cannot be believed in. Dinosaurs are not eternal. They were here. Now they're not. They were a form of the divine, temporary and fleeting, like the earth suit you and I are wearing that we call a human body. Temporary.

Anything science proves is temporary. Why? Because the eternal is always happening. It's a becoming, an eternal becoming. It is forever and continually creating Itself anew. What's true today about our world, our solar system and our place in it could radically change 1,000,000 years from now. Indeed, it has radically changed in the last 400,000,000 years that we now know the earth has been here. We certainly haven't been here 400,000,000 years, and we, in all likelihood, considering what earth does, will not be here 400,000,000 years from now. Something else will be here. This is the every changing nature of the 3rd dimensional world in which we humanly inhabit. Such is the nature of everything we think is true about it too. Such is the nature of all our dogma and doctrine and holy held beliefs. They're all temporary.

Where does that leave us? Belief-less?

No. It points us to the very bedrock of being: the changeless, eternal, timeless, deathless, birthless, breathless divinity we call the I AM.

I AM never changes. It is forever Itself. The Holy Bible tells us "I am God. I do not change."

So while we cannot rest for more than 10 seconds or 10 years on one of our cherished beliefs as the be-all-end-all, we can rest solidly on God within as the eternal, changeless foundation of everything.

I think the reason Witnesses do not concede cherished beliefs is the same reason I'm reluctant to let go of something I believe in. My beliefs give me false comfort; I think they secure me in an insecure world. Plus, my beliefs are propped up, one against the other, a dominoes game in my mind. If one topples, what happens to all the others around it? Will they topple too? Will my whole belief system crash and fall? What would happen then? What would I believe in? Would I be safe? Would I survive?

That's the real question, will we survive knowing the world doesn't work the way we thought it did.

We were one way, then 9-11 happened, and in one day, our entire world changed. No longer were we comfortably napping on the sofa curled up with the security blanket. We were shocked out of our beliefs of how we thought the world was. Truth be told, we, in America, thought everyone loved America. We were prideful. Who wouldn't love this great country? It's the best country in the world! We're the best. And we're safe too. Yep, that's the ticket, we're the best and we're safe.

Ok. If that's what you want to believe, but soon, you will see the truth; the universe will see to that.

Which brings us to the next problem with beliefs: they distort the truth.

The paradox in beliefs is that they manifest. Many of us thus have fallen into the trap, especially religious zealots, of using the outcome or results we're getting as proof that our beliefs are true.

Your beliefs coming true are not proof that they are true. Your beliefs coming true are proof that you believe them.

I could believe I'm blessed because I have Jesus as my Lord and Savior. My life is blessed, because I believe I'm blessed by Jesus. I see other people's lives who don't appear blessed, and when I look at them, I say it's because they haven't taken Jesus as their Lord and Savior. To me, my whole belief system fits perfectly together.

Until it doesn't. Something happens. A giant finger reaches out the sky and knocks over one of your precious dominoes.

Uh-oh.

That happened to me. I was convinced of everything I learned from Witnesses. So convinced that I was a full-time minister of convincing other people that what we had was the truth, end of story, the fat lady has sung.

Until I met Kitty (stay tuned for more on that story in the next chapter...)

For now, there is one more reason coming to me why we deny truth in favor of beliefs, or why we will not concede beliefs, even when proven to be erroneous, or why we will cling to doctrine and dogma that has long outgrown its usefulness to us.

It is because of fear. We are fearful of the implications of the truth, though we claim we are not. We fear the truth, for the truth rips away every lie we've ever clung to, and many times, quite abruptly, with no warning signal.

Yes, fear keeps us in lies. Truth reveals all we think we do not want to know. The saying is: the truth sets you free, but first it pisses you off.

I don't know what to say about religion that does not concede, that perpetuates beliefs that are clearly not true, or that says we're still in charge, we just got a brighter idea than we had before.

To me, that sounds like a recipe for someone wanting to dupe me into following them forever.

That I will not do.

Kitty

I confess I never saw Kitty coming. She hit me like a series of bricks on the head, seemingly out of nowhere.

I met Kitty in a network marketing business I was engaged in through a mutual business acquaintance. I can't say it was a friend, Witnesses are careful to not have any non-Witness friends (or at least careful to never admit they do).

So I never saw Kitty coming. The first thing I noticed about Kitty (brick number one was about to fall) was that she was joyful, genuinely happy. I couldn't believe it. In my paradigm, up until then, I was taught, and was thoroughly convinced, that only Witness could be joyful and genuinely happy. Everyone else, the people in the 'world' who had not become Witnesses yet, were not happy. Nor were they joyful. How could they be? They didn't know the one true God: Jehovah. They didn't accept Jesus as the only way to God. They didn't become one of Jehovah's Witnesses. No, they couldn't possibly be happy. Any shred of happiness they mistakenly thought they had would be short-lived, a temporary fluke. How could anyone be happy and worldly? It's not possible. Dismiss the idea and never have that thought again.

This may sound woefully riddled with bigotry. That would be accurate. I must confess, I was a bigot. A big one.

Back to Kitty.

No one can fake joy. It's an energetic that can be read on a soul level. No one can convince you they're joyful. More than likely, joyful people aren't trying to convince you of anything. That's probably one of the reasons they're joyful; freedom from what other people think automatically equals joy.

So I knew Kitty wasn't putting on, she wasn't faking it. She was REALLY happy and joyful. Well, I could call her an anomaly, like the agents called Neo in the Matrix, "the anomaly." Or I could look deeper.

Something was calling me to look deeper though I confess I did not know what that thing was back then. I only knew I had to follow it. I had to look deeper into the whole idea of the happy non-Jehovah's Witness.

Pardon me if I seem downright dumb or absolutely obnoxious at this point in my life. I was. I confess. There, you have it.

Back to Kitty. Brick number two was about to fall. I was invited to Kitty's house. If it wasn't strictly for business, I would never have gone, because Witnesses, real Witnesses, don't make it a habit to go to 'worldly' people's houses. They could be demonized. They could be smokers. They could have an R-rated movie playing, or be doing a line of coke. I don't know why all the untoward things come to mind when thinking of someone's home who's not a Witness.

Maybe they're not doing any of that. Maybe they're relaxing at home, petting their dog and praying for world peace.

At any rate, that's not what we were told, warned and cautioned against. We were cautioned about all aspects of association with 'worldly' people; the basis being the oft-repeated warning of 1 Corinthians 15:33 - "...bad associations spoil useful habits" (the Witness Bible version of the text).

So I, with caution, go to Kitty's house to transact business, knowing I will get out of there as quickly as humanly possible when we're done.

I arrive at her home and I am shocked.

Not only is she not doing a line of coke, nor is she demonized, nor is she smoking, nor is she watching an R-rated movie on TV.

Not only is she NOT doing any of the things that would be reasonable proof of the belief that everyone who's not a Witness is wrong, it's what she IS doing that shocks me the most.

Her home is beautiful, well-kept and well-lit (a biggie for Witnesses, who believe evil festers in the darkness). It's clean, artfully and tastefully decorated and well arranged in decency and order. Most of all, the biggest thing I notice is the calm and peaceful air in the home (this is before I consciously know anything about mastering energy).

How could this be?!?!?

Yep, big hand out the sky, toppling my dominoes.

It was almost as if the big Voice was saying to me: "Valerie, you're too ignorant to go through life like this, we must expose you to the truth."

Funny thing, Witnesses call being a Witness being 'in the truth'. Everyone else is not in the truth. How ironic. I was, in my prideful opinion, in the truth. The reality of it was that I was living a lie. A pack of lies even.

Third brick. She was living life abundantly. She had money. She had resources. She was successful. Successful and happy and not a Witness? How could this be?!?!?

Brick four. She was a church member.

Let me explain.

For Witnesses, being a non-believer is almost better than being a member of a Church. At least non-believers have no false beliefs; they don't believe at all. The danger Witnesses warn against is the category of false religion — the leaven of the Pharisees — which they claim all the planet's religions fall into, the grouping Witnesses call Babylon the Great, (as spoken of in the book of Revelation) the world empire of false religion. This is an especially heinous place to be, for Witnesses, because it means such a one is in defiance of Jehovah God. As part of a world empire that is inherently evil, and that persecutes God's true chosen ones, they are headed for certain destruction, with no chance of redemption.

At least non-believers have a shot at redemption.

So for Kitty to be having the world at her fingertips, and enjoying all of its benefits, and clearly living blessed, and not be a Witness, and was actually a member of the world empire of false religion, it was almost too much for me to take.

And yet, I was intrigued. I was so intrigued by Kitty that I spent a lot of time around her... partly to see if there was a crack in her armor. If I could find the chink in the armor, I could stay safe in my comfy beliefs.

I was desperate for the dominoes not to start falling.

I also hung around her partly because something in me knew what she had was real and, truth be told, I wanted to find out how she had it without the Witnesses. How had she mastered the art of living free, joyful and be so blessed, by her own acknowledgment, and not be a Witness?

I had never seen her kind before, though I was a grown woman. The truth is, I had never let myself see her kind before now. Something in me would not abide another day of self-inflicted blindness.

I was baffled; almost didn't know what to do. Then I did what any good Witness would do when faced with clear evidence that what I believed was not true.

I went to my support system for an explanation. My mom was the person I chose to have the conversation with. She would understand my perplexity, and better still, she would have a perfectly good explanation, a reason for me to believe. She, of all people, would keep me safe and right.

When we had the conversation, brick 5 fell. I could hardly believe what I heard fall out of my mom's mouth, though I shouldn't have been surprised in the least. She said "Valerie, Satan blesses people, to keep them away from God."

To her, it was the perfect answer, it had a distinct that's-the-end-of-it quality. What? That's it? That's the answer? For her, the matter was no more significant than stepping on a roach.

It didn't sit well with me.

I didn't say anything then, I simply pulled further away. I knew Satan didn't bless people (even in the paradigm I held at the time). Something about that answer didn't satisfy, like having a craving and eating everything I can to satisfy it, but after each item I pop into my mouth I say *that ain't it*.

I was left empty, bereft.

It wasn't a good feeling. Especially when, for the better part of my life — which by then had been over 20 years — I had every answer I ever thought I would ever need and probably a few to spare. My head was crammed with answers.

Witnesses had answers for everything. Every possible scenario had an answer, a what-to-do, a logical Witness explanation along with what to do about it (proving the point that religion does not teach us how to think, it teaches us what to think).

To have walked around with a false cloak of certainty about everything for all those years, and now to be faced with an uncertainty about everything, was terrifying.

If the first domino falls, they're all falling. That's why I think we do everything in our power to protect that first domino from falling. We attack anyone who challenges our cherished beliefs. We know, deep down inside, that whatever needs protecting ain't the truth.

Besides, who wants to be suddenly thrust into the unknown?

For me now, that's what real faith is about. Not faith in a religion, that has to be proven by following every one of its doctrines to the letter.

No, that is not faith.

It is blind allegiance.

Faith in God is more about not knowing than about knowing. If I knew, why would I need faith? The unknown is the birthplace of true faith. The terrifying uncertainty we're all desperately trying to escape is a call to faith, deeper still.

Kitty is not an anomaly. She never was. My erroneous beliefs tried to seduce me into thinking she was, even though she was not, so I could be safe and right.

The universe doesn't care about me being safe and right. The universe cares about the exact opposite: for me to be ousted from my carefully prescribed comfort zones and walk faithfully in the mystery, the space of not knowing.

No. I do not need answers for everything. I only need to know where the answers are. They are in God. All of them. When I need to know something, I ask. Maybe I get the answer, maybe I don't. Maybe the answer is still on its way to me.

Either way, in the mean time and in between time, it's for me to walk in faith, and be uncomfortably comfortable with not knowing.

Thank you Kitty.

The Flag

I confess I always felt weird about not putting my hand over my heart or saying the pledge of allegiance during assembly in school. I felt equally uneasy, on the inside, at sporting events and everywhere it was considered important to pay homage to the United States of America and all for which it stands.

We weren't allowed to salute the flag.

We weren't allowed to speak the Pledge of Allegiance.

We weren't allowed to sing the national anthem.

The flag, we were taught, is a no-thing, not a thing at all, devoid of meaning. It is nothing. It's not that we hated the flag, or didn't like the flag, we were taught an abiding neutralism toward the flag and all things American, or all things nationalistic, for whatever country one happened to be born in.

Neutral. That was the Jehovah's Witness party line: we are neutral. We take no part in any of the worlds' affairs, good or bad. We don't join the armed forces of any country. We don't salute the flag of any country. We don't sing the national anthem of any country. We don't so much as raise a hair of patriotism toward any country, or ideal, or anyone.

Period.

Neutral is just a hair off from hate. Neutral means I don't stand on one thing or the other, I'm not necessarily for anything, yet I'm not necessarily for anything either.

I'm just sort of tepidly in the middle.

I say it's a hair off from hate because it's indifferent. Indifference is not compassion. Compassion is heated. Indifference is cold, calculated, a head thing. It's a hair from hate. It's the same energy that could turn a blind eye to a homeless person in the street or a person being mugged in the alley. Indifference makes it easy to pretend not to see, and thus easier to do nothing.

Yet the cold indifference is mitigated for Witnesses. There is the belief that God will make everything right, that God is judging all, and that the wicked will be bought to justice, and the righteous will eventually be vindicated. I cannot say I don't agree with this concept. It is true, eventually, everything will be proven to either be good or not so good. A tree is proven by its fruit.

Yet, the question is, do we wait, as bystanders, until God brings about a change, or are we responsible, as God-appointed custodians of this earth, to do something to create a just and loving society for all?

This is what takes the cold indifference to lukewarm neutrality. It would be cold to leave someone or something out of order, and not give it a second thought. To think that it will all be righted soon by God, warms the indifference to neutrality.

This is the great lukewarm pool Witnesses wade in... not hot, not cold, lukewarm. It makes getting heated over something really hard as a Witness. And in all the years I've been away from being a Witness, that insidious lukewarm tendency still shows itself at the edges of my consciousness.

Neutral, to me, is really not caring. It's an easy out. There are no outreach programs in the Witness world, other than preaching and teaching the gospel of Christ, as they understand it. They may, when disasters strike, request clothing and/or supplies for brothers and sisters in stricken areas, but only so they can be up and running spreading the gospel again as quick as possible.

Witnesses don't care what happens to governments. They don't vote. They don't get involved. To me, it is a bystander mentality. How are we to turn a blind eye to the hurts of the world, and do nothing politically or socially to create change?

We are waiting for God, when, in reality, God is waiting for us.

As I see it, the Witness party line, in essence, is: when Armageddon comes,

God will destroy everything that doesn't work. Until then, put up with it, keep your eyes on the kingdom, and ignore everything else.

Herein lies the challenge with this whole flag thing, and not being loyal to any country: people need to cluster. We are grouping beings by nature. We love to collect, to come together, especially around a cause, or something we care about. The fact that Witnesses create a culture within themselves of banding together in us-against-the-world style makes it that much more sticky, harder to leave. If you are cut off from allegiance to any group, country, race, heritage, culture or even family (if they do not believe as Witnesses do) and simultaneously you are inducted into a group that promises to love and take care of you, it's darn near irresistible.

There are people I know, who would not be Witnesses if it were not for the community. They don't want to be Witnesses, the don't really believe as Witnesses, yet, they have nowhere to go.

They've been convinced that every other group or tribe is wrong and not pleasing to God. That's a deep conditioning that makes it hard to not be a Witness anymore. The need for community, for support systems, for people around us who love us, may be the prime Witness tool in keeping people Witnesses even after the soul has beckoned them elsewhere.

Where else do we go?

We haven't made friends with people at work. We've avoided them. Now, do we all of a sudden become friends with people we've spent years saying no to? No, I won't be at the Christmas party... No, I won't be at the boss's birthday party... No, I won't be going to lunch with you today... No, I won't be coming over to your house.

We haven't made friends with our country. We don't even know what's going on in politics. Nor do we care. The first time I voted in a presidential election was for Bill Clinton, well after I had left the Witnesses. Not because I couldn't vote, or because I had consciously decided not to vote, I simply wasn't interested, as part of my past conditioning, in who was president. I didn't care. Unconsciously, I was still swimming in that great lukewarm pool of neutrality. Old habits die hard.

Years before I first voted, I had a voter registration card, obtained from answering 'yes' on papers at the motor vehicle administration when renewing my license one year. I had it, but I had never used it.

I take extreme pride in this country, America. Not because it is better than any other country. It is not. Of this I am clear and aware. I take pride in it because I believe in the ideals of our founding fathers, truth, justice, liberty and the pursuit of happiness for everyone. Corny as it may seem, I do believe that we are all born with certain unalienable rights. Even as those words were being penned, slaves were still being whipped under an almost unbearable yoke of suffering that lasted for centuries in this very country I love.

We ourselves have not held to our constitution. Which makes me that much more committed to living the constitution, to righting wrongs, to making a better world, starting with me.

When I contemplatively reflect on the hard-won freedoms the blood red of the flag represents for me and my people, I am aware I may be looking at a completely different symbol when I gaze at the very same flag my brethren look upon. Yet, it is a symbol, a symbol of freedom, liberty and justice. Even when we are not perfectly living up to it, or not living up to it at all, at least it is our ideal.

Yes, I love this country, and in no way am I lukewarm or ambivalent about the earth citizens of any and every country.

"Oh say can you see..." those words bring tears to my eyes, for I know they ring heavy with meaningful beauty to the race of humanity.

The presidents and would-be presidents of this country have a patriotic practice of ending every significant speech with "God bless America."

I say "God bless us all."

Sky God

As long as you believe in a sky god, your spirituality will be compromised.

I used to believe in a sky god. I was taught His name is Jehovah God, He lives in heaven, and no matter how good I am, or aspire to be, or how well I live, even if I live according to all the rules of the Bible, I will never see, meet up with, nor be in the presence of the sky god.

Never.

Ever.

I was taught He's too high above us to ever reach. His ways are unsearchable, who can know them? His thoughts are not our thoughts. Besides, in the Witness paradigm, only 144,000 are going to heaven, and I'm not one of them. So even if I die, I shall have no chance of ever seeing God.

I cannot thing of anything more hopeless.

There must be more to the God story than this.

I don't believe in a sky god any more. A sky god never did anything but smote, send pestilence, judge, maim, burn and drown, in addition to generally letting bad stuff happen to everybody, everywhere. What good is that? Let me be an atheist right now if that's what God is.

Now, I have an intimate, visceral, abiding, devoted, doting relationship with the Keeper of my soul, God within, the I AM THAT I AM, the immanent, eminent, imminent Guardian of my life and Sustainer of my every breath. The Creator and Sustainer of my life is closer to me than my "neck vein" as the Koran puts it. I love how the Koran puts it. YES! God is closer to me than my neck vein; not somewhere up in the sky.

This God I AM I love. This is no sky god.

We used to teach our children, when I was a Witness, that Jehovah God lived in heaven, and that heaven is an actual place. When we taught our children this doctrine, we taught them to point up to the sky when we asked where Jehovah God lives. When they complied, we applauded them with praise and adulation. Another child convinced of the sky god. We're doing our job.

For me, everything about that has changed. It took years for it to change, yet change it did.

Today, I teach my grand children that God lives within and they simultaneously, live, move, breathe and have their very existence in God. When I ask them where God lives, my prayer is that they point to their own hearts. I pray they never deny the knowing they came here with: that God is the fiber and essence of their being, the breath in their lungs, the power in their legs, the resident love energy pumping through their hearts. God is what they are made of.

No, there is no sky god for me any longer.

When I believed in a sky god, my spirituality was sorely compromised. How intimate could I get with an invisible being whom I will never meet, never get to see, never be in the presence of and whom I think committed the most shocking crimes against humanity? How could I fall deeply in love with a vengeful sky god that kills its own creation with impudence? What difference is there between that idea and a cannibal or a hungry polar bear father who eats his cubs? Not an endearing thought. Not only is it not endearing, it is impossible to fall in love with a god we fear.

We were taught the sky god was busy watching my every move, taking note of each thought, inclination and action in a really big book, tallying them all scrupulously. Eventually, the sum total of all the deeds I've done, and thoughts I've thought, will end in a pronouncement from the sky god that will either carry me into the favor of my Father, or into the realm of Satan the devil where everlasting death awaits (Witnesses do not believe in a burning hell for sinners, more on that later.)

No.

I do not believe in a sky god of any kind.

Sky gods are not helpful for spirituality, though they are immensely useful in religion.

If there is a sky god, and you or me, being lay people, members of the religion, can never get in touch with said deity, he residing high above our heads, we will always need someone (the keepers of the religion) or something (the religion itself) to connect us to the sky god. Sky god doctrine leaves no room for the average person to ever hope to connect with the divine in a meaningful, intimate way. It leaves us just a tad hopeless, or even worse, completely so, or, worst yet, resigned to a lot of never truly knowing God as present as He Himself informs us that He is: nearer than our very breath.

I never got that when I was a Witness. I never got the *realization* of God being closer to me than my breath.

Now, thankfully, I grow deeper in the understanding and realization of this truth every day, that God is my skin, my nails, my breath, my next divine idea, the hairs on my head and everything that comprises me.

I don't think I so much fought the idea of a sky god when I was there as I sort of filed it in a box labeled 'well, if they say that's how it is, that must be how it is.'

What's more, the people who make up doctrine always give a basis for why they are the ones who get to make up doctrine. It's like declaring yourself the boss then coming up with a reason that makes you the boss. If you believe it hard and strong and long enough, chances are you can get other people to believe it. The more people who believe it, the easier it will become for more people to believe it. Religion is born.

The ones in charge, the ones who are the self-proclaimed keepers of the sky god, have an 'in' that the rest of us don't have. They are privileged. Elite. They know and we don't. They have special entrance into places we don't. It's not surprising that the people who make up the doctrine are the people who tell you they have been specially set up by God to make up the doctrine and that disobeying them is tantamount to disobeying God.

I never heard God say this to me, though I've heard it from people (from the Pope to the Faithful and Discreet Slave) more times than I care to think about or remember.

This in no way implies disrespect of the Pope, or the Faithful and Discreet Slave. Both are regarded as the be-all-end-all authority for God by a group of religious people. While I respect the belief they hold, I decline to hold the belief that any person on this planet is more in touch with God for me than I am for me.

We must unplug from the Matrix.

The sky god doctrine is force-fed to initiates and adherents. It must be, as it is a linchpin for the rest of what Witnesses will attempt to get you to believe. It is taught, oft-repeated, and never challenged. It is the law of the Witness world: God lives in heaven. The vast majority of Witnesses have no hope of ever having an intimate experience of God, directly or personally. He's not meant to be a personal god. He's meant to be approached only through Christ. Though the doctrine of Jehovah God being a sky god is taught alongside the doctrine that one should always strive for a personal relationship with God through prayer, I wonder how the two can happen simultaneously. I don't know that they can. They never did for me.

Once belief in a sky god is locked firmly in place, the rest of the doctrine can be methodically installed. One would need an intermediary, a way of reaching the unreachable One. If he's a sky god, you'll need a ladder. The intermediary is Jesus Christ, the only way, as taught by Witnesses (and many other Christian denominations) to reach God. He is, after all, called in the Bible "the way, the truth and the light." What does that mean if not that he is the only way?

I love Jesus as much as the next person, that's for sure.

Yet, I also know that there are billions of people on this planet who do not at all subscribe to the Jesus doctrine. Some of them never heard of him. Others have heard of him and are just as convinced that their way is *the* way.

While Witnesses take it as their personal aim and mission to spread the 'good news' of Jesus Christ to every nook and cranny of the world, and have devised organized systems for methodical precision in execution of this aim, I am not on board with the teaching that everybody must accept Jesus as Lord and Savior in order to be in God's favor.

Even after all my years as a Christian.

I think my turning point came when I went to Hawaii in 2004 to marry my then sweetheart.

Shortly after checking into the magnificent Halekulani resort, I did what I always do when I check into a hotel: pull open the nightstand drawer looking for — and fully expecting to find — the Gideon Bible. It's okay if I see other books in the nightstand drawer too, like a phone book, or a book that tells me about the town I'm in, or a booklet about the local eateries and sights. As long as I see a Gideon Bible in addition to whatever else is there in the nightstand drawer, I'm good. I can sleep well while I'm there. I may never pick up that Gideon Bible. Opening the drawer and seeing it there is enough for me. I usually close the drawer after discovering the Bible and settle into my hotel room with a strange sense of safety and comfort, feeling a little more eased and at home. *The Gideons were here*, I think, *they did their job, they put a Bible in here, I can go to sleep now, resting soundly.*

To my shock, dismay and horror, not only did I not find a Gideon Bible in the nightstand drawer when I slid it open for my usual investigation, I found something completely unexpected.

Something I had no idea would change my life forever.

Something I could have never predicted I'd come across, nevertheless, something my soul was more than ready for me to come across.

It was the holy book *The Teachings of Buddha*.

WHAT??!?

No Gideon Bible!?!?!?!

Who's responsible for this?!?!?!?

What kind of hotel is this anyway?!??!?

I thought it was one of the best in the world!!!! Obviously, I'm mistaken!!! How can I sleep soundly in this place?!??!

I slump down on the bed next to the nightstand that holds the strange contents in its top drawer, shocked, taken aback, miffed even.

I look at it.

Then I think to myself, *I'm in another country. Up until then, I thought Hawaii was part of the United States. They call it a state. We all agreed. It was signed and dated, and it was done. But now I see that's just not true. I am not in the United States of America at all. I am in another land. I am in strange territory, alien territory, where people do not believe in Bibles.*

This is what I tell myself.

I feel so far from home. More thoughts race to my mind in the form of questions...

How could this be?

How can all these people sleep in this hotel without Bibles? And who told them they could just replace the Bible with whatever they felt like putting in the drawer? Is there a protocol? A vote? A democratic way of putting holy books in hotels? And who took it upon themselves to decide that the Gideons were wrong?

This was all way too much for my mind to wrap itself around.

Which is why, when I slump dejected, shocked and horrified onto the bed, thankfully, a deeper heart wisdom takes over, gently whispering in my ear, *pick it up.*

Shocking and horrifying as it may be, I must confess the book is appealing to look at, I think to myself, it has the most beautiful picture of a sunrise on the cover that I may have ever seen on the cover of a book.

Pick it up.

As my hand stretches out toward the drawer to take hold of the renegade replacement, the judgments in my head do back flips and yell in a thunderous and tumultuous inner command: *WHATEVER YOU DO, DO NOT TOUCH THAT BOOK! I REPEAT: DO NOT TOUCH THAT BOOK!*

The loud voice is always the rogue one.

The still small voice is always pointed, and pointing, in one direction: true north.

I decide to go with the quieter voice, coming from a distant place deep in my soul, a place I may not have, up until that point, visited often. A place now poised to take a forward position in my consciousness. I call this place *unconditional love-acceptance-non-judgment.*

In a word: Compassion.

Wow. I am having a first hand experience with non-judgment. Non-judgment had spoken about the book, softly and surely, urging me to simply *pick it up*.

Could I? Could I betray the Bible like this? What about my tribe? What if they found out? What about the man I was about to marry, the devout Baptist, what would he say? This is heresy.

I push past the loud voices and pick up the renegade replacement. I look at the back then flip it open, part scared, part bewildered, part curious, part skeptical, part indignant, part open.

The open part wins.

Thank you God.

The first thing I notice about the renegade replacement is that the pages are thin, white leaves, just like the Bible.

At that precise moment, one of the louder judgment voices makes her presence more than known with the loud declaration, *I hope they don't think this is as good as the Bible. IT'S NOT.*

Ok voices, I hear you, but you'll have to stop screaming if I'm going to read this book and hope to get anything out of it.

Thankfully, I knew enough to silence the big voices and side with the still small one.

I read on.

And on.

And on.

Suffice it to say, coming up on a decade after making that shocking discovery in a Hawaii hotel room, I still have that book. Yes, I lifted it out of the hotel and took it home with me, just like one would help themselves to a Gideon Bible, if one really needed it. *The Gideons would understand.* This book had a similar note in its front, that if I felt compelled to take it with me, I was more than welcome to do so, and if I would be so kind as to send a small check to cover the cost of getting another one to the next beleaguered soul who would make their way into that very same hotel room, it would be much appreciated. There is, however, as with all holy books, no obligation.

Don't you just love people who leave holy books in hotel rooms?

When I got back home, where my checkbook was, I wasn't at peace until I got a check into the mail to the kind people who had left that book for me. Though I don't think the check ever got cashed, I read every word in that book. Several times. It's one of my most cherished holy books.

Back to Hawaii. After picking up the book, and reading one or two pages, I was hooked.

That holy book became my new traveling companion. My traveling companion up until I saw the book in the nightstand had been my sweetheart. He and I were together. He and I had come together. He and I were there to get married, and he and I would leave together.

All that happened, as planned.

But something else happened that I hadn't planned: I got a new traveling companion. The book went everywhere with me, even to places my human traveling companion didn't.

While we were away, it went with me to the swimming pool, to the beach, on drives we took to the far reaches of the Hawaiian island of Oahu, and with us on the Hawaiian cruise we honeymooned on the week after our stay at the Halekulani, the ship that sailed us to Kauai, Maui, the Big Island and Kona. In the moments when my sweetheart wasn't with me, the book was. In a sense, the book become a closer companion than him. While I still have the book, he and I have long since gone our own ways.

How could sliding a drawer open so change my life?

There's more.

How could the book replace not only the Bible, put a whole person?

My husband-do-me was not happy about it. He asked, with a bit of agitation around the edges, but never outright mean, "when are you going to put that book down? Do you have to take it everywhere?" He may have sensed a change was under way.

As I reflect on it, I was having a soul opening experience in Hawaii; me, that book and the still small voice. Hawaii was the perfect healing context in which this could unfold, a place that opened my spirit, arrested my senses, stilled some of the bigger voices enough for me to connect with the still small one, and caused me to know, beyond any shred of doubt, that God has spots on this earth She has kissed.

Yes, the healing context of Hawaii melted my edges, opened me deeply, got me to drop defenses, constructs, and preconceived notions on how things should be and my indignation when they were not that way just enough for Spirit to slip in *The Teachings of Buddha*.

On a deeper level still, Hawaii, my soul and spirit, and *The Teachings of Buddha*, all conspired to wean me, once and for all, from the flawed and limited belief that Jesus is the only way to God.

While he is *a way*, he is not *the only way*.

I discovered for myself, more deeply than ever before, that we make direct connect with God right where we are, where ever that is, whether it be from, or on, a mountain top, or in the ocean wave lapping up over my foot on the beach, or in a bird singing outside the window, or in a cockroach and how it lands, or in a leaf falling from the tree in autumn, or in a snowflake, or a lake, or a blade of grass.

All of us can reach God anywhere, at any time, in anything, with anyone, and without it all too.

Why?

Because God is in us, and we in God. God is imminent. God is reachable. God is touchable. God is here now. God is omnipresent. God is in the mountain, and at the mountain top. God is in the lava flowing from the mountain top. God is the wave lapping up over my foot on the beach. God is the bird singing to me outside my window. God is the cockroach, and the snowflake and the leaf and the lake and the blade of grass.

God is all. All is God. God is in all. All is in God.

There's not a spot where God is not.

This was my revelation.

I have not pointed up at a sky god since.

7 Days With the Goddess

I confess I'm an Ocean witch.

When I have a tangly problem I can't make heads or tails of, I go to the Ocean.

When I'm at my wits end, I go to the Ocean.

When I want or need that particular brand of inspiration in wave and water form, I go to the Ocean.

When I want to feel better, rejuvenate and remember myself, I go to the Ocean.

And when I want to do nothing at all, I go to the Ocean, one of my favorite do-nothing places on the planet.

In the middle of the manifestation of the funding for Diva House, our new home, I feel pulled to the Ocean. I happen to be living right now in Ocean City, 3 short blocks walk from the Ocean.

When I feel the pull, I go.

I walk over, on a breezy, 50-something-ish degrees November morning. I get close and hear the roar.

She's roaring loudly today I think, louder than I think I may have ever heard her roar before; I can hear her from a good block away.

Maybe she always roars like that, and I hadn't paid attention, or didn't hear the roar above summer fun, babies crying, children's footfalls on boardwalk wood and grown-ups unloading cars.

This morning, her roar is loud, and I hear all of it. I can drink it in.

I walk over across the boardwalk, straight onto the sand. I don't know what I'm about to do, only that I'm answering the call to the Ocean. I'm on a mission, so I restrain myself from getting distracted by all the curious looking seashells on the sand, the ones I would normally go through for intriguing specimens that I would take home to add to my ever growing collection of Ocean oddities.

No time for that now. I'm not here to collect shells. I'm here to answer the call to the Ocean.

I look up the beach to my left and see not a soul. I look as far in the opposite direction, all the way to the impressive Ferris wheel, not a soul in that direction either.

I am completely alone.

There's a shell, really close to the water's edge, that's different from the others. It's almost like this shell is looking at me, expecting me to pick it up. I bend over and oblige it.

A step or two beyond that, just before reaching the dark, curvy line in the sand that marks the whereabouts of the last wave that sloshed in, I remember that I don't have an offering for the Goddess.

I go closer to the water's edge.

I feel led to start praying, something there has inspired me, so I begin yelling out loud:

"Yemaya! Yemaya! This is your daughter! You know I'm your daughter! I need you! I need your bounty to flood my life! I need your abundance to flood my life! I need you! This is your daughter! I need your nurturing to flood my life! I need your abundance to flood my life! Your abundance to flood my life!"

Somewhere in the prayer I involuntarily toss the shell in the water, asking her if she would accept it as my offering back to her of the gifts she had given.

Then I got down on my hands and knees to prepare for an answer.

There was a loud roar, a huge wave was coming, bigger than all the others. I almost started to stand and run, but something held me still. It washed up on my feet and pants.

She said to wash my hands, face and feet in the Ocean water.

I did.

The water feels freezing to me. Then I confess how afraid I've been. How afraid I am of living my path and calling as a priestess, how afraid I've been of my own power, and that I'm not willing to live afraid, not even one minute more.

"I'm ready!" I yell. "Ready to live my path as a Yoruba priestess!"

She smiles. She tells me to come back every morning for 7 days. I agree. (Here are passages from my journal during 7 Days With the Goddess).

Day 2 – Wednesday, November 21, 2012

Today, I know to bring an offering. When I left the beach yesterday, I made a conscious decision to never again come to the Ocean empty-handed.

I have an apple from Panera Bread. Normally I take a second or two of deliberation when ordering, between apple and chips, the proverbial angel on one shoulder, devil on the other. I know I'm supposed to be eating the apple, but I want the chips. There was no deliberation when ordering this time around, only a sudden and swift response: "apple".

Apple it was.

I didn't get to eat the apple then. I didn't know then the apple wasn't for me; it was for the Goddess.

It dawned on me later, call me a slow learner, it settles in eventually.

So I have my fresh apple firmly in hand, ready for my meeting with Yemaya this morning.

I walk directly across the boardwalk out onto the sand like before, but unlike yesterday, there are people on the beach, one or two souls scattered here and there.

I feel pulled to the rocks, jutting out into the Ocean, so I head there without hesitation or delay, both of which signal fear and have never been my friend.

The one thing I've learned from working with subtle energies is trust, to trust what I'm receiving, to trust and move forward in the direction I'm being led/guided to or in, and to not hesitate.

He who hesitates is lost.

I get closer to the rocks and just before approaching, I hear to wash my hands, face and feet again with the Ocean water. I kick off my Nike's, I have on no socks today, and walk close to the dark line in the sand. The waves come in, but they're nowhere near me. I walk further out, still no water. I go further still, and nothing.

Finally, I go well past the dark line toward the Ocean bidding her to give me enough water to wash with, and here comes a wave, all of a sudden, that rushes toward me, laps me up and my pants and washes completely over my empty sneakers that I've left several feet behind me.

"You got me!" I laugh hysterically, not knowing why.

In that moment I learn the Ocean is a Temptress.

On my way over, I feel the presence in the Ocean treasures under my feet of mermaids and sirens, the beautiful temptresses of the Ocean, none other than the daughters of the great Temptress herself.

She got me.

After getting over my laughing fit, I wash my hands, face and feet. This time, I open my mouth and the sweet salty taste of ocean water tickles my tongue.

I pick up my shoes in my right hand and approach the rocks. I step up on the first one and feel my feet go cold. They're freezing. In a second, I start praying, and instantly, my feet start warming up, on their own. Nothing's changed about the environment, or the rocks, or the weather, but my feet are comfy and warm, though still completely bare in November on the face of a black slab of rock.

My prayer today is: "Thank you! Thank you! Thank you! Thank you! Thank you! Thank you!"

I spread out my arms to the left and right. I feel so good, better than I've felt in I don't know how long. I feel amazing. It's a miracle. I look up at the sky and continue the prayer:

"Thank you! Thank you! Thank you!"

The scene and everything about it is glorious.

It is heaven on earth.

She bids me closer. I walk across the rocks, gentile and steady in my steps, to be sure to stay upright. The rocks I'm on at first are dry and solid. The closer I get to the Ocean, the wetter the rocks, and I sense they're slippery, though I don't detect any slipperiness under my feet. I'm solid.

The closer I get to the Ocean, the more I'm aware that I'm in territory I've never covered before, and the thought comes to me that I could slip and fall and conk myself out on these rocks. If anybody found me, they wouldn't even know who I was, I have no identification on me, and no wallet. I dismiss those thoughts. Fear rises up in the form of trepidation about going farther. I get to the middle of the rock outcropping and another huge wave comes in, this one splashes me and the rocks. It's like a kiss from the Ocean. I go farther, seeing the rock She's calling me to, it's way out there, in my mind.

She's clear that she wants me to come sit on it and talk with her. I don't quite make it that far. I get close, really close, but these rocks are wetter and farther apart than they were a few steps ago, more jagged and more perilous looking to cross. Not to mention they're covered with green furry stuff. I opt not to go all the way out.

I about-face and feel a sense of relief.

I feel that the Ocean let me out of coming to the rock today, that I'll make it one day. On my exit, I look down and see a shell with a tiny baby shell right behind her, almost like it's on her back, both wedged between the rocks. I get the guidance to pick them up. I reach down and wriggle the two shells free and cradle them in the palm of my hand for inspection. I hear: "mother and daughter", which means a lot to me considering that my mother and I are somewhat estranged and me and my daughter are also experiencing more separation than we ever have before. (Little did I know then that my mother was nearing the end of her earthly life and would pass on in just a few short weeks.)

Hmmmmmmm.

Back on the sand, I brush my warm feet off and slide them into my wet sneakers to leave. When I reach the boardwalk, there's a white cat there, to my left, staring at me with pink eyes. She doesn't move an inch, to the right or to the left, she's frozen, arrested, right there, in the middle of the boardwalk, staring at me, deeply into my eyes. I feel something. I keep walking. Her gaze doesn't shift. She follows my every move with her eyes.

I wonder why she's looking at me like she's seen a ghost. I wonder why she doesn't move. I wonder if the Goddess has shape-shifted into a cat. I wonder how I know the cat is female.

I don't know what the white haired, pink-eyed cat does after I leave.

P.S. - I get the inkling to put the shells under my pillow when I go to sleep that night. I do, and sleep like a baby.

Day 3 – Thursday, November 22, 2012 – Thanksgiving Day

It's Thanksgiving morning and I'm at the beach, romping around with Yemaya. She's beautiful. The sky is clear, and I remember, again, that I have no offering.

Before approaching the water's edge, I take off my shoes and pick up several choice baby shells and ask her if she would accept them as my offering. I toss them in the Ocean before I pray.

I re-commit to not ever coming to the Ocean empty-handed.

My prayer is *thank you*. Simply *thank you*. *Thank you for my home. Thank you for this man. Thank you for my gifts. Thank you.*

The Miracle Zone

I'm in New York, visiting family, on the heels of finding out my Mom has passed on. It happened on a Saturday, in January, and with her wish to be cremated, I spent the day after on an emotional roller coaster between thoughts of her not being here and thoughts of her body being burned in a fire. Every time that image flashed in my head, it was almost unbearable. Thankfully, as grace would have it, that image no more popped into my head than once or twice, and after that, I was in the weepy place for her, her life and all it meant.

I don't even know if that's true. I don't think we weep for the dead so much as we weep for ourselves, the ones left here to carry on where that soul left off, and wondering how we're going to do that.

So here I am in New York, really happy to be here, and feeling so much better now that several days have passed since the news.

Mom was sick for a while, so I cannot say it was a surprise. It was not. It was not expected right then; still, it was no surprise.

My finances are doing something interesting right now and I'm watching. Watching how my life is always abundant, with everything I need, and then some. Every day it's that way, thanks to God in heavenly consciousness. The work I've been doing for years around building and maintaining an abundance consciousness has finally paid off.

Even still, when looking at the 3rd dimensional plane, I become aware that I want more money. I don't ever have this feeling when I'm looking within. When I'm there, there's only abundance, nothing missing, pure paradise. When I look outside of me, at bank accounts and pieces of paper that randomly, and sometimes not so randomly, show up in the mail, I think, *I really want more money.* In those moments, it seems more money would make so much difference in my life. I wonder about that. Would it really? Would things really be so different with lots more money? Maybe not so much. Money isn't creating my reality; I am. With that said, I do notice that I always have the money I require to do what's before me in any given moment, my life has taken on a sort of Jesus manifesting quality, and I'm not mad about that, that's for sure. That Jesus manifesting quality is exactly what I prayed for, thinking and sensing that it was the answer to life on the 3rd dimension and living it richly. Just do it like Jesus did. He seemed to have everything he wanted, with plenty to spare and share. He didn't seem to ever concern himself about what he was going to wear or eat or sleep. He made it up as he went along, and being the master he was, what he made up was pretty darned good.

Yes, I'll have that, that Jesus way of manifesting things, like extra fish and loaves when everybody's hungry, or a home to stay in that night, or figs on a tree or a glass of wine. Whatever. It doesn't really matter the nature of the manifestations, all things coming from the same space in the universe, the No-thing-ness, formed and shaped according to the patterns we're holding in consciousness.

We're literally squeezing energy through the portal of our consciousness, and consciousness being shaped one way or the other, squeezes our 3rd dimensional reality into some form or shape, always according to the mold we're holding in mind.

I figure if I can get my consciousness more closely in the mold of Jesus' consciousness, I should be good to go. Everything I require to live my destiny on this 3rd dimension will show up, and indeed it does. And much more than what I require. A whole lot of what I desire shows up too, in addition to what I need, which is quite the juicy part.

Which almost makes me not know what to do with money. On the one hand, it's a wonderful energy, God in motion. On the other hand, something in me knows I don't need it to receive what I truly desire. My heart's desires and all of what my life requires show up, whether I have money or not. So

I guess it's safe to say that money is an entity not unlike all other forms of beneficial energy, the more, the better. And I would also venture to say that it is a tool, a very beneficial one, that can be used for immense good. And, like any other tool, it's effectiveness in making life better for self and others largely depends upon the tool-bearer. You can take a hammer and build a house for you and your family, or you can take it and clock someone on the head with it and spend the rest of your born days behind bars. Such is the nature of tools, they depend almost entirely upon the user for the outcome. Money, being no different than any other tool, can be used to feed a village in an underdeveloped nation or it can be used to buy another line of coke. You get to choose.

I also see money as a magnifying glass. To me, it just magnifies who you really are. If you're broke, and we ask you for $50, chances are, you may say no. We may attribute your 'no' to broke-ness, but maybe your 'no' really is stinginess. Later, you get a windfall and it's become common knowledge that you have money, loads of it. We put forth the same request, and the answer is 'no', not because you don't have it, but because you didn't want to share it. More money just magnified who you are.

Money doesn't change people. It shows us who we really are. The more money you have, the more magnified it becomes, by how you use the tool, who you are, and what's important to you.

No judgments.

Just awareness.

Christ said where your treasure is, there your heart will be also.

So when I look at my money situation in the days leading up to the trip to New York, I wonder how it's all going to come together. There is money in my accounts, thank God, yet I wonder, as I said earlier when I look at 3rd dimensional reports, if it's going to be enough.

I'm on the Eastern Shore of Maryland, and I need to get to New York City, which, to me, seems no easy feat without a car. Yet I know I'm taking public transportation, and I'm fine with that. I go online and start looking around, mapping out, what I think, is the very best way to undertake this mission, with elegance (the least amount of effort, with the greatest results/rewards) excellence (my very best) and abundance (more resources than I need, overflow).

I decide to hop on the $3 bus from Ocean City to Salisbury, where I'll hop on another bus for $3 to the Salisbury bus station, where I'll pick up the Greyhound bus to Annapolis. From there, I'll hop on another $3 bus to the Annapolis Mall, where there's a regular shuttle (for $5) to the New Carollton Metro Station, where, for about $4, I can catch the Metro to Union Station, where I'll board a Megabus to New York for about $16.

I thought I had it all figured out. I thought I had the best possible route mapped out, for the best possible pricing. I've done these steps before, not altogether, but in increments, so it's not completely unfamiliar.

The day comes and I pray, thankfully, for a magickal day, filled with miracles, with me living solidly in the miracle zone.

Make it happen Angels.

I leave and to my surprise, there's snow everywhere. There's a veritable blanket of white, so beautiful, so hushed, that it almost elicits tears. Serene. Still. Fresh. Crisp. This is a snowy morning on the beach. Not so bad, except that I'm walking about a mile to the bus stop. I walk all the time, more than a mile at a time, so it probably would have been an easy feat on a good weathered day.

This was not a good weathered day.

I trudge through snow pulling my wheeled luggage behind me amid gently settled piles of snowflakes, an occasional car, and the obligatory snow trucks, brushing snow to the side with one sweep, and spewing salt with another.

I walk to the bus.

I'm there early, the bus leaves at 7:58 AM. It's 7:55. Yes, I timed this perfectly. The fleeting moment of feeling proud of my early morning accomplishment ended when I didn't see the bus, called the dispatcher and got the news that the buses were behind schedule.

Hmmmmmmmmm, did I pray for miracles?

Yes, I did, I remind myself.

Finally, the bus comes. I'm happy. It's warm. I hop on, pay my $3 fare and ask about a transfer for the next bus.

"No, we don't give transfers for that bus" the driver informs me.

"Ok." I was getting ready to mutter a complaint to myself when another passenger on the bus said "You can walk to the Greyhound bus station, that's where I'm going, it's only about a 10 minute walk."

"Thank you!"

With that, I sit down with a smug look on my face. I just manifested $3.

We get off at Salisbury and the other passenger takes off ahead of me. I follow him. Trudging through the snow is not fun, but seconds after I start out, I see a crisp, new $20 bill in the snow in my path.

YES!!!! I scoop it up swiftly, happy as a clam, and stuff it in my pocket.

YEP, it's a magickal day alright!

I give a wink and nod to the Angels.

We get to the Greyhound. It's cold outside, biting cold. In New York when I was growing up, the old people used to say "the hawk is out!" I remember looking up every time I went outside after listening to those old people, for a glimpse at this very elusive, may even invisible, hawk. I never saw him.

Well, on this morning, the hawk is out.

But no worries, right on time, at a few minutes to 10:00 AM, a Greyhound bus pulls up.

Funny thing, the bus sign says New York. Hmmmmm, this bus is supposedly headed for Annapolis. Something in me says "You're going to New York, aren't you?"

Yes! Out of the cold and on to a nice warm bus.

I gather with the other expectant passengers around the bus, eager to get the luggage in the belly and us on board, in the warmth, when I find out this is not my bus.

"This bus is going to New York, not Annapolis. Your bus will be along soon." the driver announced.

Feeling a little dejected about standing in the cold a little longer, me and my luggage slink back to the outside bus shelter to fend off the hawk for a few more minutes.

The bus driver gets all his rightful passengers on board, who are going where he's going, then he sits there for a few minutes.

Soon after, he gets off his bus, comes over to us and says, "I hate to be the bearer of bad news..."

I don't do bad news is the thought that runs through my mind.

"but your bus is not coming, it's broke down in Ocean City."

Now here's the magickal part....

When making my reservations, something told me not to pick that bus up in Ocean City, but to pick it up in Salisbury, the next town over. It's the very same bus.

Now it makes sense.

Then the next magickal thing happened.

He continues, "I don't know when the next bus is coming, and I don't want to leave you out here in the cold, so I'll take you to Wilmington, Delaware. It's the next bus depot, and they can work out something for you there."

Yep, that sounds like a winner, even though I already know this bus is taking me all the way to New York.

I love the miracle zone.

Sure enough, we get to Wilmington, Delaware, and when I ask the driver about my ticket, he and I having become chatting chums on the road, my front seat positioning having given him the golden opportunity to regale me with stories from his bus driving 'you'll never believe this' collection, answered me with a "don't worry about it."

Miracle number 3 – he has yet to ask for any ticket from me, though I have one, it certainly isn't one all the way to New York, which is my destination.

It turns out that the Angels got me to New York straight away, without having to take the other $3 bus in Annapolis, nor the $5 shuttle, nor the $4 metro ride, nor the Megabus.

They conveniently cut out multiple steps, several dollars, several hours of time, excess energy and attention. I did ask for elegance.

I was in New York lickety-split, straight from Salisbury on the Eastern Shore.

The funny thing about it is, I never even knew there was a bus that went to New York from those parts.

Go figure. The universe knows so much more than I do, and even when I'm off in the bushes, actually trying to make plans, that seem somewhat good to me, if not ideal, it never fails, the Universe has a better, faster, more elegant, more abundant way to do it.

Thank God.

So here I am, riding happily to New York, which is what I wanted in the first place.

We arrive safely, and I'm richer for the experience, since I've made a new friend, and have been introduced to the world of the bus driver, who lives in Norfolk, Virginia with his wife, after 20 years in the Navy, and 3 more years to go before retiring from this job, which he held as a childhood dream, growing up in the South, that he was going to drive one of those buses one day, the very same buses that he dare not, back then, sit in the front of. He actually proclaimed to himself, as a little boy, that he would one day drive one of those buses.

And here he is.

In New York, I go to the ladies room, then head to the subway station to take the #1 train uptown to my Mom's block. I'm staying with my brother, who lives up the street from Mom and Dad, on 158th Street between Broadway and Amsterdam.

I stand in front of the giant machines in the subway station almost not knowing what to do. How much is the fare? I haven't done this in so long I don't even know what buttons to press.

Something in me nudges me to move over.

Not so much in a voice as in a general feeling of this-is-not-where-I'm-supposed-to-be-let-me-move. I move to the next machine.

No, this is not it either.

Finally, I move to a machine clean on the other side. The second I position myself in front of the machine to study its workings in an attempt to find out what I'm supposed to to, a man comes up to me on the left. He's speaking in such a thick Hispanic accent that I almost don't understand him at first. I apologetically tell him I don't speak Spanish. He presses his point.

"This is unlimited card, I finished, you can have"

I make out that he's giving me an unlimited fare card that he's done with for the day.

Miracle zone.

"Thank you! Thank you very much!"

The more thankful I am, the more things the universe gives me to be thankful for.

I receive the fare card, swipe it and walk through to the train platform.

I still can't tell you how much the fare is. I guess I don't really need to know.

I hop on the train.

A word about trains in New York: they are interesting, entertaining, lively and usually packed.

First I hear a marine who announces, "Ladies and gentlemen, I'm a United States Marine..." the rest gets drowned out by the churn on the train engines, but my guess is that he's pitching for money.

Then something unusual happens.

We pull into a train station where I see an unusual fellow, wearing a royal blue and gold Mardi Gras mask, a black Fedora, a fleece blue jacket with a multi-print miniskirt, fishnet stockings, black ankle socks and a pair of Nike Air Jordan's on his feet, pushing a colorful suitcase on 4 wheels and playing a Ukelele.

I promise I'm not making this up.

He steps onto the train amid gentle smirks, smiles and eye-brow raises. Nothing really strange for the New York City subway, just your very run-of-the-mill humorous loon.

He gently strums his Ukelele as we pull out of the station. At some point, I expect that he's going to hit us up for some change or something, except he never does. He just strums his Ukelele. That's apparently all he wanted to do, provide us with a little gentle background music, that we could barely make out above the train engines, to soothe us at the end of a day.

How nice of him.

I smile at the judgments in me that want to call him crazy or strange or the part of me that just wonders what happened to him and what would come over a person to make them put that get up on and walk out the house. Not two of the things he had on actually went together. Well, maybe the Mardi Gras mask and the fishnet stockings, on a good day, or a bad night, you decide.

The non-judgmental aspect of me knew that there was something in him that told him to do what he's doing, and there's not a thing wrong with that part of him, or him. He's doing exactly what he thinks he should be doing. Who am I to judge?

That little release from judgment of my friend in fishnets is my next miracle. Non-judgment is a miracle, especially when we consider the almost compelling urge of the ego mind to judge everything and everyone.

I arrive at the 157th Street station, button up and go outside, where the next miracle unfolds.

I look down and see a penny on the street. I get so happy! Pennies are my messages from Angels, they mean everything is good, that I'm right where I'm supposed to be, they're a cosmic YES.

I scoop up the penny.

Yes, life is good, especially when lived squarely in the miracle zone.

Ridiculous Faith

A big part of magick is *knowing*.
Not just believing.
Knowing.

Knowing, to the core of your soul, that your magick is working, that your word is the power to create and that it goes forth and does what you say it will, that your will, set into motion, activates supernatural forces that most certainly bring intentional results, every time.

If you are to be a magician, you must *know*.

If you are to successfully practice magick, you must *know*.

If you are to successfully manifest, you must *know*.

Which is where it gets tricky for humans. No matter how many miracles God has done for us, and no matter how many times we've been saved by grace, there's something in us that says it may not happen the next time.

Somehow, when we're faced with the ferocious issues of life, we think this one won't be solved, even though all the other ferocious issues of life we've ever met with somehow got solved. Every single one.

Still, something in us tells us it might not happen this time.

We think that the particular thing we're facing is somehow different, or worse than before, or nothing like we've ever seen before, which engenders fear, worry and doubt.

As far as I can tell, worry has no redeeming value.

Fear has some redeeming value, it informs me when I've reached my personal edge and bids me to stay safely in the bounds of what I know. At least fear has a purpose, several purposes really, one of which is not to do something stupid to throw my life away needlessly.

That's helpful. So for the alarm-sounding properties of fear, I am grateful.

Doubt is the devil, if there be one. It robs us of every dream we could ever hold, and leaves us bereft of hope. No, doubt is not helpful, it is most unhelpful.

Worry, when viewed side by side with fear and doubt, is the most needless thing in the world. At least fear is helpful at times, if nothing but an early warning system, and though doubt be the devil, it is not entirely useless, as it shows us where to bolster our faith. Worry, on the other hand, is never warranted, period. Which makes it completely useless. There is absolutely no redeeming value to worry. There is never anything helpful that will come of it or from it. It is altogether problematic to everything that's beneficial to you.

With that said, it would behoove us to have at our ever ready disposal spiritual practices guaranteed to move us out of the energies of fear, worry and doubt as swiftly as we notice we're in them.

For me, the tried and true spiritual practice is FAITH.

RIDICULOUS FAITH. For me, that means that the conscious mind will protest that the faith I'm walking in is just ridiculous. It will scream in vain attempts to get me to look at 'reality' and it will try to convince me to stay safe. As I approach the edge of my comfort zone, the protest becomes deafening loud. The alarm sounds: DANGER! DANGER! DANGER! I've found that the second my conscious mind says my faith is ridiculous, is the precise moment I know I am going in the divine direction.

RIDICULOUS FAITH.

There's no substitute, and there's no thing you can practice that can do for you what Faith will do for you. There is nothing more required of you than your absolute, unwavering, rock solid, ridiculous faith in the Supreme within you, and all of what that entails. Think about it, God made it really simple for us, have faith. Period. That's really what the whole Bible is about.

Have Faith that God is.

Have Faith that God becomes what you seek.

Have Faith that God is active and alive in you and is doing it (whatever 'it' is.)

Have Faith that God loves you and couldn't not love you.

Have Faith that right now God is cooking up something so delicious for you, it will astound you when it shows up, even though you've been asking for it.

Have Faith that there's nothing in your life that could ever appear that God could not conquer on your behalf.

Have Faith that nothing in the universe is more powerful than the power you have inside you.

Have Faith that no matter what your 5 senses tell you, you're really alright, and you're always going to be alright.

Have Faith that nothing is impossible with God.

Have Faith that God will do it.

Have Faith that God will see you through.

Have Faith that you are never alone.

Have Faith that life is incredibly FOR you.

Have Faith that all the stuff in your life that you don't understand will one day make sense, or you'll make peace with it not making sense.

Have Faith that all your dreams and desires are registered in the universe and that the universe is right now contriving the best possible way to deliver them all to you, harmoniously.

Have Faith that all you have to do is have Faith, and the way will be shown.

Then have Faith in the Way that is shown.

That's really all we have to do to live magickal. Have a rock-solid, never wavering, never faltering, deep and abiding Faith... in God and all God can do and is doing, in us, through us, and as us.

If you have Faith the size of a mustard seed, you're good to go. I'm sure you could muster that much if you really tried. And if you knew how incredibly important it is to manifesting everything you've ever wanted, you'd find a way to muster it now.

Proof

This story is intended to provide proof that your magickal path is paved for you by Spirit, step by precious step, moment by moment, without fail, always with your highest and best good and the highest and best good of all as the reason and purpose.

You never have to be concerned about what steps to take, or when, or with who.

You only have to trust that the next steps will always be revealed to you. The path of the solitary witch may have taught me this lesson deeper than any other walk I've had with Spirit.

When I was a Jehovah's Witness, there wasn't much left to wonder about. Everything was planned out. My spiritual practices were given to me by somebody else. My time was scheduled by somebody else. It was told to me what my next steps were at any given time. First, have a home Bible study, to learn the 'truth'. Next, answer the 80 questions in the book with the elders and see if you are ready to get baptized. Next, get baptized. Next, expand my service to auxiliary pioneer or full time pioneer.

There was nothing left to my own soul and spirit. It was all planned out for me in a carefully scripted religious code that did not abide non-compliance.

When leaving traditional religion behind to follow the heart and beat of one's own soul, there's no blueprint, no plan of action, no clearly defined pattern of steps to take.

It's all being created new and fresh, you in concert with the divine, especially for you, especially for your magickal walk, especially for your soul's journey and all it must learn, discover, know and heal through. It's all new. No one gets to make up your walk with spirit but you.

This can be a scary place for some.

I heard something alarming years ago that stuck with me: that 97% of people need written or oral instructions daily.

For the most part, people don't know what to do with themselves.

We need to be told what to do. This is true. We want to be told what to do.

The question is: by whom?

We could let religion tell us what to do, or we could choose to be guided by the Inner Voice that is both our essence and core. You, and only you, can choose.

One day years ago I was on a walk outside thanking God that I had been rescued from the box I had been in, the religion. I was whipped up about it. I started praying that everyone come out the box and be free. I thought it was an appropriate prayer.

Just then, I heard the Voice say "some people need the box."

Wow.

The Voice has a way of righting me in a split second.

YES! Some people do need the box! I needed it for all those years, until I didn't anymore. I get to respect and honor everyone's process, and what it looks like, without judgment that it should be some other way.

After that, I stopped praying for people to come out the box. Instead, I choose to pray for enlightenment, and soul ascension for every being, however that happens, and however that path unfolds for each soul.

Yes, we need written or oral instruction daily. Some of us receive that instruction directly from God/Goddess and act on it with divine results. Some of us need religion to tell us what to do until we figure it out. Be patient with yourself. It took me 26 years of religion to be willing to walk my own path.

With that said, your path is ALWAYS paved, beforehand, by Spirit. There's no surprises to God. There's nothing that will pop up on your path that God won't know what to do with. That cannot happen. Therefore, you can trust. You can be still and know.

As you walk your magickal path, know you will receive your next steps, your next teacher, your next book, your next magickal training, your next magickal implement, your next _____ (fill in the blank), at the perfect time, in seemingly miraculous and amazing ways.

We don't know how the divine does what it does, we only know it's good!

At the perfect time for me, I received each wand, each Tarot deck, each crystal, each magick book, each teacher, each workshop, each retreat, each program, each community, each Facebook group, each Youtube channel, at the perfect and precise moment for my unique walk with Spirit as a Christian Witch.

I've learned to trust the process.

I've learned to be okay with not seeing more than 1 or 2 feet in front of me, and I've learned to be okay with zero visibility.

I've learned to be okay with not knowing how to do something, knowing that when I need to know how to cast that particular spell, or when I need a particular incantation, these will come to me.

As if by magick.

Indeed it is.

A few years back, I appeared at a Barnes and Noble store in New Jersey, hundreds of miles from where I live. The magickal story of how I got to this particular Barnes & Noble is recorded in a video on my channel, so I won't tell you all the details here. Suffice it to say, how I arrived to this particular Barnes & Noble was a miracle.

When me and my 3 kids left home that morning for a road trip to Maryland to New York to visit grandma and grandpa, I declared to them that I would be going to Barnes & Noble. Since we were headed for New York, I thought I would be at a Barnes & Noble location in New York City.

But no, fate would not have it that way.

I told my kids resolutely "I'm going to Barnes & Noble."

I knew intuitively I had to get to Barnes & Noble.

I didn't know what was going to happen when I got there.

I didn't care.

We got on the road later than we had anticipated, and made multiple stops along the way, which pushed our arrival time later. We were in communication with my parents, so they let us know that they were going to be having dinner while they waited for us. They told us where to meet them.

When we arrived, there was a Barnes & Noble right next to the restaurant.

My kids looked and me and said "Mom! You gotta stop doing that! You're freaking us out! How did you know a Barnes & Noble would be here?!?!? You really are a witch!"

I don't know why people are still surprised, even after I've been telling them the same thing for years.

Anyway, I go into Barnes & Noble and promptly head directly to the section I'm led to: paranormal, magic and supernatural. I know I'm going to find something magickal here, I just don't know what it is.

I look through the magic books. I pulled out, one by one, over a dozen or so books. None of them is it. What am I looking for? I know I'm in the right place, still I don't see anything that speaks to my soul. Because I love the look and feel of it so much, I pull out the book *Secrets of High Magic*. I decide to dig deeper into it over a nice warm drink in the cafe. I head downstairs and step up to the cafe. The man behind the counter, youngish looking, asks "is that Secrets of High Magic?"

A dash of astonishment swirls around with curiosity when I look at him. "Yes.

"Well if you like that, you'll LOVE this."

And he whips out, as if by magick, a book, seemingly out of nowhere. Is the youngish guy behind the Barnes & Noble cafe counter a magician? Nah, can't be!

He holds up the book Enochian Vision Magick.

I see the angel wings on the cover and know I HAVE to have that book. I have never heard of Enochian Vision Magick before. I wouldn't know an Enochian Vision Magician from the man in the moon. I don't care.

I HAVE to have that book.

I buy it right on the spot, without so much as flipping pages, on the youngish man's recommendation. The way he speaks to me is otherworldly, and he says this book is for me.

Holy smokes.

I sit down with the book and hot chocolate and know I am in heaven. Spirit has done it again. It has bought me the perfect book, at the perfect time, especially for me and my path, as if by magick.

That book was waiting for me at that Barnes & Noble.

And Spirit got me to that Barnes & Noble store, with that man behind the counter, holding that book for me.

How do I know it's perfect? Because that's what happened. There are a million other ways that day could have gone. From that morning, I knew I was going to Barnes & Noble, and I knew I was getting the next key on my magickal path. The rest was anybody's guess, but I trusted Spirit. Trust in Spirit has never failed me.

Yes, I am cared for.

I am watched over.

My steps are ordered by the divine, even when they seem catastrophically out of order.

My every blessing on the magickal path is prepared for me in advance, awaiting my arrival to the scene, as are all your blessings.

This you must hold as a knowing on the path of magick, especially if you are a solitary practitioner, who does not have a rule-book or someone telling you what steps to take and when.

This you must trust: **your steps are ordered by God/Goddess**. Your tools are on their way to you, along with instructions on how to use them. You are being supplied with everything you need. You are being watched over, looked after, protected, guided, inspired, all from the inside.

You are loved.

Ones who are loved are always taken care of. Everyone is loved. Not everyone recognizes that they are loved.

Once you know how deeply loved you are, and that your magickal path was paved before the beginning of time, though you are only showing up to it now, and that the angels have been dispatched to your left and right and front and back, and that God has left no detail of your soul's unfoldment to chance, once you know this, and once you embody all the implications of being unconditionally loved, you will immediately let go of trying to secure instructions in order to make yourself 'feel better' or more secure, you'll stop trying to find a playbook that has all the right moves in it that you can hopefully follow so you don't have to trust as much, you'll stop trying to find that just-right list of do's and dont's that will always tell you just what to do, or don't do, and you'll stop trying to secure an outside authority to tell you what to do in some secret hopes of taking you off the hook for personal responsibility.

Though you'll have teachers, books, communities and more that provide you with very useful and effective tools, you will understand the ultimate Authority is within you.

Follow your heart.

Trust that it's leading you on a path and to a destination that's so good it will astound you.

II

Magickal Resources

*Magickal Resources from the Heart & Soul Grimoire of
S.S. White Cosmic Wizard.*

How Do I Start?

O ne of the most oft asked questions about the path of being a Christian Witch is "how do I start?"

The question has many forms and faces. Some ask if there's a spell that can help them make the entry into the magick kingdom from the Christian world. Some wonder if there's a process, and if it is, what is it? This question seems to beg formulas, when, there really are none. Some wonder when, how and where to take the first step.

Here's what I know and can offer you about your path as a Christian Witch: TRUST GOD.

That's it. Your Spirit Self — God/Goddess/I AM — will lovingly, unerringly, consistently, patiently guide you on your path of magick and alchemy, giving you the perfect books, websites, teachers and magickal implements at the perfect time, in ways that have proven to be more surprising and miraculous than I could have ever expected or anticipated when first starting out on this journey to honor my magickal Self, in all its dimensions.

To answer the question fully and honestly:

- there's no 'starting' place – begin where you are
- there's no 'right' way to do it – do what your Spirit leads you to do
- there's no 'wrong' way to do it – you can't mess it up
- there's no way you 'have' to do it – should's are judgments that lock up the soul
- there's no 'forbidden' places – if you're drawn to it by your Master Self,

it's for you, whether that's a deck of Tarot cards or crystals or a magick wand

With that said, treat it like the grandest adventure you've ever undertaken, indeed it is, what journey could be more full of adventure and discovery than the journey of your own soul? What could profit you more? The Christed One advised against trying to gain the whole world (getting the approval of others) and in the process, forfeiting your own soul. It's not worth it.

He also taught to leave mother, father and houses behind to follow him (the Christ spirit within every being) and be rewarded with 100-fold as much as a result. If you think the 100-fold blessing comes after you're dead and have successfully arrived in heaven, think again. Heaven and hell are states of consciousness. You are either choosing heaven or hell right now, thought by thought.

The journey of your soul cannot be lived out while you're trying to do what other people told you to do. It cannot be lived out to its divine potential while you are sitting obediently in a church pew, doing whatever you are told. It doesn't work that way.

The second you are ready to strike out and do something seemingly illogical and downright crazy — that being following your inner guidance on a path that seems foreign (and even of the devil) to the people you've spent most of your formative years and beyond with — that is the very second you open to an amazing grace...

The grace to be true to you, no matter what it costs. Of this you can be more than sure of: walking your authentic path will cost you, dearly.

The grace to stand with strength and power on Who you are, what you know and to live how you know you are called to live. How you live has universal and eternal import.

The grace to call up the courage to hold your head high, always, regardless of who's looking or what they're saying, and to never be moved, neither by the people who adore you, nor in the face of those who vehemently oppose you (and don't mind making that fact known at any given opportunity).

Quite simply, it is the grace to dance to your own heart beat and to dance that dance like no one's looking.

As Above So Below

A great magickal maxim, given to us by the mighty mage Hermes Trismegistus (the Greeks called him Thoth), states: 'as above, so below.'

Now one wouldn't think that the key to the universe is in a simple little 4 word maxim, but I've found that the most poignant, profound, powerful pieces of wisdom in the world are hidden in tiny little packages, so insignificant and seemingly simple, that the fool will pass them right on by, dismissing them for simplicity's sake.

But a fool is simple.

Once you understand this, and I mean, REALLY understand this, you become the most powerful Magus in the universe. When you understand and practice right use of Universal Law, you can do anything, your power is infinite.

This universal law, *as above, so below*, means that everything in the physical manifest world has a correspondence in the world of spirit, on the astral plane. It's the divine blueprint, or idea, that makes possible that the thing can exist in physicality. If there were no divine counterpart for the thing above, it could not exist below. That's the Law.

Christ prayed, and taught us to pray, for God's will to be done on earth, as it is in heaven. As above, so below.

A Word About the Will

As magick is an act of the will, two dynamic charges come into play for the working/practicing Magician:

To strengthen your Will, located in the Solar Plexus, the Central Sun, the nexus of energy and power,

To align your will with the Will of the Highest Most Holy Self.

Let's address both now.

Will is an interesting thing, it can lead you down a path of sheer destruction, or it can lead you to heavenly bliss. It's your choice.

What makes the difference in where your will leads you?

Alignment.

Alignment makes all the difference. If you are aligned with the Light within, which seeks only good, only Love for all beings, your Will is pure.

If your will is unfettered, freely roaming, without any foundation in law and spirit, it is like a wild rabid dog: sure to cause harm.

Before undertaking the practice of any magick, examine your will. Examine yourself. The prime directives for a Magician of the High Order are:

Know thyself.

Quit the night and seek the day.

What do these directives mean for the Wise Ones?

These mean we no longer function from the unfettered, untamed, unpurified free will, which could very well be the base desires, needs, aspirations and urgings of the lower self, which are always centered on selfish and carnal desires, which, out of the control and dominion of the Master Self, could lead to utter and complete ruin. I cannot state the magnitude of the ruin we're talking about here: ruin of self, others, property and legacies that have been built up over decades. When I say 'BE CAREFUL' I pray you take heed and if you get even a whiff of the lower self in your magickal operations, STOP and PRAY.

One of my favorite Magicians, John Dee, prayed like his life depended on it. It did. When you are in magickal territory, with access to Ancient Mysteries and Hidden Secrets that are not revealed to the untrained, unprepared, unready or unwise, you have a weighty responsibility with the Power.

You are held accountable for that Power, and its right use.

Knowing such, we choose, therefore, to function on a higher plane, according to the Law of Love, the Highest Order of Magick, in complete alignment and harmony with the Cosmos. Remember, there is no aspect of God that is in conflict with Itself. All God means all Good. If your magick in any way conflicts with Life, you are not in alignment.

How do you know if you're in alignment? 3 keys:

Intention – what is your intention, with using magick and with any particular magickal operation? Why are you doing what you're doing?

Ruthless and continuous examination of motives, and self as a whole, always leads to greater awareness. And as Magicians, the more awareness we have, the better. You can never be too aware.

Feelings – how does the thought of what you are about to do feel? Is it to bring harm to anyone anywhere? Is it possible that it could cause harm? Is it for the highest good of all? Or if you can not know the answer to that question, is your intention for the highest good of all? Your feelings will guide you well, as they will alert you when you're not on the path of Cosmic Love. Feelings are not the same as emotions. To be ruled by emotions is a deeply unhappy experience. Feelings, in this context, refer to the subtle messages we receive from Spirit... spine tingles, hands heating up, skin crawling, and all manner of signals in the body temple (which is a high functioning antenna) that alert us as to what to do, and just as important, what NOT to do.

Results – what are the results of your magick? Did you examine your outcomes? Were they good for you and good for others? Maybe even better than you thought? Did blessings flow from your work? Were your needs supplied, and then some? Were others benefited in ways you could not have known when you began? Are you in a better place now, in consciousness, than you were before the operation? The results will reveal if your magick is appropriate and beneficial, and hence, aligned with Spirit.

The Broom Closet

I must confess I had an excruciating exit from the broom closet. I was in there bumbling around for years, harboring far too much fear and far too little courage.

I hid my crystals and Tarot deck from my Baptist husband. He was hotter than a wet cat when he found out I went to a Tarot workshop.

I was trying to hide in plain sight.

Maybe that's you.

One of the most oft-asked questions I receive about this path is: *how do I come out?*

Associated questions include:

How do I let my Christian family/friends know about what's going on with me?

How do I stop living in fear?

How do I stop hiding my gifts, and stand up to do what I really want to do... what my soul is yearning to do?

Associated fears include:

My family and friends may think I'm working for the devil.

My family and friends won't/don't understand me.

They'll be shocked. They'll think I'm weird. Some of them already think I'm crazy.

I was always different.

I really love God and I secretly wonder if God will judge me for being on this path. I feel guilty.

I keep my Tarot decks and magickal tools hidden from the people I live with. If they find out, I would be in big trouble.

The questions and stories I hear from magickal folks who have painstakingly hidden their Tarot decks (in newspaper or brown paper bags), or other magickal implements, so as not to be found out, are varied, yet carry a common theme:

Fear vs. Love

That is the question. It is the only question that matters: *Am I living from fear or am I living LOVE?*

Once you answer that question, within yourself, definitively, everything else will work itself out divinely.

You have to make a choice. You cannot live both. Fear and love cannot occupy the same space. Your consciousness will either be dominated primarily by fear, or governed largely by love.

You get to choose.

Are you going to live from fear or from love?

If you're living from fear, I pray this book will support you in, right now, making the choice and stand for love.

If you're committed to living LOVE, I pray this book arms you with resources, information and inspiration to do just that.

Either way, you get to choose. I recommend opting for love, but only you know when you're fully ready and able to give yourself to Love.

I gave myself to Love.

I do not belong to myself. I never did, though I thought I did. You don't belong to yourself either.

You belong to Love.

I belong to Love.

So no matter what people say, no matter who agrees with me or who doesn't, no matter what people call me, or who people say I'm working for, I made a commitment to be Love.

And nothing on this planet, or on the next, is getting me to change my mind.

Once you make the commitment to BE LOVE, the next step is asking yourself, moment-by-moment, in every aspect of your life, and in every motivation you uncover within yourself: *is this love or is this fear?*

The ritual and practice of gently checking yourself with an easy question (*is this love or is this fear?*) will do something huge for you: it will make you crystal clear on where you spend most of your time, in the land of fear, or in the land of Love.

And isn't that the awareness you want? If you're spending way too much time in fear land, wouldn't you want to know it? You can't change anything you're not aware of, so becoming aware of how much time you spend away from Love land is the first key to returning home to your true essence: LOVE.

Because I had such a traumatic exit from the broom closet myself, I can feel you if you're having pain, fear, trepidation or hesitation about coming out.

I confess I was so committed to staying hidden that I almost didn't know how to operate openly and authentically.

I had to learn.

I confess I was afraid of being marginalized, not taken seriously, or even worse, being outcast. The old abandonment story was playing an active role. I had to melt the fear — in the form of an abandonment story that 'might' happen again — with LOVE.

I engage in the practice and ritual of pouring love on me.

Living magickal isn't easy, especially if you're just coming out and haven't found kindred spirits yet.

It seems kindred spirits don't show up until you get sick and tired of the people you've been traveling with. You somehow know you're with the wrong bunch, not because there's anything wrong with them, or you. You know you're with the wrong bunch for you because you are a vibrational mis-match to the people you're with. There's nothing wrong in that. You simply don't match.

It's like peanut butter and jelly. They go well together. They are a vibrational match. Peanut butter and mayonnaise may not be a vibrational match, nor a pleasing one. Peanut butter and butter may not be a match either. Peanut butter and ketchup may not go well together either.

There's not a thing wrong with peanut butter, jelly, mayonnaise, butter or ketchup. You may love them all. But you may not put them all together. We've elected to put peanut butter and jelly together because it's a pleasing match.

If the matches you've made aren't pleasing, make new matches.

Stop putting peanut butter with mayonnaise and trying to make it tasty. It's not. It's never going to be. Accept that.

Then get about finding your jelly.

Finding new people, a new circle of kindred spirits to be around, is not about making the people you're with wrong. It's not about making you wrong either. It's not a matter of right and wrong at all. It's a matter of match or mis-match. That's all. Don't make it more than it is. Don't find reasons to villainize people, unless you want to be villainized.

A new circle of kindred spirits arises attracts to you out of your love and appreciation for you. You'll then attract people just like you whom you love, appreciate and vibe with.

People who are being critical of you, or judgmental of you, are only around because you're being critical or judgmental of you, on some level, somewhere inside your own consciousness. Your inner state of being is a match to the people who magnetize to you.

If you don't want to be judged by the people in your life, love yourself. Don't judge yourself.

If you don't want to be criticized by the people in your life, love yourself. Get rid of — or greatly silence — your inner critic.

Too many magickal people try to get non-magickal people to understand and accept them.

If you're doing that, I have a question for you:

What purpose does that serve?

Why try to convince people who do not understand you to accept you? Why try to convince anybody of anything? Life is not about convincing.

Rather than waste your time in a pointless and painful undertaking of making yourself right or trying to convince people, why not shift your focus and attention to loving you?

Why not accept yourself?

Why not approve of you, as God approves of you?

If there's any convincing to be done, why not convince you to love you, as you are?

That's a worthy and fruitful undertaking. Once you've convinced yourself of your inherent lovability and fall deeply and rapturously in love with you, naturally and totally accepting you, what's left for other people to do but the same? Or exit?

That's the law. People are doing to you what you are doing to you. Want to change what people are doing to you? Change what you're doing to you.

Want to change what people think of you? Change what you think of you.

Want to change how people treat you? Change how you treat you.

It's that simple.

Not only is the Law simple, if not easy, taking total responsibility for you, your world, and everything in it, is *required* in magick.

You are responsible for you. You are responsible for who shows up in your world, as they are a vibrational match to something you're holding. You are responsible for what you allow in your world, and you are responsible for what you allow the people in your world to do, including how you allow them to treat you. Any blame you lay outside of you is an automatic and sudden reduction in power and a recipe for weakness.

In the magickal life, you need ALL your power.

From my own path of hard-won self-love and self-acceptance, and from the many letters I receive from you, my dear friends and magickal folks from all over the world, I offer you a simple formula to come out the broom closet.

I pray it serves you in living LOVE.

Out of the Broom Closet in 4 Simple & Self-loving Steps

1. Tell yourself the Truth about yourself. Acknowledge you are:

Divine – a child of the Most High.

Divinely designed – God uniquely designed you. You did not create yourself, nor did you arrive here by accident. There was a specific pattern in Divine Mind that created the unique blueprint that is you. You are a one-of-a-kind divine original. You could search the entire cosmos and not find another you. Don't insult God by thinking/wishing/believing you should have been created some other way.

Uniquely gifted – God gifted you with all you have and all you are. Appreciate and apply your gifts, whatever they are, no matter how 'strange' they may seem. Some have gifts of insight, psychic ability, telepathy, clairaudience, clairvoyance, claircognizance or clairsentience, and more. We have all kinds of gifts. Honor them all.

* * *

2. Acknowledge, discover, accept and embrace the Divine plan & purpose for your life (what you're here to do):

Your soul's Destiny, which includes:

Your purpose

Your mission

Your service

The Vision of how you live and serve

God has a purpose and reason for summoning you into existence now, here, on the earth plane. You and God made a deal before you came here. You agreed on the purpose for this incarnation. You have the honor of discovering that purpose and fulfilling it. It will be the most joyous unfolding you could ever engage in. Give yourself a chance to be spectacular.

Regardless of what people around you say, think or believe about you, remember, you and God have a deal. The deal is for you to fulfill your divine assignment, and be spectacular at it.

Don't let fear cheat you out of your joy.

* * *

3. Communicate your Truth & your path with loving power to those who are important to you, with the intention of standing in the Truth of who you are and being of vital service to the global community and beyond.

This is where you tell the truth to everyone else and come out the closet with your head held high.

Remember:

You are not seeking approval. You don't need it.

You are not seeking agreement. You don't need that either.

You are not seeking acceptance. You already have it, if you've given it to yourself.

You are not asking for permission. God already gave you a heavenly seal of approval and all the permission you require.

You are not asking forgiveness. There is never a need to apologize for who you are.

You are simply stating your truth, to the people you love, with an intention to be authentic, honest, soulful, and at peace, whether they accept you or not.

My Jehovah's Witness mama didn't accept my path until she crossed over to the other side. It's all good.

* * *

4. Let go and confidently leave the rest to God in faith and trust (that includes everyone and everything).

Your inspired and set-free heart will surely, gently and steadily guide you in every aspect of your magickal life, including training, teachers, books and path.

Follow your heart. Tune up your inner ear and heed your intuition *unerringly and unswervingly.*

Everything about your magickal life — including your every step on the magickal path — is ordained by Spirit. It will all be revealed to you at the appropriate time, in the most divine and mystical ways, always for your highest and best good and for the highest and best good of all.

Trust God for that.

Trust God with your whole magickal life.

Trust God.

Christian Witches Creed

I wrote this Christian Witches Creed several years ago to stake my claim as a Christian Witch and to set down in writing what was swirling around in my spirit. I published it on Issuu with the recommendation that one recite it daily at 11:11 for 40 days and watch the miracles unfold. Feel free to use the Creed as it best serves you!

I am a witch,
and proud of it,
free to be
as God created me,
Living my Soul's Destiny…
Magickal,
Mystical
Mysterious me,
I am Love, exceedingly.

I am not here to please anyone.
I need no one's permission
to be who I am,
nor do I seek approval
or require validation.

I am only here for Love.

I am a Christian Witch;
I love my cross and my wand.
I consult my Tarot deck and my Bible.
I adore & am devoted to Christ &
the Goddess.

There is no conflict in what
I do, what I say or who I am.
Like Yin & Yang, I am perfectly integrated on all levels of my being:
spiritually, mentally, emotionally
and physically.
I am aligned with Divine Mind.
I walk in the Light.

I use my magickal powers for the eternal Good of all...
for Healing in love,
for transforming consciousness,
for shifting energy and changing conditions that are not beneficial,
for delivering messages from the other side,
for casting spells to attract and keep love,
and for drawing closer to God/Goddess through the
rich & potent power of the elements...

Fiery passion stirs my heart!
Air lifts me to new heights!
Earth grounds and centers me.
Water cleanses & purifies my spirit.

Magick is in my blood.
I was born this way, and I love it!
It feels good to be me!
Whether I'm walking in nature hanging out with Faeries,
or in high consciousness communication with Angels,

or commanding demons & spirits,
or stirring a healing remedy
in my cauldron,
or pulling herbs for a tea,
or speaking a spell
or dressing a candle,
where ever I may be,
and whatever I may be doing,
I am never confused
and I am never in denial.
Though others may not fully 'get' me,

I know who I AM.

I am clear and certain.
I was sent here by God for God's good purposes.
My path is flooded with Light.

I have a powerful calling on this planet.
I am gifted for my unique purpose.
Gifts of psychic insight,
or the ability to commune with departed souls,
or the gift of channeling higher beings,
or the gift of being an empath or healer, like all gifts,
come from God/Goddess,
to be used in service,
for the highest good of all.
I know my gifts are doing nothing to help anyone if I hide out, terrified,
in a broom closet.
So I set my true intention & make the conscious choice
and empowered decision to be **FREE**,
to serve my brothers and sisters by honoring the Divine in me.

I am a Christian Witch,
and proud of it,
forever free to be me!

I claim my Divine Self-hood in this very moment…

**YES, I BOLDLY STEP OUT THE BROOM CLOSET AND
INTO THE LIGHT, TO LIVE MY GLORIOUS CALLING AND TRUE
IDENTITY AS THE MAGICKAL, MYSTICAL, MIRACULOUS
INFINITE BEING OF LOVE & LIGHT
I AM!**

In the name of the Holy Christ Presence, it is so, and so it is!

Ase & Amen

Gospel Magick Spell

This spell is for use when you feel conflicted between the magickal self and the Christian self, and the inner conflict is getting in the way of your peace. You know this spell is for you if:

- you experience inner conflict around magick and the Bible
- you have an inner standoff going on, with the witch/magickal self on one side and the Christian on the other
- you're in the 'broom closet', afraid to come out and be your full magickal self for fear the Christians around you may not understand or approve
- you want your inner conflict resolved

This 44-Day Magick Spell is designed and intended to:

- align your resonance with the Christ within
- resolve inner conflict around being a Christian Witch
- release fear
- release judgments
- and most of all, usher in the PEACE OF GOD

The spell is simple. Anyone who desires can do it. Here it is:

Step 1 - Set your intention to be FREE, mentally, emotionally, spiritually, physically. Pray this prayer: LORD CHRIST, SHOW YOURSELF! THANK YOU!

Step 2 - In your mind, set your ENTIRE religious belief system in a beautiful box to the right of you (you can always come back and pick it up later). Put a lid on the beautiful box and put it on a shelf.

Step 3 - At the same time each day (preferably during the 'witching hour' of 3 am to 6 am) read 2 chapters of the Gospels in order.

(The only exception to this is the first day, in which you will read 3 chapters – the first 3 chapters of Matthew).

There are 89 chapters in all 4 Gospel books of Matthew, Mark, Luke and John. This spell is to be done in 44 days, 44 being a master number.

Step 4 - Prepare to be amazed.

WARNING: THIS SPELL IS NOT FOR THE FAINT OF HEART. DO NOT PERFORM THIS MAGICKAL OPERATION IF YOU ARE NOT READY TO EXPERIENCE THE RESULTS. ASK YOUR INNER GUIDANCE, AND FOLLOW IT IMPLICITLY.

My experience with this spell is that it is one of the most potent and powerful spells I've ever performed on myself for aligning the magickal self with the Christian self. I perform it fairly regularly, as required.

Reading the magickal workings of Christ daily, and living and breathing this energy, will amp up your magickal powers and align your mind with your calling and walk as a magus.

The Gauntlet for Decision Making

T he Gauntlet is a tool for decision making, especially when you don't know what to do or you feel conflicted or you're experiencing confusion and would love clarity.

The negative ego is tricky, and, given its way, would keep us in confusion; a confused mind says NO, when your best life only happens when you say YES.

Clearing confusion is a MUST for the spiritual seeker and practitioner of magick. You must at all times seek to be as clear about all major issues and decisions as you can be, and this tool was created to support you in doing just that.

Run all decisions that are important to you through the Gauntlet. A Gauntlet is a test, a string of obstacles, that must be successfully passed in order for the one running it to win. This Gauntlet is designed to weed out ego tendencies and negating energies, those that are not helpful on your soul's journey.

This tool will also support you in being clear about your intentions, and will uncover motivations. When you know clearly what your intention is, and what's truly motivating you to go in one direction or the other, you have self-knowledge that will yield you tremendous insight.

Before using the Gauntlet, which is a series of 8 questions, set your intention that the truth will be clearly seen, all human and ego considerations will become apparent (and thus easier to pluck off) and your way will be made clear and well lit.

Before beginning, have a journal and pen ready to record your answers.

Step 1 – Set the tone. You can do this in your magickal circle or in your prayer space or any sacred space you create. DO NOT do the Gauntlet while you are riding on a bus or watching T.V. This is a powerful tool that deserves your full attention. Do it where you do your magickal operations, with your altar lit, or where you pray and meditate, or other sacred space, such as in the park or at the beach (when not heavily populated) or other nature setting. Light candles or incense.

Step 2 – Pray. Lift your vibration in heartfelt prayer. Use one of the prayers in this Grimoire or use prayers that feed your spirit and are effective at lifting you into a higher vibration consciousness, an ascended level of awareness where you have access to answers that you don't currently have access to. This is your invocation to access the wisdom of the Higher Self.

Step 3 – Evoke. Call in angels. Use the Archangel Invocations in this Grimoire or your own. Proceed with the Gauntlet only after the angels you've summoned are present.

Step 4 – Ask. Ask each question, be still, listening silently for the answers within your soul and spirit, then record your answers for each:

Is this for my highest good? How will it affect me?

Is this for the highest good of those closest to me? My spouse/mate? My children? My parents? Friends? How will it affect them?

Who benefits from this? Or Who stands to benefit? (This is a question that is sure to uncover ego tendencies. If you are the only one who stands to benefit from a particular choice, this could be a red flag, as Spirit led decisions always benefit the greater whole, not just one person.)

Does it align with principle? (Principles such as authenticity, integrity, truth, honestly, etc.) Is it a principled centered choice? Does it reflect excellent character?

Does it align with Law? Which Laws? How? (Laws such as the Law of Cause and Effect, the Law of Polarity, the Law of Correspondence, etc.) If it is unlawful, don't even think about doing it, the karmic consequences could be disastrous.

How would I feel if everyone knew about this? (Eliminates covert operations and clandestine activities.)

How would I feel if no one knew about this? (Eliminates the egoic need for aggrandizement, validation and recognition.)

Have I shared this and run it past my elders, teachers, coaches, mentors and/or prayer partners? (A wise senior could provide valuable guidance without making the decision for you or telling you what to do.)

Step 5 – Statement of closing. After you've recorded the answers, you more than likely now have a good handle on the issue and may have already come to a conclusion about to what to do. If not, sleep on it and read your answers again in the morning. If you're still not clear, do the exercise again, and again, if required, until you are clear. Conclude this session with a deep sense of gratitude as you make the following statement:

Only the pure, true and highest good, aligned with my divine purpose, will get through the Gauntlet.

My way is well lit with Truth and the love and light of God.

I am grateful for the guidance of Spirit, now pouring through my mind. This treasured guidance I swiftly and accurately follow, for the highest good of all involved.

May I have peace on my journey.

I am grateful for wisdom, knowledge and understanding and I expect the very best!

And so it is

III

Prayers for the Christian Witch

Prayers and an Isis Invocation from the Heart & Soul
Grimoire of
S.S., White Cosmic Wizard

A Witch's Prayer of Confession

To align with the confessions in this book, here's a prayer that energetically bolsters the release! State the prayer with an intention to be FREE, CLEAN and CLEAR:

Father/Mother God, my Creator, my Breath, my Life, my Heart, my Skin,
my Hair, my Being, my All-in-All,
I Am as You created me.

There is nothing missing, nothing lacking, nothing wrong,
with me or in me.
I Am as You created me.

I confess fear.
Right here and now, I let it go. It served me for a while, now it doesn't. I'm done with it. Gratefully, I take all the lessons it showed me, and carry them forward into my glorious life of magick and mystery.
I Am as You created me.

I confess lying.
I tried to hide from myself.
I tried to hide from you God, but you had another idea.
Thank goodness.
I lied to try to cover up the magnificence and brilliance that is me. I thought I was doing it because I was afraid of other people.

307

What I know now is that I was afraid of myself, my power, my majesty and my divinity.

I didn't know what to do with these, so I hid them under a bushel basket. They were too powerful to unleash, I thought.

So I tried to shrink myself into something that could fit into the boxes I had created about myself. What I didn't realize is that I was trying to shrink You, God.

It didn't work. You cannot be shrunk.

I Am as You created me.

I confess need for external validation and approval from people who never were going to give it to me anyway.

What I didn't realize – while striving to please, appease, cajole and pacify the people around me – was that I was crippling my own soul with assaults on its very nature.

I was raping myself.

Holy Father/Mother God, besides that, it didn't work. Me trying to fit in only caused the people around me to have the sense that they were smelling a rat, and they were…

the inside rat that sprawls in dark, dank crevices, cowers in cesspools and gutters and alleys and eats from the trash.

That's not me. I was created for much more. So I got sick of doing what I was doing, and even though I didn't know what I was going to do instead, I knew I wasn't going to do that anymore.

I Am as You created me.

I confess I let myself be sized up by other people's measuring sticks.

That didn't work either.

I could never measure up. Half the time, they didn't know what they wanted, so the measuring stick kept moving, and the other half of the time was spent trying to keep sane.

I don't feel like doing that anymore.

It's too tiring to be something I'm not.

I am not here to measure up to anybody's ideas.
I Am as You created me.

Thank you God, for saving me from myself.
I Am as You created me.

I confess judgment.
I judged people without know I was judging them.
Because I didn't accept me as You created me, Holy God, I projected my judgments on other people and called them wrong.
My judgments and projections showed up in my world as Christians who cursed me.
They could only show up because I had cursed me. They were following the same trail through the woods that I had cut.
It hurt when people told me I couldn't be a Christian Witch.
It hurt when they told me I was working for the devil.
It hurt me when I felt judged.
I realize now, my blessed and sweet Spirit, that I had hurt me by not being true to me, the worst hurt there is. I had inflicted the most painful stab on my soul. Others only followed suit.
So I decided to not do that anymore. I decided to stop hurting myself.
Thank you for saving me from myself.
I Am as You created me.

I confess guilt.
It's been a slow inner leak of the zest and zeal that are used to create and fulfill dreams. The inner enthusiasm has been dampened by guilt.
The guilt carried with it punishment, and so the ride of the 4 Horsemen was complete: guilt, shame, judgment and punishment, bent on sending us all to hell, right here on earth.
No. I will not abide a living hell.
I Am as You created me.

I confess pride and arrogance.

The pride and arrogance that I used as a false front to hide painful and deep feelings of insufficiency, not enough, unworthiness and less than.

Funny how I made that up in my head God, that if I wasn't good enough, I was going to damn sure pretend that I was better than anybody else. In some twisted way that I must confess I myself do not fully understand, I thought that that would be the solution.

I thought acting superior was the solution when I was really feeling inferior.

I thought acting better-than was the solution when I was really feeling less-than.

I thought that acting like I knew was the solution when I felt dumb as heck.

No more.

I'm done with that. It doesn't feel good and I don't like it.

I Am as You created me.

I confess disobedience.

I have felt like Jonah more times than I can shake a stick at God.

You guided me to tell the Truth about being a witch, to use the word witch with love and complete absence of fear, to break myself free of limiting beliefs, and in the process, to help others break free too, of all we thought "witch" means.

Witch doesn't mean what I thought.

Witch may not mean what any of us thought.

You taught me that witch means wise one, powerful one.

That's it, and nothing more. Everything beyond that, I made up.

When you lovingly led me to share my story Mother God, I trembled and ran the other way. I tossed myself on an ocean of uncertainty, whipped up by winds of confusion.

Just like my brother Jonah, I knew I was the cause of the storm.

All because of one big little word – 'witch' – a word loaded with more meaning than I can recount in a million years.

And why?

310

Why so much meaning on one 5 letter word?
That word has burned people alive.
That word has ripped mothers from babies.
That word has chopped off heads.
That word has started holy wars.
No, God, was my first unconscious thought, *I don't want to use that word.*
Instead of doing what I was being invited into by my Inner Being, I wanted
to change things up, to use words like Intuitive Adviser or some other
watered-down version of 'witch'.
A watered-down version of the message you put in my heart, Holy God, is
not the same message.
I do not take it upon myself to disobediently, faithlessly and recklessly alter
the message from Spirit.
I know who I Am.
I know why I'm here.
I Am here to change the world, not make it feel comfortable about it's
dysfunction.
I Am as You created me.

I confess doubt.
The insidious thief in the night who sneaks up on the unwary snatching
away dreams and hopes and desires is the demon of doubt who never
walks the day.
I have met this inner demon more times than I care to count.
Over and over, I thought I vanquished him.
Yet, he kept coming back, nagging me, whispering nasty nothings in my
ear, *maybe it won't work, are you sure?, what if…*
He's never overt. He's not that kind. He's never been in my face. He's too
cowardly for that. He sneaks up from behind, trying his best to go
unnoticed until he's right up on his prey and its too late; there he is again,
implanting a nasty little notion that what I'm dreaming about and
visioning won't work.
Except he had beaten me so many times, that in all the encounters, I got to

peep his game. I found him out, and how he operates.

I prayed up real good and put an end to him.

I thrust him through with the sword of Trust. Staring in my eyes with a look of absolute horror on his pale face, he knew he had been mortally wounded. I didn't shed a tear.

I Am as You created me.

I confess and release all these energies, and any and all energies that are not the blessed offspring of Love, the Truth of my soul.

In the void created, I ask for a fresh indwelling, in-pouring and infilling of

LOVE

TRUTH

AUTHENTICITY

INTEGRITY

HONESTY

SELF-ACCEPTANCE

RESPONSIBILITY

OWNERSHIP

HOLINESS

HUMILITY

EQUANIMITY

FAITH

OBEDIENCE

&

TRUST

I surrender to the Allness I Am!

I celebrate the witch I Am!

And I am grateful beyond all good sense!!!

I Am as You created me.

Amen

Forgiven Prayer

This prayer is to forgive all the instances when we've made promises to self that we didn't keep. It's a prayer I find most helpful for letting go of any and all guilt and/or shame.

I forgive.
Forgiven. Forgiven. Forgiven. Forgiven. Forgiven. Forgiven. Forgiven.
Forgiven. Forgiven. Forgiven. Forgiven. Forgiven. Forgiven. Forgiven.
Forgiven. Forgiven. Forgiven. Forgiven. Forgiven. Forgiven. Forgiven.
Forgiven.
For all the times you said something out of your mouth that you knew was out of order the minute you said it (or even before you said it) but you said
it anyway,
you are forgiven.
For all the times you lied to yourself and to someone you love,
you are forgiven.
For all the times someone hurt you and you briefly (or not so briefly) entertained ways to do them in, and even considered how you would
dispose of the body,
you are forgiven.
For all the times you were so angry at yourself, and turned that anger toward yourself and created depression and felt like, or considered taking
yourself out,
you are forgiven.
For all the times you said you were going to:

go to the gym,

stop eating cookies and/or midnight snacks,

lose 25 pounds,

stop drinking soda,

stop drinking,

stop sleeping with him,

stop sleeping with her,

or, fill in broken promise here: _____

you are forgiven.

For all the times you yelled at your kid,

you are forgiven.

For all the times you drank too much,

you are forgiven.

For all the times you knew better and did it anyway,

you are forgiven.

For all the times you ended up in bed with somebody you KNEW you had
no business being in bed with,

you are forgiven.

For every red light you've run,

you are forgiven.

For every time you should have spoken up but instead opted to keep your
mouth shut, and people got hurt behind it,

you are forgiven.

For every time you succumbed to fear,

you are forgiven.

For every time your intuition said "LEFT" and you went right, or it said
"STOP" and you lunged ahead anyway,

you are forgiven.

For any and every thing you have ever done _____ (insert your
name) in any and all lifetimes, in all dimensions, that is in any way not
wholly and completely aligned with Love,

you are forgiven.

Go in peace and s.i.n. no more.

314

(s.i.n. - self-inflicted nonsense)
Thank you!
Thank you!
Thank you!
Thank you!

Amen

P.S. - No one's holding anything over your head, except you. Guilt is a killer. Let yourself off the hook. Forgive you.

Miracle Inducing Prayer

This prayer was written when I needed a miracle, and FAST! I was in a precarious situation that called for an instant miracle. I wrote this prayer to remind myself of my true identity (divinity). With the remembrance of true identity, miracles occur naturally. Use this prayer to remind yourself of the truth when you require or desire an instant miracle.

I AM THE BELOVED OF GOD.
I AM THE BELOVED OF GOD.
I AM THE BELOVED OF GOD.
I AM THE BELOVED OF GOD.

The beloved of God is good and worthy and pure, worthy of ALL-GOOD. I AM the child of the Most High, perfect and pure and holy in every aspect and way. I De-SERVE God's best.

I COMMAND GOD'S BEST NOW.
I COMMAND GOD'S BEST NOW.
I COMMAND GOD'S BEST NOW.
I COMMAND GOD'S BEST NOW.

I command the very best for me, for mine, for all, for God's name sake. I do not walk in shadows. I do not rest in the status quo. I do not accept business as usual. I do not accept what is thrown at me as if I were a mere dog accepting scraps.

I CAST ALL SCRAPS ASIDE AND CLAIM MY HOLY INHERITANCE, HERE AND NOW, FROM THE DEPTH OF MY SOUL TO THE OUTERMOST MANIFESTATIONS IN MY WORLD. I KNOW I AM THE BELOVED CHILD OF GOD, PERFECT AND HOLY IN EVERY WAY, NOW AND FOREVERMORE MANIFESTING GOD'S HIGHEST AND BEST FOR ME, FOR MINE, FOR ALL. I AM GRATEFUL FOR THIS KNOWING. IT LIFTS ME FROM EVERY PIT OF DARKNESS. IT LIFTS ME TO A NEW IDEA. IT REVEALS THE PERFECT AND HOLY AND ACCEPTABLE WILL OF GOD, EVER SEEKING TO BE KNOWN, TO BE SEEN, TO BE ADOPTED AS THE BEAUTIFUL LOVE CHILD OF THE DIVINE FATHER/MOTHER.

I ACCEPT THIS PERFECT AND BEAUTIFUL AND HOLY WILL OF GOD NOW. I ACCEPT THIS AS MY VERY BEST. I ACCEPT GOD AS THE PERFECT SCULPTOR OF ALL MY PERFECT LIFE'S AFFAIRS NOW AND ALWAYS.

I ACCEPT AND KNOW I AM LOVED.
I ACCEPT AND KNOW I AM LOVED.
I ACCEPT AND KNOW I AM LOVED.
I ACCEPT AND KNOW I AM LOVED.
I ACCEPT AND KNOW I AM LOVED.
I ACCEPT AND KNOW I AM LOVED.
I ACCEPT AND KNOW I AM LOVED.

I ACCEPT MY PRIZED POSITION AS A CHILD OF THE MOST HIGH. A DAUGHTER OF THE DIVINE, IMMACULATE, BEAUTIFUL, PRISTINE, CONSECRATED FOR GOD'S HOLY AND DIVINE PURPOSE, BRINGING FORWARD THIS HOLY KNOWING INTO MANIFESTATION NOW IN EVERY AREA OF MY LIFE'S AFFAIRS.

ALL IS WELL.

I AM PERFECTLY AND BEAUTIFULLY PROVIDED FOR. I AM
WATCHED OVER. I AM TAKEN CARE OF. I AM CHERISHED. I AM
THE DAUGHTER OF THE DIVINE, PERFECT AND HOLY IN EVERY
WAY. I AM DESERVING OF MY UNIMAGINABLE GOOD, THE GOOD
GOD PROMISES ME IN MY EVERY WAKING HOUR. THIS GOOD IS
THE GOOD OF MY FATHER EXPRESSING ITSELF POWERFULLY,
ETERNALLY, INSTANTANEOUSLY AS ME, IN ME, THROUGH ME
AND FOR ME. THIS IS THE GOOD I LIVE, BREATHE, ACCEPT,
WEAR, EMBRACE, EMANATE, RESONATE, EXHALE, INHALE, SWIM
IN, WALK IN, DIVE IN, LIVE IN.

THIS GOOD IS MY FATHER'S GOOD PLEASURE. IT IS THE
KINGDOM OF HEAVEN, WHICH HE DELIGHTS IN GIVING TO ME.
I ACCEPT THE KEYS TO THE KINGDOM. I CHOOSE TO ACTIVATE
THEM NOW, IN RADIANT, ALL-ENCOMPASSING LOVE.

THE POWER OF LOVE NOW HEALS OLD OUTWORN, DATED,
NON-PRODUCTIVE, LIMITING BELIEFS OF ALL KINDS,
INCLUDING LIFE IS HARD, LIFE IS EXPENSIVE, WHAT I WANT IS
TOO EXPENSIVE FOR ME, I CAN'T, I DON'T KNOW HOW, WHAT IF
IT DOESN'T HAPPEN, I MUST SUFFER, I'M BAD, I MUST BE GUILTY
AND DESERVE TO BE PUNISHED, I BELIEVE IN PUNISHMENT,
AND ALL SUCH ERRONEOUS THOUGHTS, BELIEFS, CONSTRUCTS
AND ISSUES, GENERATIONAL, AND BEYOND. THESE ARE NOW
HEALED IN A HOLY INSTANT OF THE REVELATION OF GOD'S
IMMENSE LOVE AS ME, IN ME, THROUGH ME, EVER FOR ME.

I AM FULL AND OVERFLOWING LOVE. LIFE AND GOOD.
I AM FULL AND OVERFLOWING LOVE. LIFE AND GOOD.
I AM FULL AND OVERFLOWING LOVE. LIFE AND GOOD.

I AM SUSTAINED BY THE LOVE OF GOD.
I AM SUSTAINED BY THE LOVE OF GOD.
I AM SUSTAINED BY THE LOVE OF GOD.
I AM SUSTAINED BY THE LOVE OF GOD.
I AM SUSTAINED BY THE LOVE OF GOD.
I AM SUSTAINED BY THE LOVE OF GOD.
I AM SUSTAINED BY THE LOVE OF GOD.

I NEED A MIRACLE NOW. I ACCEPT A MIRACLE NOW. A MIRACLE IS NOTHING MORE THAN THE EXPRESSION OF GOD'S LOVE SHIFTING MY PERCEPTION. THIS IS NORMAL, FOR ME AND EVERYONE. I DO NOT BELIEVE IN THE FANCIFUL. I DO NOT HOPE OR WISH. I HOLD FAST TO WHAT IS TRUE AND RIGHT AND PURE. GOD'S LOVE IS TRUE AND RIGHT AND PURE.

I ACCEPT MY MIRACLE NOW.
I ACCEPT MY MIRACLE NOW.
I ACCEPT MY MIRACLE NOW.
I ACCEPT MY MIRACLE NOW.
I ACCEPT MY MIRACLE NOW.
I ACCEPT MY MIRACLE NOW.
I ACCEPT MY MIRACLE NOW.

THANK YOU O PERFECT LORD OF MY SOUL!
THANK YOU O PERFECT LORD OF MY SOUL!
THANK YOU O PERFECT LORD OF MY SOUL!
THANK YOU O PERFECT LORD OF MY SOUL!

AMEN

Prayer of Extreme Faith

Kabbalah is a spiritual technology that teaches we're here to become more *certain*, and less doubtful, fearful or wishy-washy. The key is to have certainty about our Creator, and certainty that everything before us is here to make us better in some way, even when we cannot directly see how. Certainty means we know we're here for a reason, and that our soul purpose — hence our total fulfillment — is assured. This prayer of extreme faith makes us more *certain*.

God of Love, God of Peace, God of Grace, in me, as me, through me, always for me,

I NEED EXTREME FAITH.
I WANT EXTREME FAITH.
I CALL UP EXTREME FAITH.
I ACT IN EXTREME FAITH.
I BREATHE EXTREME FAITH.
I WALK IN EXTREME FAITH.
I SPEAK EXTREME FAITH.

I HAVE FAITH THE SIZE OF A MUSTARD SEED, MORE THAN THAT IN THIS MOMENT IS PUSHING IT, BUT I KNOW IT'S ALL I NEED TO MOVE THE MOUNTAIN IN FRONT OF ME.

I CALL UP EXTREME FAITH.

I ACT IN EXTREME FAITH.
I BREATHE EXTREME FAITH.
I WALK IN EXTREME FAITH.
I SPEAK EXTREME FAITH.

I AM EXTREME IN MY FAITH. I NEED ONLY THE INTUITIVE
KNOWING OF THE DIRECTION TO HEAD IN AND I
CONFIDENTLY GO THAT WAY.
I DO NOT NEED EXPLANATIONS FROM GOD.
I DO NOT EXCESSIVELY QUESTION GOD AS TO WHY I'M BEING
LED THE WAY I'M BEING LED.
EXCESSIVE QUESTIONING, ASKING FOR EXPLANATIONS,
HESITATION AND WAVERING ARE ALL EARMARKS OF A LACK OF
FAITH.

I DO NOT LACK FAITH.

I AM FAITH FILLED, ROCK-SOLID, AND UNMOVABLE.
THERE IS NOTHING THAT CAN SWAY ME FROM THE GOOD
PURPOSES OF GOD MY FATHER.
I KNOW I GET ALONG REAL WELL WITH MY LIFE WHEN I WALK
IN, SPEAK AND ACT FROM EXTREME FAITH.
THEREFORE, I CHOOSE EXTREME FAITH NOW.

I'M HAPPY TO MAKE THIS CHOICE, AS EVERYTHING GOD HAS
EVER ASKED OF ME HAS BEEN FOR MY EXTREME GOOD AND
FOR THE GOOD OF EVERYONE IT TOUCHES.
I HAVE NO REASON TO DOUBT. WHEN THE MIND MAKES UP
DOUBT, I CHOOSE TO SQUASH IT.
I HAVE NOTHING ON EARTH TO FEAR. WHEN THE MIND MAKES
UP SOMETHING TO FEAR, I CAST IT OUT.
I HAVE NOTHING IN THE WORLD TO WORRY ABOUT. WORRY IS
ALWAYS UNWARRANTED, AND I DO NOT CHOOSE TO WASTE MY

PRECIOUS TIME, OR VITAL LIFE FORCE ENERGY, ON ANY
THOUGHT THAT DOES NOT TAKE ME STRAIGHT TO HEAVEN.

I CALL UP EXTREME FAITH.
I ACT IN EXTREME FAITH.
I BREATHE EXTREME FAITH.
I WALK IN EXTREME FAITH.
I SPEAK EXTREME FAITH.

FOR THE FAITH OF A MUSTARD SEED, I AM GRATEFUL TO MOVE
THE MOUNTAINS BEFORE ME.
THERE IS NOTHING I CANNOT DO WITH YOU GOD, AND THERE
IS NOTHING I WANT TO DO WITHOUT YOU GOD.
I AM FAITH-FILLED,
RIDICULOUSLY HAPPY,
RADIANTLY WISE,
SUPERNATURALLY SUPPLIED,
AND
MIRACULOUSLY LED IN ALL MY UNDERTAKINGS TO THE
EXTREME GOOD ONLY GOD CAN PROVIDE.

GOD IS ALWAYS TICKLING MY FANCY WITH NEW AND
WONDERFUL MANIFESTATIONS OF BLESSED GOOD!
FOR THIS I'M ETERNALLY GRATEFUL!
FOR THIS I'M ETERNALLY AND EXTREMELY FAITHFUL!
IN THE NAME AND NATURE OF THE
HOLY CHRIST PRESENCE

AMEN

Risen Witch Resurrection Sunday Prayer

A couple of years ago on Resurrection Sunday, the inspiration came to me for this Risen Witch prayer. It feels a bit like a call to arms, because I believe it is. It's a clarion call for witches to rise. It's fitting that the clarion call to rise would come on Resurrection Sunday.

On this day, as Christ rose from a tomb sealed with a
Heavy stone, I rise from the sarcophagus of my former
Self into the glorious revelation of Who I AM: A Risen Witch
I AM the Phoenix, the living proof, that what was
Once burned was never lost. We live on triumphantly!
I AM the Voice that calls in the darkness: "COME, all
Ye who are thirsting and drink life's waters free!"

I AM a Risen Witch

I AM the hope of magickal Beings who have long since
forgotten their innate powers or have not the courage tb
Summon them. I call with a gentle unabating whisper to the
Fiery cauldron of your Immortal Heart : RISE WITCH RISE

I AM a Risen Witch
I am not ordinary.

I am not normal.
I do not fit in.
I do not shrink.
I do not cower.

I do not hide in broom closets.
I do not attempt to stifle the Power coursing through me in futile wishes to make others comfortable.
I do not squat on my divine gifts because others seem afraid of Who I AM or what I can do.
I do not hesitate as the Truth is set ablaze upon my tongue.
I do not seek or require approval from anyone other than my own magickal Self.

I AM a Risen Witch
I bring healing to the ailing, wisdom to the willing,
Light to the groping and comfort to the mourning.
I AM an Avatar, a Miracle-worker, a Bright Shining Star
Beckoning you Home to your DELICIOUSLY IMPOSSIBLE,
WICKEDLY POWERFUL, PASSION-DRENCHED WITCH SELF!

I AM a Risen Witch!
Hallelujah!
SO MOTE IT BE!

Isis Invocation

This is an invocation to embody the Archetypal energy of the Goddess. Enchant this invocation with GREAT FEELING each day at high noon (when the sun is highest in the sky) for 40 days:

ISIS
Queen of Magick
Mother
Protectress of loyal souls
I implore thee
TURN TO ME
EMBODY ME
EMBODY ME

ISIS
Creatrix of Sun, Moon, Stars, Cycles, Rhythms of Nature,
Seas, Trees & Mountains,
I implore thee
TURN TO ME
EMBODY ME
EMBODY ME
With thy mighty presence
There is a bold power untold in your rapid wings of protection and fight to
the highest heights.

I desire to unleash this power for good!

I desire to focus and direct this power for High Magick for the greatest

good of all creation

I implore thee

EMBODY ME

EMBODY ME

I want to feel your wings enfold me.

OH ISIS

ENFOLD ME

ENFOLD ME

I want to feel the presence of your power and magick inside me.

OH ISIS

ABIDE IN ME

INSIDE ME

ABIDE IN ME

INSIDE ME

I want to know and remember I am imbued with divine power that can:

Raise the dead

Bring forth new life

Heal the sick

Correct errors

Make amends

Unite lovers

Rekindle flames of love long thought dead

Open the eyes of the blind

Free hearts, spirits and minds

This is my holy prayer

This is my invocation

ISIS

Mighty and Divine

Creatirix Sublime
I implore thee
EMBODY ME!
EMBODY ME!
EMBODY ME!
ENFOLD ME!
ENFOLD ME!
ENFOLD ME!
ABIDE IN ME!
Inside me
ABIDE IN ME!
Inside me
ABIDE IN ME!
Inside me

AMEN

IV

Soul-stirring Letters & Comments

Letters, emails and comments from our global audience on the
Christian Witches Facebook Fanpage, the Valerie Love YouTube
Channel and more.
THANK YOU FOR TRUSTING ME ENOUGH TO SHARE
YOUR INNERMOST EXPERIENCES.
I love and appreciate you.

Comments From Our Global Community

Help for New Witches

"Blessed be)O(

I have recently found you on you tube and it has been magnificent. I was born a witch have always felt it, but raised Christian. I have a request, I want to know who and where I have been, my past lives. Is there a possibility you can create a video to help us new witches with doing this?

Namaste"

* * *

"Don't Want to Upset Jesus"

Facebook Message 2/20/2014:

"Hello good afternoon, long time no see. Boy have I been on a beautiful journey. I got saved at Evangel Cathredral, I got baptized and I felt the heat of the holy ghost. I would like to speak to you. I want to be a Christian enchantress witch but I don't want to do anything to upset Jesus."

* * *

Condemnation & Depression to Joy & Love

"Hi Valerie, I love this article! I had a very bad fight with my sister over our conflicting religious views last month. She's a "TV Christian", I'm a Christian Witch. She got into the "it's from the devil" stuff & I tried to defend my views & it blew up! So I was searching on the web for info & help me understand my own views. I went to YouTube one day, searched Christian Witch & I found you! The first video I watched you said that if I'd found that video it was because I was meant to. You couldn't have been more right! I've watched a lot of your videos since that day & still am. I found this web site & the articles. And I got your book on Amazon, "God is in love with you". I can't tell you how much you have helped me & brought joy & love back into my life where before I just had condemnation & depression. Thank you SO MUCH!! Now I'm learning to live in awareness of God's love, in me, around me, everywhere, in everyone & everything. I realize I did not speak to my sister in love & I intend to change that. I have not loved myself either & I'm changing that. Keep doing what you are doing! Thank you, thank you, thank you!

Love, Cindi"

(Public comment on my former blog on the post *Transcending Religion*)

* * *

"You have to believe in Jesus, not fairies!"

"I really do hope you read this :D

I just watched your video "How I Became a Christian Witch" and I must say I got emotional for a moment cuz I feel exactly the same thing.

Personally, I'm a pagan witch, I believe in fairies and Celtic gods, they're like my kin and my "higher self" if you can call it xD. But i really enjoyed your Christian point of view in the matter cuz there are lots of Christian "witches" - (how they call them so) that still think that paganism is satanism and don't respect the other gods and beliefs. So I did really like your respect involving other beliefs such as Buddhism.

My mom got really shocked when I told her what and how I am, but then I explain it to her and she understood everything and she accept it :). But sometimes she still says "You have to believe in Jesus not fairies!" Well I do believe in Jesus but I'm more attracted to the Irish and Celtic world since I was a child, I can't help it xD. Maybe cuz in my past life I was a healing plants Irish woman, I don't know xD.

Well I would love to keep in touch, if possible and excuse my English (I'm Portuguese).

Blessed BE!"

* * *

"Confused"

"Hi...I wont make this long but I came across your video just now and WOW and I'm just eating this up. You see all of my life I have 'known things' and they are always right. I have always had a natural attraction to witches and witchcraft but because of my Christian upbringing I have been too afraid to look further into it. But I have been so confused because I have all of these natural gifts and desires that I believe are from God and yet if God gave them to me WHY would He condemn me to Hell for having them!!???!! Confusion! So, I go back and forth my entire life (by the way I am 43 years old) of being drawn to things then withdrawing because it's wrong. But the past couple of years I have allowed myself to grow and question things and to research things....still never the witch part. Then just the other day as I was quiet within myself, I heard a voice say you are a natural witch... you were born a witch. I am like WHAT!!!???? Crazy....then there's the dreams I have all of the time that I am flying...but not like superman like on a broom...and not flying high just around tree level (sometimes I get higher). Anyways....could this be true? Could I be a natural born witch and not know it? Could God have made me this way and it's okay if I explore things?

I am sure you are so busy but if you could please take a moment to answer this I would be so grateful.

Very Sincerely,"

(Name withheld here.)

* * *

"Sad and Frustrated"

"I just want to say Valerie that I loooove your videos so much! Your energy is soo very great! Can't wait until you post more. I was feeling very sad today, and didn't do any magick which I should have. Your video not only made me happy :) but also made me want to get up and get my dream magic started! I just get frustrated sometimes because I live in a household where it's the bible and that's it! so a lot of my magic is done in private. Thank you so much love, love, love you!

Merry meet, Valerie!"

* * *

"There's something sleeping with me"

"Hello! I imagine that you're quite busy and I don't mean to bother you but I wanted to ask you a question in regards to coming out of the broom closet.

I've known for a long time that I've been able to sense things that others cannot. Most recently when I go to bed at night I feel something walking around in the bed and lay next to me - for the longest time I thought that this something was something bad. I've heard all kinds of stories of people 'dabbling' without knowing what they were doing and evoking evil or negative entities and I'm very afraid of doing this so I've never pursued or answered anything that's tried to talk with me. It was only about a week ago that I realized the something that's been sleeping with me each night was my cat who died two years ago and I was really mad at myself for not realizing this sooner as I was too caught up in worrying that it was something bad.

I'm just very afraid of invoking the wrong spirits or spirits who will do harm and I was wondering if you had any advice on this or any experiences you could share as I took note in your video when you said you had been taught to believe if anything is talking to you it's a demon because angels don't talk to anyone anymore. How did you overcome this belief? How often do negative entities reveal themselves? Is it just a risk that will always exist?

Thank you, I really appreciate you taking the time to read this and answer me.

Thank you!"

* * *

Abused Christian

"I feel like God definitely led me to your videos. Thank you for sharing your insight and your experiences. I can identify with so much of what you're sharing. I was also born with certain gifts and abilities that I was taught to be ashamed of because they were "of the devil" and didn't fit with the warped sense of ideals that my parents had. I had a really abusive upbringing, but for months or years on end they did attend church and identified as Christian. The only positive thing that came out of that for me was a love for Jesus Christ, and feeling so loved because I knew that God cared about me. I still have that belief, but have struggled at times with the inner conflict you described. I am beginning to reconcile those feelings and I am a much happier person. Thank you."

(Comment on Youtube, BOOST! Morning Show Episode: *The Devil and Magic*)

* * *

Daydreaming Witch

"Love, you have brought a true light into my soul. I was supposed to see this - I prayed and meditated that I would find some reassurance that the pull on my soul was love and just and right for me. I have studied so much about Wicca and the craft, but could never justify turning away from the God I always knew and loved to worship something different. But the pull of the craft has had a grasp on my heart since I was a small boy. I

335

remember everyone asking me "are you ok?" … I was just daydreaming. Every parent-teacher conference was "_____ (name withheld) is a joy to have in class and he's every teacher's dream …. he just daydreams a lot" … I saw spirits no one else did. I communicated with them even. And my favorite thing to do while playing alone was to be a witch. This was no mistake. I was … I am. And from the bottom of my heart, I thank you for allowing me to step towards the love and forget the fear. You have an intoxicating aura and I feel so blessed to have found you."

(Comment on the Youtube Video: *A Witch is Born & Not Made*)

* * *

Born Witch?

"I've slowly started to become more and more drawn to the craft it started when I like you, stumbled across a book on Wicca and I began to read and it intrigued me, and then near enough straight out of this people I talked to in passing conversation would mention witches not even realizing. The coincidental nature of the events really freaked me out and I started to wonder if this is something telling me I've found my path? I'm scared to start this path but I feel like something is drawing me to it, something that I don't yet understand, does this make me a born witch?"

(Comment on the Youtube Video: *A Witch is Born and Not Made*)

* * *

"A gift and a pain"

"I have had my gift since a child, my mom was an intuitive and my grandma was a tea leaf reader with 100% accuracy. I had touched an Ouija board playing with my family in our cottage when I was a teen; boy was that a trip. I have been into tarot and crystals and scrying.

My family was catholic but spiritual and no one understood that; I had to hide my gifts because people said it's the devil so I kept it to myself. I always had the gift of spirits letting me know they are around. My friend, a minister, when we met knew I had this gift and showed me how to discern and get rid of them....

I always get visions when there is a message for someone but only if it is truly needed for them. I am very strong in vibrations from people good and bad and it can definitely drain me until I learned how to protect myself. Images pop into my head about someone and they would say how did you know that, who told you...lol...it has been a gift and a pain....

I am confused though because my path is broader than my Christian friends, and they say it's the work of the devil.....so still working on it..."

(Comment on Youtube – BOOST! Morning Show Episode: *The Devil and Magic*)

* * *

Spiritual High

"Oh... oh my goodness. This video has spoken to my soul in a way that I can not even begin to explain. I've been struggling with my beliefs, and this just.. it's like you collected all of my thoughts and feelings that my soul has that I have been struggling to understand and even realize I have, and presented them to me. It's like you've reminded me of what my soul knows, but that I mentally couldn't tap into, like I had barrier between my mental thoughts and my soul's thoughts, and you turned it into a window, where now both my mind and soul can understand each other and connect once again. I haven't felt the "spiritual high" I'm feeling right now in such a long time. Being reconnected to it after all this time is such a profound beautiful thing. Your words, they truly are magick. So many spiritual people online seem to have such a disconnect between physical reality and their spirituality. They try so hard to be profound, where it does not feel genuine. Yet, you, you mesh them perfectly without contradiction, then project that onto me through your words and personality. You are beautiful, thank you.

(Comment on the Youtube video: *How I Became a Christian Witch*)

* * *

"I have been fighting with this"

"I have been fighting with this. I have always been drawn to the craft, the light side of course. I have been raised to be a Christian and I love the Lord above all things. As a woman who has been in my shoes you know that when you say the craft and Christianity it doesn't match up. God is too good to me. I just prayed about walking into God's will for me and I was on youtube searching other how to videos and this video showed up.

I thank my Supreme Being for you and this video. Thank you for being you.

(Comment on the Youtube video: *How I Became a Christian Witch*)

* * *

"I've shed this... armor"

"I'm not even sure you'll see this as I know you're probably busy. I just want to start off by saying, thank you. I was born into a Christian household and I've known ever since I was young I am not like the religion I was raised in. I've always had an affinity to crystals, and herbs and spells. For a long time I thought something was wrong with me. That I was some spawn of satan. Watching your videos has really helped me realize I can still read my bible and believe in what I believe. You've drawn tears from my eyes and you've touched my life in such a way that I don't feel as ashamed to be who I am. I feel like I've shed this…armor. Thank you for your message and I wish nothing but fantastic things for your life."

(Message on Youtube)

* * *

"Draw towards voodoo"

"Dear Val,

I grew up in a southern christian household in New Orleans. Ever since

338

I was little I always felt a draw towards voodoo. Ever since I heard about it I always had a desire to look more deeper into it. Whenever I asked the relative that I stayed with at the time about it she would say that it's of the devil this that and the other. So I would drop the topic. But I could never forget about it. Fast forward some years I was in college and I was told by my best friend's aunt who is a palm-reader that my grandmother passed voodoo down to me and wants me to pick it up. I also found out from my best friend's aunt that I am an empath. So over time I started looking into Wicca magic and anything esoteric that I could get my hands on.

Over time I also learned that I am a very skilled tarot card reader. What I mean by that is its almost as if the interpretations come natural to me. But I am conflicted inside about whether I should continue the practice or not. Because of the verse in Deuteronomy.

Yes I feel a really strong draw and pull towards the voodoo practice. But at the same time I do not want to do anything that would harm my chances of getting into heaven. I have did all the studying on Voodoo that I could. I was also able to dispel some things that they think about voodoo.

So what is your opinion on the matter? Because like you I still believe in god I still believe and Jesus and that will never change. I would really appreciate your advice on the matter." (Public comment posted to my former blog.)

* * *

"I was so conflicted"

"Hi! Miss Love,

My name is _____ and I am 36 years young and mother to the most awesome teenage daughter amongst so many other titles I hold.

Where do I start? I am at work and I am listening to all of your videos on YouTube. Never in my life have I been able to truly identify with someone on so many levels. I couldn't wait until later to send this email. Just to give you a snap shot about me… Here are a few things… Maybe a bit random but I feel in my spirit you'll understand…

-From around the age of 4 or 5 I remember just wanting to heal the world and not just physically

-Around the age of 10 I experienced astral projection

-At 12 is when I truly discovered Christ for myself... My connection with God...

-At 18-my early twenties I studied different religions, magic... All things spiritual... I was on a quest... My spirit desired more... My mind...

-In my mid-20's I was studying to become a minister but felt like as much as I love Christ am I completely true? What about all the other things I've learned and practiced?

For a while I was so conflicted how could I speak of Christ and minister to others on being conscious too... Your video about being a Christian Witch... I am unable to articulate what that did for me today all I can say is... It was a blessing.

-In my mid-20's to now I've witnessed myself manifest situations, materials items, money, experiences but sometimes I am not sure how to harness my power... When I'm on I'm on... And the times I was off... The mental chatter would creep in... Then I'd 2nd guess myself... Right now I am in the mist of reprogramming my subconscious... I know I am close...

Like you I've worked in the financial field and I was a Credit Analyst for quite some time. I own a few online stores and in the midst of writing a couple of guides but I feel like something is missing. I know I can do a whole lot more. My businesses started to see success and I was in a space I've never been and now I put everything on hold... How can one desire success but be apprehensive when it's right there for the taking?!

What I love to do is edify one's spirit. People are always telling me maybe you should be a therapist or something of that nature... I have a knack for getting people to open up... I've even did free business coaching in the past.

My purest intention is to help others... To spread love... Healing in every sense of the word... That's who I am...

Stay encouraged! I love every video I've watched today! I now know for sure I am on the right path. I thank God for you."

Name withheld.

(Email message reprinted here by permission of the author.)

* * *

"Withcraft has always had a pull on me"

"Hi there,

I am a Christian, have been since I was 5 or so, a daughter of a protestant minister. But witchcraft has always had a pull on me. Even as a kid. I have read the book by Adelina St. Clair, and it seems so perfect. I have a bunch of books to research, but due to my upbringing, I'm kind of afraid to. Do you have any advice or could point me in a good direction? There's no one here locally classes wise, or any covens that would be accepting of a christian witch, I'm afraid, so this would be a solitary type path. I just feel so overwhelmed and not really sure where to start.

Thanks for your time,"

(Name withheld here.)

Facebook Community Page Comments

Our Facebook community has always been highly engaged from the very beginning, with content and comments on all aspects of being a Christian Witch, from a vast variety of community members. Here's a smattering of comments I hope you'll enjoy!

"You've no idea how long I've searched for something like this. Thank you."

* * *

"As a new witch and a lifelong Christian I'm glad, no, relieved that I'm not alone."

* * *

"Nice to see a site on Facebook for Christian Witches. I was raised Christian but it never worked for me, at least the kind of Christianity that was being spoon fed to me. When I became a Wiccan things fell in place for me spiritually. Even though I'm no longer a Christian I can say that I am closer to understanding the mind of the Christ and his teachings. Not so different from Wicca… just worded a little different."

* * *

"I finally feel like I have found my home with God's grace. I love Jesus and I love my craft. I was constantly told by family that I couldn't be both a witch and love Jesus. Now I know differently. I have no words to express my joy and inner peace. Thank you."

* * *

"I'm not a witch (I don't think) but I love witch energy!"

* * *

"Thank you for this page/community. I didn't know there were others who believed in Jesus and wicca."

* * *

"I am very happy to be a part of your community! For so long I have never really quite fit into any "category" or belief system. I cannot tell you how nice it feels to find people who understand and relate to what I feel. Peace to all!"

* * *

"Blessings to everyone here. I am a liberal Episcopalian who has always wanted to be a witch and practice magick but without having to step outside of Christianity. I'm not into heavy ritual. I like to keep my practices very simple and basic. Or, as some Episcopalians might say, I like the via media between Catholic ritual and Protestant simplicity.
I welcome any advice on how I might "become" a Christian witch, or perhaps rather, how I might integrate basic practices of witchcraft with an exclusively Christian context and setting. Again, blessings be."

* * *

"Ok so I have a question. This group says christian witch. I have the pain of believing in Jesus. Yet I was born as a witch. I can never fit into either world. It took me nearly 40 years to accept this. I see lots of beautiful posts for witchcraft. Where does Jesus come in? I would like to learn to incorporate them together."

* * *

"Wonderful page... God who created the elements and is known by many names is a God of love... no creator wishes to destroy what he has created... the elements give us our power... we bring it all together with our intent. Let us seek love and care for each other and this world as it was meant to be.)O("

* * *

"Hi. I am very new to all this but I feel I'm being called to it. I love the spirituality of Wicca... the ritual... I believe I was born to be a witch even though I'm getting a late start at 44. I've been trying to figure out how to do what I'm called to do as well as keep my belief in the good I've always known and Christ as well. I'd love to talk to some of you."

* * *

"Hi... I am very new to all this but i feel I'm being called to it. I love the spirituality of Wicca.. the ritual. ..I believe i was born to be a witch even though I'm getting a late start at 44. I've been trying to figure out how to do what I'm called to do as well as keep my belief I'm the good I've always known and Christ as well. I'd love to talk to some of you."

* * *

"As a new witch and a life long Christian I'm glad, no, relieved that I'm not alone."

* * *

"It is difficult being Catholic and a 'born' witch. I am hoping to meet like minded (not same minded necessarily) to connect with and talk of all things witchy."

* * *

"Loved your Christian Witch manifesto, Valerie Love. Perfect! So helpful."

Recommended Reading

For books on magick, the occult, Christian Witchcraft, metaphysics, grimoires and more, go to KAISI's Amazon Store where a carefully curated selection awaits you:

https://www.amazon.com/shop/valerielove-kaisi

More Books You May Love:

A Practical Guide to The Runes – Their Uses in Divination and Magick by Lisa Peschel

Drawing Down the Moon – Witches, Druids, Goddess-Worshippers, and Other Pagans in America Today by Margot Adler

Life Magic – The Renowned Psychic Healer Shares Her 7 Keys to Finding Your Power and Living Your Purpose by Laura Bushnell

Magick in Theory & Practice by the Master Therion by Aleister Crowley

Magick Without Tears written as letters by Aleister Crowley

Necronomicon – Edited with an Introduction by Simon

The Modern Guide to Witchcraft – Your Complete Guide to Witches, Covens, & Spells by Skye Alexander

The One World Tarot: Astrology, Tarot and The New Age by Crystal Love

The Tarot Speaks by Richard Gardner

The Tarot Spellcaster – Over 40 Spells to Enhance Your Life With the Power of Tarot Magic by Terry Donaldson

The Wicca Bible – The Definitive Guide to Magic and the Craft by Ann-Marie Gallagher

Transcendental Magic – Its Doctrine & Ritual by Eliphas Levi

Podcasts, Blogs & YouTube Channels

Podcasts:
Black Sheep Experience
Glitch Bottle
Modern Hermeticist
Rune Soup
Speech in the Silence

Blogs:
Bad Witches Blog by Carolyn Elliott
Christian Witches Patreon Blog

YouTube Channels:
Balthazar's Conjure
Behati Life
Christian Witches

About the Author

Rev. Valerie Love (aka KAISI) is the author of 17 books on practical spirituality, metaphysics, and Christian Witchcraft. As a student of the occult for nearly 3 decades and a practicing Christian Witch, Rev. Val's soul mission is to inspire and to catalyze transcendance for self and others.

As the founder of the Christian Witches Facebook Community and the Covenant of Christian Witches Mystery School, Rev. Val enthusiastically takes on her charge to serve, share wisdom and teach ancient mysteries so that all who desire to do so can apply TRUTH principles in such a way that complete fulfillment in every area of life is created and manifested, as ordained by Source.

You can connect with me on:
- 🌐 https://www.christianwitches.com
- f https://www.facebook.com/ChristianWitches
- 🔗 https://www.youtube.com/c/christianwitches
- 🔗 https://www.instagram.com/christianwitches

Also by Rev. Valerie Love

Hello Love! If you enjoyed this tome (and I pray you did), here are a few of my other books that may inspire you on your path as a Christian Witch and in transcendence. Enjoy! And please do remember to kindly leave a review on Amazon to help future readers make a choice to enjoy this work. I appreciate you!

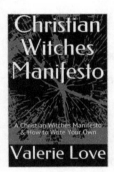

Christian Witches Manifesto

This 10-Tenet Manifesto for Christian Witches is for you if you're anything like me... I had ideas in my mind of what I knew to be true as a Christian Witch, and what I hold dear to me on my path. I knew it had to be in writing. Just as all great documents, such as the Constitution and the Declaration of Independence, this manifesto codifies my walk as a Christian Witch and I pray it provides inspiration for you as you walk your unique calling.

40 Money Mantras

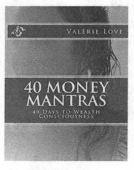

ONLY if you're READY to ACTIVATE WEALTH CONSCIOUSNESS, dive in… Your intention created the experience of connecting with this book, these mantras, here and now. Each divinely inspired mantras on one side of the page (40 in all), with journal lined pages on the opposite side of each page, to journal your experiences with each of the 40 money mantras. Of extreme help and support in DISSECTING each mantra for maximum power is the 40-Video Playlist on YouTube in which the author, Rev. Valerie Love (aka KAISI), goes into detail for each mantra in a daily show she filmed live with her audience. Grab the book and head on over to YouTube for much more than you could have ever imagined… Welcome to your new money world!

40 Money Spells

This is a book of 40 short, powerful, practical, proven spells for WEALTH CREATION the WORK. Not included here is fluff, hype, gimmicks or platitudes, nor is anything here unnecessarily complicated, or hard to understand or difficult to implement. The spells here are quite simply alchemy of the soul. As with the book 40 Money Mantras, this book is also accompanied by a 40-Video Playlist on YouTube in which the author, Rev. Valerie Love (aka KAISI), gives detailed instructions on each spell in a daily show she filmed live with her audience. Enjoy!

The Bible 11:11 Code

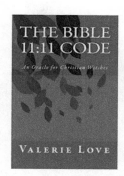

Is there a code in the Bible related to 11:11 that can be tapped in to for answers to burning queries? It turns out, YES, there is, and YES, it can be used to answer life's burning questions. The Bible is a code book, a book of allegory, myth, legend, and can be understood on many different levels, prophetically, metaphysically, allegorically, symbolically, and more. To glean the wisdom of the Bible 11:11 Code in a way that answers important questions, it is here arranged in a series of 31 scriptures passages, in order from the Bible, along with the accompanying answers. Follow the protocol at the beginning of the book for any questions that may haunt you and prepare to receive powerful answers from Spirit.